"Make it Yourself"

This work is a partial representation of *"Make it Yourself"* by Sarah A. Gordon, a multimedia work of scholarship published in the Gutenberg-e online history series. As such, this print edition does not include the images, maps or the index contained in the online edition. The Gutenberg-e series is part of our commitment to create new kinds of scholarly and educational publications through new media technologies. Our mission is to make these works as innovative, efficient, and cost-effective as possible. We encourage reviewers and readers to also consult the complete work online at the free access site: http://www.gutenberg-e.org/ or through ACLS Humanities E-Book (HEB) at: http://www.humanitiesebook. org/series_GUTE.html

The online version of this work contains all the printed text here, in addition to digital images, artwork, audio, video, and hyperlinks that allow the reader to experience the full meaning of this scholarly work. The organizing structure, content, and design of the online work was created by the author in collaboration with a team of editors, web developers, and designers in order to give the richest meaning to the historical narrative and argument. The intellectual content of this work is designed to be read and evaluated in its electronic form. This text is not a substitute for or facsimile of the online version of this work.

"*Make it Yourself*"
Home Sewing, Gender, and Culture,
1890–1930

Sarah A. Gordon

www.gutenberg-e.org

COLUMBIA UNIVERSITY PRESS

NEW YORK

Columbia University Press
Publishers Since 1893
New York   Chichester, West Sussex

Library of Congress Cataloging-in-Publication Data

Gordon, Sarah A.
Make it yourself : home sewing, gender, and culture, 1890–1930 / Sarah A. Gordon.
p. cm.
Includes bibliographical references.
ISBN 978-0-231-14244-1 (cloth : alk. paper)—ISBN 978-0-231-51225-1 (e-book)
1. Sewing—United States—History—19th century.   2. Sewing—United States—History—
20th century.   3. Home economics—United States—History—19th century.   4. Home
economics—United States—History—20th century.   5. Sex role—United States—
History—19th century.   6. Sex role—United States—History—19th century.
7. United States—Social life and customs.   I. Title.

TT715.G67 2008
646.20973—dc22
2008043642

www.gutenberg-e.org

References to Internet Web sites (URLs) were accurate at the time
of writing. Neither the author nor Columbia University
Press is responsible for URLs that may have expired
or changed since the manuscript was prepared.

CONTENTS

ACKNOWLEDGEMENTS

I have received support from so many people and institutions that it is a daunting task to thank everyone. I will begin with the Rutgers University History Department, which provided financial resources and was a welcoming community of professors and graduate students. Nancy Hewitt's gracious support as my dissertation advisor made the process a pleasure, and my committee members Alice Kessler-Harris, Jennifer Jones, and Jim Livingston provided encouragement and an indispensable range of ideas. Norma Basch, Paul Clemens, Dee Garrison, Charles McGovern, Nicole Pellegrin, Dawn Ruskai and Virginia Yans helped me as well. I especially appreciate the friendship and insight of my graduate school colleagues Sara Dubow, Justin Hart, Dan Katz, Lia Paradis, Jennifer Petit, Jennifer Tammi, and Charles Upchurch.

I am also very grateful to the Winterthur Research Fellowship program, the Hagley Library's "Beauty and Business" conference and "Consumption as Social Process" workshop, Carole Turbin's fashion history workshop, the Rutgers Works in Progress seminar, and the Columbia University Oral History Summer Institute. Phyllis Magidson at the Museum of the City of New York shared her love of the social history of clothing and taught me how to read and handle garments. Joy Emery of the Commercial Pattern Archive at the University of Rhode Island helped me understand patterns, and Barbara Burman encouraged me to pursue oral history interviews. I appreciate the editorial help of

Philip Scranton and Stephanie Gilmore with two of my articles. Wendy Kozol and Carol Lasser continued to be interested in my work long after I graduated from Oberlin. I also appreciate the companionship and perspective provided by my non-graduate-school friends.

It has been a pleasure and an honor to be part of Gutenberg-e project. I would like to thank the American Historical Association, EPIC (Electronic Publishing Initiative at Columbia) and Columbia University Press for their generous funding and good-humored patience. I could not have wished for a more sympathetic and constructive editor than Kate Wittenberg. I have truly enjoyed working with Sharene Azimi, Robert Darnton, Elizabeth Fairhead, Nathaniel Herz and Robert Townsend. And I am grateful to the Gutenberg-e authors for their welcoming collegiality and scholarly imagination.

One exciting element of the Gutenberg-e project has been the opportunity to include far more images than a traditional book would allow as well as audio excerpts and a photographic essay. Obtaining those photographs, and permission to use them, was a significant amount of work, and I had assistance from a great number of people, many of whom went out of their way to help or shared their own personal photographs. I'd especially like to thank Jacalyn Blume of the Schlesinger Library; Delight Dodyk; Sherry Onna Handlin of the Butterick, McCall's, Vogue Pattern Archive; Ellen and Julie Land-Weber; Kelly McCartney of the Hermitage; Margaret Ordoñez and Susan Jerome of the University of Rhode Island; Jeanne Solensky and Emily Guthrie of the Winterthur Library; and Kathy Woodrell of the Library of Congress. Thanks to Susan Shaw for her help as the good-humored and knowledgeable star of my sewing photo essay. I also wish to extend my appreciation to the friends and colleagues who connected me to the women who generously shared their memories with me. Those women are Winifred Byrd, Jane Dunn, Margorie Durand, Florence Epstein, Patricia Gordon, Marian Goodman, Jean Gulrich, Edith Kurtz, Elizabeth Nagle, Dorothy Orr, Helen Schwimmer, and Roberta Thourot.

Most of all I'd like to thank my family. My in-laws Peter and Karen Flint have been supportive and introduced me to Winterthur and Hagley. My parents Ben and Suzanne Gordon have encouraged me in innumerable ways, most of all teaching me to pursue my interests and not my "shoulds." My brother and Man of Honor Josh, who began and graduated from law school while this book was being written, calls me from sunny California. My husband Peter listens to me, serves as in-house technical advisor, takes me on adventures and makes me laugh. And last but hardly least, our daughter Ruthanna has given me blissful perspective.

INTRODUCTION

In 1889, a young teacher named Blanche Ellis read *Uncle Tom's Cabin*, attended church and a "gym," visited with friends and did housework. Among entries about an "exciting debate with Fred on 'Women's Rights'" and disciplining her students, Ellis made numerous comments in her diary about her sewing. She was one of millions of turn-of-the-century American women for whom sewing was a part of daily life.

Ellis appears to have been a typical white, middle-class woman of her time, and the effort and money she spent sewing is probably representative of others in a similar socioeconomic position. She had help from family members, occasionally went to a professional dressmaker, recorded the precise amounts she spent on fabric, made over hand-me-down dresses, and took pleasure in her accomplishments. It did not take her long to make a dress, provided she worked on it steadily. Eleven days after purchasing ten yards of fabric and a few entries of "been sewing on dress nearly all day," Ellis wrote "wore my black dress today first time."[1]

The material for that dress cost $7.64, but the effort, expertise, and pride represented by wearing it were far more valuable. Blanche Ellis' sewing is an intriguing way to understand her and, by extrapolation, other women and girls in the late nineteenth and early twentieth centuries. How did Ellis feel about the items she made? How did sewing factor into her daily routine? What economic and cultural roles did home sewing play in her life? In the context of changing domestic roles and shifting power dynamics, developing economic patterns, and changing fashions, Blanche Ellis and her sewing offer insight into women's lives at the time.

Home sewing is laden with multiple meanings about femininity, labor, family, creativity, sexuality, identity, and economics. It blurred boundaries between work and leisure, and yet was different from many forms of wage work because women wielded a degree of control over the process and products. It satisfied traditional ideas about women's roles, engaging in ideas about thrift, housekeeping, maternal love, sexual attraction, and familial duty. However, these ideologies were themselves shifting in reaction to larger cultural changes and sewing moved with them, acting alternatively as a tool for adapting to or challenging new ideas.

This book will explore the cultural meanings of sewing in the late nineteenth and early twentieth centuries, examining the dynamics and persistence of home sewing as clothing became increasingly available for purchase and more women worked outside the home. Over several decades, home sewing was challenged by a growing ready-to-wear industry. As mass-produced clothing became more accessible and desirable and more women had money of their own to spend, the symbolic meanings of sewing became apparent. Depending on the circumstances, home dressmaking could be a chore or a pleasure, a survival skill or a means of personal expression. By studying home sewing and the tensions inherent in its different meanings, we can gain a broader comprehension and appreciation of changing gender roles, cultural dynamics, and women's household labor at a critical time in American history.

HISTORIOGRAPHY

In her introduction to *A Midwife's Tale,* Laurel Thatcher Ulrich describes how a diary of an eighteenth-century midwife was long dismissed as "trivial and unimportant" because it was "filled with trivia about domestic chores and pastimes." Ulrich argues instead that "It is in the very dailiness, the exhaustive, repetitive dailiness, that the real power of Martha Ballard's book lies."[2] The experiences of Ballard and Ellis are wildly different, but the records of their daily lives share a great deal for the historian interested in daily choices and routines.

Fortunately, the economic function of housework has received important scholarly attention in recent years. Jeanne Boydston and Christine Stansell have demonstrated that housework supported capitalism by providing vital support services for workers. Essentially, women's domestic labor supported men's wage labor in a culture that valued visible and paid labor rather than invisible and unpaid labor. Sewing was a key component of that domestic support, but unless it earned a wage, home sewing was housework, not legitimate employment.[3] This bias against unpaid labor persists, of course, discounting many money-saving labors done in the home, from cooking to maintenance to childcare. Glenna Matthews has argued that as domesticity has diminished in social importance since the mid-nineteenth century, women's household skills have lost cultural currency. Likewise, Susan Strasser describes a woman who considered the unpaid work she did for her family, including sewing, to be "junk." [4]

Of course, women have been paid for their sewing skills. There is a wealth of scholarship on the garment industry, professional dressmakers, and piecework done in the home.[5] The boundaries between paid and unpaid sewing blurred when dressmakers, garment factory operatives, and pieceworkers sewed their own clothing. Home sewing was certainly part of the gender-specific domestic upkeep that supported exploitative industrial homework.[6] While this study will touch upon women who used household sewing skills to supplement a family income, it will not focus on sewing as wage-earning work. Instead, I will look at how sewing functioned as part of everyday domestic labor and household dynamics.

While historians have examined industrial sewing and related work, *home* sewing has received relatively little scholarly attention. One exception is a collection edited by Barbara Burman that reveals various dimensions of home sewing, from the professionalization of home economics to what Army officers' wives made in the American West.[7] Another study by Nicole Pellegrin of needlework in pre-Revolutionary France concludes that sewing and related needle work can be seen both as an area of expertise and influence and as a means of marginalization.[8] These studies demonstrate the exciting range of topics that are revealed by an examination of home sewing. Most scholars, however, have focused on the business end of sewing, looking, for example, at the development of the sewing machine or pattern industry.[9] While these studies are important and many inform this book, I take a larger view of home sewing, seeing it as an important and often fascinating way to understand a variety of historical issues, from domestic work and material culture to class and race dynamics.

While there may not be much focus on home sewing in the historical literature, there is a wide variety of work exploring the cultural and social dimensions of dress. Scholars from a variety of disciplines, including history but also sociology, art history, and anthropology, have studied the relationship between clothing, gender, and culture.[10] One consistent theme concerns the power of dress to embody the values of a particular culture. In *A Perfect Fit: Clothes,*

Character and the Promise of America, Jenna Weissman Joselit describes how early twentieth-century reformers were concerned about dress because "what one wore was a public construct, bound up with an enduring moral order."[11] Like most scholars who look at the role of clothing, Joselit focuses on ready-made clothing, but clothing made at home, and the labor that went into it, offers a particularly interesting way to examine how women sought to satisfy and challenge that very "moral order."

The changing economic structures that facilitated the simultaneous growth of the ready-to-wear industry and a growing female workforce are embedded throughout this book. In a sense, this book considers what James Livingston has called a "political economy of gender" as it relates to an entire body of literature that examines the relationship between gender, culture, and material goods.[12] It is important, however, not to become too focused on sewing solely as a form of "consumption" since home dressmakers were simultaneously producing and consuming. One scholar, in fact, sees no "straightforward shift from one cultural system to another nor a neat dichotomy between 'producer' and 'consumer' culture."[13] While sewing is certainly a consumer behavior—after all, home dressmakers were major purchasers of fabric, machines, patterns, and advice—they were buying those goods in order to subsequently produce a product. It was often the element of creation that elicited pride and pleasure in the work of sewing. Meanwhile, many women sewed because they were, to a degree, excluded from a growing consumer culture. The farm women who made children's clothing out of chicken feed sacks or remodeled donated dresses were still consumers but were hardly the middle-class shoppers sought out by the mass-market magazines.

While this book addresses large-scale concepts of culture, consumption, production, and gender, it also engages with ideas of identity, among them age, region, ethnicity, race, and class. While most women used the same techniques, their reasons for and experience of sewing might vary dramatically. A teenaged Jewish immigrant garment worker, a middle-aged African American mother, a ten-year-old farm girl, and Blanche Ellis all sewed, but their particular understandings of the task varied. For example, African American and immigrant women both used sewing as an economic strategy, but a student at Spelman College countered the notion that she was promiscuous by wearing especially proper clothing while young Jewish workers chose bright colors as a way to feel glamorous.

When addressing socioeconomic class, it is important to consider rural women who, because they rarely earned wages, might not be seen as members of the "working class." Whether they earned cash or not, their agricultural and domestic labor was central to maintaining their families. In fact, their relative isolation, compared to women in urban areas with more access to affordable clothing, made rural women's sewing essential to their household economies. Sewing was an important part of rural women's identities and was supported by institutions such as agricultural extension services and state fairs. I hope that this book will help to expand conceptions of class to include rural homemakers and agricultural workers as well as urban wage earners.[14]

In the end, however, this is not solely a study of domestic labor, sewing and clothing, or consumer culture. It is also an exploration of how those issues interconnect to help us to understand how gender functioned at a particular time and place. The period of the late nineteenth century through the early to mid-twentieth century saw such drastic changes in the experiences of many American women that it is a crucial period of study. In this sense, this work builds upon scholarship that examines all sorts of experiences, from women's political activism to girls' education, by looking at a very rich period in American history.[15]

SOURCES

This book will speak to a variety of schools of thought relating to gender, domestic work, consumption and production, material culture, education, and business practices. To that end, I have built on a range of scholarly work in those and other fields. While the secondary literature is critical, at the heart of any historical study are the primary sources that breathe life into what would otherwise be abstract ideas. Many of the sources used in this study are familiar to historians. Newspaper and magazine articles, fiction, advertisements, business archives, organizational records, and letters and diaries all come with their own peculiar caveats but are generally understood as "normal" sources for historical research. Others, such as oral histories, need to be approached with caution, but they also provide valuable, and in my view irreplaceable, insights. Obtained and used responsibly, oral histories offer some of the most evocative material.[16] In addition to these sources, I also use more unusual forms of evidence such as dresses, sewing patterns, workbooks, and toys. Following are some notes on a few of these sources.

One familiar type of source used in this study is prescriptive literature such as popular magazines and advice columns. All are tools for understanding what a particular group of people thought another group should do. Two less familiar forms of prescriptive literature also play a role in this study. I use school textbooks and lesson plans aimed at teaching schoolgirls how, what, and *why* to sew, teaching basic skills alongside cultural values. However, perhaps the most entertaining of the sources aimed at a young audience are the toys—namely dolls, doll clothes, and paper dolls. These toys, clearly aimed at teaching children adult skills and values, can be used to demonstrate the cultural power of sewing and clothing among young girls.

There is no guarantee that people paid much attention to what the "experts" thought they should do. One way to discover what people actually *did* sew or wear is to look at photographs. While photographs can be staged (the posed photograph of Hampton Institute students in Chapter Three is an example of how images can be used to promote particular ideas), they can also show how women did or did not listen to the advice they were given concerning what was appropriate, attractive, and feminine clothing. Photographs can serve as evidence of what women chose to purchase and what they were capable of producing.

Historians are accustomed to using letters and diaries to get close to an individual and understand her perspective, but if a letter can tell us a great deal about a real person, her dress can also connect us to the role of sewing in her life. I use garments from museum collections throughout this study. Like a diary, I found these garments to be a compelling link to actual individuals and crucial to supporting my argument. In this work, I was aided by museum curators who answered my questions concerning construction details, context, and background information.[17] Garments must be studied with certain constraints in mind. For example, middle- and upper-class people wore much of the clothing that makes its way into a museum collection.[18] Used judiciously, however, garments demonstrate the particular choices of an individual as well as denote similarities and differences between what was suggested and what was made and worn.

Another unorthodox type of source used in this study is the tissue paper dress pattern. I wanted to investigate first what kinds of garments the commercial pattern industry expected women to want and to be able to sew; second, how patterns were developed with ample room for personal interpretations; and third, how women interpreted those options when they sewed their own clothing. Again, I was helped by experts who know how to read a pattern, many of which were manufactured in a way no longer used today. Most of the information I used came from the pattern envelope, which typically explained the contents and usage of the proposed garment to the consumer as well as providing directions. However, the delicate, crumpled tissue pieces themselves evoked the process—choosing a pattern, laying out and carefully cutting into the fabric on the floor or table—that is the real work of sewing.

Workbooks created by little girls more than a century ago are also an unusual and evocative source. These workbooks, filled with childish handwriting, rusted pins, and meticulous samples, hit a nerve. Sitting in an archive looking at strips of flannel demonstrating different stitches and doll-sized petticoats, I felt a connection to the girls who, whether they intended to or not, created miniature pieces of art.[19] I hope that others will find these less-than-standard forms of evidence as compelling as I do.

Most immediately, artifacts such as dresses, patterns, and workbooks offer a way to understand what women and girls made and wore. Sewing is a tangible activity and it serves us to get as close to that hands-on work as possible, but these objects also operate as windows into a variety of expectations and experience. Why did a young woman choose to alter patterns? How did an adolescent girl feel about making a graduation dress? This idea of moving from a physical object to the context of its creation and the social relationships associated with it is in keeping with what folklorist Michael Owen Jones has called "material behavior." Jones expands the notion of material culture to include the actions and ideas that surround objects:

> [Material behavior] includes not only objects that people construct but also the processes by which their artificers conceptualize them, fashion them, and use them or make them available for others to utilize. It consists of the motivations for creating things, . . . sensations and bodily movements involved in their fabrication, and reactions to the objects and their manufacture . . . . It also comprises ideas that people associate with objects, the meaning they attribute to them, and the way in which they use them symbolically and instrumentally.[20]

The artifacts discussed in this book provide concrete links to the values that are at the center of this study. How did sewing function as a social process? How did that process change over a particular span of American history? How did those changes resonate for American women of a variety of social and cultural backgrounds? I hope that the objects examined here go beyond illustrations and become an important base for our understanding of the cultural meanings of home sewing.

CHAPTER OVERVIEW

Chapter One, "'Sewed Considerable': Home Sewing and the Meanings of Women's Domestic Work," explores the range of reasons why women sewed. It shows how sewing was one of many tools women from a variety of backgrounds used to fulfill their domestic roles. Middle-class, working-class, and affluent women often had different motivations for sewing at home. For example, an African American sharecropper's wife had few options other than to sew for her children, whereas a wealthy white woman's choice to sew her children's clothing signaled to others her motherly devotion. Home dressmaking came with a set of values that applied to women of different classes, ethnicities, races, and regions. The two women contrasted above may have sewn for different reasons, but both participated in a set of ideas about women's work, family, and domesticity. The first chapter therefore considers some of the ways sewing upheld traditional ideas about women and domesticity.

In contrast, Chapter Two, "Boundless Possibilities," looks at how home dressmaking challenged accepted views of women's behavior and appearances and provided a space for pleasure and individual taste. Sewing skills provided a way for a poor woman to defy preconceived notions about how someone in her circumstances "should" look: African American women stressed propriety and Jewish garment workers dressed "above their station." Commercial paper patterns encouraged consumers to make individual decisions about their dress by offering multiple options, and women with sufficient skills could copy designs they saw in department stores and adapt them to their own budget and style. In a culture that equated long skirts with good character, one could shorten a hemline as a challenge to established mores or counter racist stereotypes with starched propriety. Sewing became a way to test the boundaries of modesty, confront race and class bias, and invite creativity and pleasure.

Chapter Three, "When Mother Lets Us Sew: Girls, Sewing, and Femininity," examines how and why girls were taught to sew at a time when sewing was gradually waning in popularity. Girls of different backgrounds—Native American, middle class, African American, rural—were all taught to sew, but while they were taught the same skills, it was rarely for the same reasons. For example, minority girls were often taught skills with the goal of training a servant class and middle-class girls sewed in clubs reminiscent of their mothers' charitable societies. However, while many of those mothers admitted that they sewed less and less, they also wanted their daughters to learn the skills they themselves used infrequently. How, then, did an increasingly symbolic domestic education mesh with a rapidly changing social structure?

Another theme of this book is how a "private-sphere" practice functions as part of the larger economy. Chapter Four, "Commodifying Domestic Virtues: Business and Home Sewing," examines this question from the perspective of business practices. The extent of business investment in home sewing drew attention when women began to buy more ready-made clothing. It was one thing to sell tissue paper patterns, sewing machines, or fabric when home sewing was considered a regular part of domestic work, but what about when it declined in popularity? This chapter looks at the variety of ways in which businesses sought to encourage women to purchase their products, whether it was to reinforce traditional ideas associated with sewing or suggest that making clothing at home was a way to express modern individuality. Ultimately, the chapter argues that while many businesses supported a traditional mindset about women's work, it was in the businesses' interest to keep up with larger social changes.

One way to see how a number of these themes interact is to look at a specialized type of clothing that, because it was relatively new and marginal, was subject to significant personal interpretation. Chapter Five, "Clothing for Sport: Home Sewing as a Laboratory for New Standards," serves as a case study for the idea that sewing was both a way to conform to social norms *and* to challenge mainstream views. It demonstrates how, by making their own clothing for newly popular physical activities, women helped renegotiate standards of femininity. As a niche market in proportion to other clothing styles yet worn by a wide range of women, sport clothing was a "safe" place in which to experiment with clothing design. By making decisions about how they would dress, women challenged dominant ideas about their bodies and behavior.

I myself am a mediocre sewer, so I took a class at a small fabric and crafts store in Brooklyn. We learned to make a shirt with a yoke, collar, and cuffs from a commercial pattern. Over the four sessions, I learned not only how to sew buttonholes and attach a collar but also experienced the back pain and pricked fingers that can accompany time bent over a garment. I experienced a frustration experienced by many seamstresses—my shirt turned out much too big. I also felt the satisfaction that many of my long-gone subjects expressed. I added fruit-shaped buttons and wear my shirt at the beach with pride. I am sure it is the only beach cover-up on the East Coast with French seams.

This experience was gratifying not only because of its tangible, if imperfect, result. It also showed me both how much work goes into a garment and how satisfying it can be to create something from a bolt of cloth. I was reminded of sewing lessons by my mother and home economics teachers and of the doll clothes I made as a child. Moreover, the shop that offered the lessons has since gone the way of so many home sewing-oriented businesses—it is closed. Perhaps the most appealing dimension of the class was that it connected me to generations of women who learned the same skills and used them for a fascinating variety of reasons. These women, their sewing talents, and their reasons for making clothing at home are explored in the following chapter.

NOTES

1. Blanche M. Ellis, Diary, 1889–1890, entries of 29 June, 28 January, 29 August and 7 September. Joseph Downs Collection of Manuscripts and Printed Ephemera, Winterthur Museum, Garden and Library. Ellis was eighteen and originally from Cleveland; she was probably teaching in Ohio.

2. Laurel Thatcher Ulrich, *A Midwife's Tale: The Life of Martha Ballard, Based on Her Diary, 1785–1812* (New York: Vintage Books, 1990), 9.

3. Jeanne Boydston, *Home & Work: Housework, Wages, and the Ideology of Labor in the Early Republic* (New York: Oxford University Press, 1990), and Christine Stansell, *City of Women: Sex and Class in New York 1789–1860* (New York: Knopf, 1982).

4. Glenna Matthews, "Just a Housewife": *The Rise and Fall of Domesticity in America* (New York: Oxford University Press, 1987) and Susan Strasser, *Never Done: A History of American Housework* (New York: Pantheon Books, 1982), 4. See also Sarah A. Leavitt, *From Catherine Beecher to Martha Stewart: A Cultural History of Domestic Advice* (Chapel Hill: University of North Carolina Press, 2002), and Ruth Schwartz Cowan, *More Work for Mother: The Ironies of Household Technology from the Open Hearth to the Microwave* (New York: Basic books, 1983). More specific topics such as cooking have also come under study; see for example Sherrie A. Inness, ed., *Kitchen Culture in America: Popular Representations of Food, Gender and Race* (Philadelphia: University of Philadelphia Press, 2001) and Laura Shapiro, *Perfection Salad: Women and Cooking at the Turn of the Century* (New York: Farrar, Straus and Giroux, 1986.

5. See for example the work of Alice Kessler-Harris, including *In Pursuit of Equity: Women, Men, and the Quest for Economic Citizenship in 20th-Century America* (New York: Oxford University Press, 2001), Eileen Boris, *Home To Work: Motherhood and the Politics of Industrial Homework in the United States* (Cambridge: Harvard University Press, 1994) and Carole Turbin, *Working Women of Collar City: Gender, Class, and Community in Troy, New York, 1864–1886* (Urbana: University of Illinois Press, 1992).

6. Boris, *Home To Work*, 2.

7. Barbara Burman, ed., *The Culture of Sewing: Gender, Consumption and Home Dressmaking* (Oxford: Berg, 1999). Other studies include Joan L. Sullivan, "In Pursuit of Legitimacy: Home Economists and the Hoover Apron in World War I," *Dress* 26 (1999) 31–46 and Amy Boyce Osaki, "A 'Truly Feminine Employment': Sewing and the Early Nineteenth-Century Woman," *Winterthur Portfolio* 23 (1988): 225–241.

8. Nicole Pellegrin, "Les Vertues de 'l'Ouvrage' - Recherches sur la Feminization des Travaux d'Aiguille (XVI-XVIII Siecles) (The Virtues of 'Work'—Research on the Feminization of Needlework (16th-18th centuries)," *Revue D'Histoire Moderne et Contemporaine*, 46-4 (Octobre-Decembre 1999): 747–769.

9. Two important studies of the sewing machine are Marguerite Connolly, "The Transformation of Home Sewing and the Sewing Machine in America, 1850–1929," Ph.D. diss., University of Delaware, 1994 and Ruth Brandon, *A Capitalist Romance:*

Singer and the Sewing Machine (Philadelphia & New York: J. B. Lippincott Co., 1977). The pattern industry has received substantial attention; see for example Joy Spanabel Emery, "Dreams on Paper," in Burman, *The Culture of Sewing*, 235–253; Carole Anne Dickson, "Patterns for Garments: A History of the Paper Garment Pattern Industry in America to 1976," Ph.D. Dissertation, Ohio State University, 1979; Claudia Kidwell, *Cutting a Fashionable Fit: Dressmakers' Drafting Systems in the United States* (Washington, DC: Smithsonian Institution press, 1979) and Margaret Walsh, "The Democratization of Fashion: The Emergence of the Women's Dress Pattern Industry," *Journal of American History* 66 (1979): 299–313.

10. Some of these works are encyclopedic, such as James Laver's *Costume & Fashion: A Concise History* (reprinted London: Thames and Hudson Ltd., 1982). Others consider dress across a number of cultures and are hardly limited to western dress, such as the collection edited by Ruth Barnes and Joanne B. Eicher, *Dress and Gender Making and Meaning* (Oxford: Berg Publishers, 1992) or see it as a sociological study, as Fred Davis's *Fashion, Culture and Identity* (Chicago: University of Chicago Press, 1992). Others more immediately pertinent to this story look at gender, dress and culture, such as Jenna Weissman Joselit, *A Perfect Fit: Clothes, Character, and the Promise of America* (New York: Henry Holt & Co., 2001); Anne Hollander, *Sex and Suits: The Evolution of Modern Dress* (New York: Alfred A. Knopf, 1994); Philippe Perrot, *Fashioning the Bourgeoisie* (Princeton: Princeton University Press, 1994, trans. Richard Bienvenu); and Claudia Brush Kidwell and Valerie Steele, *Men and Women: Dressing the Part* (Washington, DC: Smithsonian Institution Press, 1989).

11. Joselit, *A Perfect Fit*, 2.

12. See James Livingston's *Pragmatism, Feminism and Democracy: Rethinking the Politics of American History* (New York: Routledge, 2001) and *Pragmatism and the Political Economy of Cultural Revolution, 1850–1940* (Chapel Hill: University of North Carolina Press, 1994). For a range of views on consumption and culture, see Warren Susman, *Culture as History: The Transformation of American Society in the Twentieth Century* (New York: Pantheon Books, 1984), Jennifer Scanlon, ed., *The Gender and Consumer Culture Reader* (New York: New York University Press, 2000); Susan Strasser, Charles McGovern and Matthias Judt, eds., *Getting and Spending: European and American Consumer Societies in the Twentieth Century* (Cambridge: Cambridge University Press, 1998); Roger Horowitz and Arwen Mohun, eds., *His and Hers: Gender, Consumption, and Technology* (Charlottesville: University Press of Virginia, 1998); Victoria de Grazia and Ellen Furlough, eds., *The Sex of Things: Gender and Consumption in Historical Perspective* (Berkeley: University of California Press, 1996).

13. Rob Schorman, "Ready or Not: Custom-Made Ideals and Ready-Made Clothes in Late 19th-Century America," *Journal of American Culture* 19 (1996): 111–120, 111.

14. Two recent studies of rural women are Lu Ann Jones, *Mama Learned Us to Work: Farm Women in the New South* (Chapel Hill: University of North Carolina Press, 2002) and Rebecca Sharpless, *Fertile Ground, Narrow Choices: Women on Texas Cotton Farms, 1900–1940* (Chapel Hill: University of North Carolina Press, 1999). For the perspectives of immigrants (albeit mostly Jewish and Italian) see Nan

Enstad, *Ladies of Labor, Girls of Adventure: Working Women, Popular Culture, and Labor Politics at the Turn of the Twentieth Century* (New York: Columbia University Press, 1999); Susan A. Glenn, *Daughters of the Shtetl: Life and Labor in the Immigrant Generation* (Ithaca: Cornell University Press, 1990); Kathy Peiss, *Cheap Amusements: Working Women and Leisure in Turn-of-the-Century New York* (Philadelphia: Temple University Press, 1986); and Elizabeth Ewen, *Immigrant Women in the Land of Dollars* (New York: Monthly Review Press, 1985). Two studies of African American women's culture are Tera W. Hunter, *To 'Joy My Freedom: Southern Black Women's Lives and Labors After the Civil War* (Cambridge: Harvard University Press, 1997) and Stephanie Shaw's *What a Woman Ought to Be and to Do: Black Professional Women Workers During the Jim Crow Era* (Chicago: University of Chicago Press, 1996), while for Hispanic and Indian women see Sarah Deutsch, *No Separate Refuge: Culture, Class, and Gender on an Anglo-Hispanic Frontier in the American Southwest, 1880–1940* (New York: Oxford University Press, 1987) and Devon A. Mihesuah, *Cultivating the Rosebuds: The Education of Women at the Cherokee Female Seminary, 1851–1909* (Urbana: University of Illinois Press, 1993). Meanwhile, three perspectives on girls' culture are Jane H. Hunter, *How Young Ladies Became Girls: The Victorian Origins of American Girlhood* (New Haven: Yale University Press, 2002); Joan Jacobs Brumberg, *The Body Project: An Intimate History of American Girls* (New York: Random House, 1997); and Miriam Formanek-Brunell, *Made to Play House: Dolls and the Commercialization of American Girlhood, 1830–1930* (New Haven: Yale University Press, 1993).

15. Many important studies of women's history and gender meanings focus on this particular time period. A few examples are Nancy A. Hewitt, *Southern Discomfort: Women's Activism in Tampa, Florida, 1880s-1920s* (Urbana: University of Illinois Press, 2001), Margaret Finnegan, *Selling Suffrage: Consumer Culture and Votes for Women* (New York: Columbia University Press, 1998). Gail Bederman, *Manliness and Civilization: A Cultural History of Gender and Race in the United States, 1880–1917* (Chicago: University of Chicago Press, 1995), Evelyn Brooks Higginbotham, *Righteous Discontent: The Women's Movement in the Black Baptist Church, 1990–1920* (Cambridge: Harvard University Press, 1993) and Nancy F. Cott, *The Grounding of Modern Feminism* (New Haven: Yale University Press, 1987).

16. I would like to thank the leaders and participants in the 2001 Columbia University Oral History Summer Institute for their insights on the use of interview materials.

17. I'd like to thank Phyllis Magidson of the Museum of the City of New York; Margaret Ordoñez and Joy Spanabel Emery at the University of Rhode Island; Diane Barsa, Tunde Horvath and Coralee Cummings at the Hermitage Historical Society; and Alexandra Kowalski at the Metropolitan Museum of Art Costume Institute for their help with garments. For more insight into using clothing as a resource, see Nancy Bradfield's *Costume in Detail, 1730–1930* (1968; reprinted New York: Costume & Fashion Press, 1997).

18. In her technical study of early nineteenth century fabrics, Susan Greene reiterates this point, writing that museums "boast all kinds of pretty dresses. Made of lace,

taffeta, velvet, chiffon, lawn and muslin—they evoke visions of teas and operas, weddings and balls. Conspicuous by their absence, or nearly so, are the early nineteenth-century printed calico dresses worn in kitchens and barnyards, seldom valued enough to have been stashed in family trunks with baby clothes and outdated dresses." Susan Greene, "Service with Style: Indigo, Manganese Bronze, and Hoyle's Purple Dress Prints, 1800–1855," *Dress* 26 (1999) 17–30, 17.

19. One such workbook is that by Florence Loop, Graded Sewing Exercises, Joseph Downs Collection of Manuscripts and Printed Ephemera, Winterthur Museum, Garden and Library.

20. Michael Owen Jones, "How Can We Apply Event Analysis to 'Material Behavior,' and Why Should We?" *Western Folklore* 56 (1998): 199–214, 202–203.

1. "SEWED CONSIDERABLE"

Home Sewing and the Meanings of Women's Domestic Work

In 1934, a Mrs. H.S. from Illinois wrote to the editor of the *Woman's Home Companion* to ask for advice on how to arrange her furniture in the house she shared with her railroad engineer husband and seven-year-old son. She went on to explain that she "reads everything" in the magazine as she "tries to be a good wife and mother."[1] Part of her efforts included sewing, even though by the 1930s, she could have easily purchased clothing for her family. Mrs. H.S. ostensibly lived in a comfortable home; after all, she had furniture and a living room and dining room to arrange. She was probably white, had one school-age child, and does not mention working for wages herself. From this short letter in a women's magazine, we have a snapshot of a member of the middle class.

Mrs. H.S., however, was anxious about her class status and her ability to fulfill her domestic role. After all, she was asking for advice from "experts" on setting up her house and found it necessary to say how hard she tried to fulfill her roles. As a member of the middle class, she was the target market for the rapidly expanding ready-made clothing industry and could probably afford to purchase her family's wardrobe. Nonetheless, she still did some sewing at home and evidently believed that this work was an integral part of fulfilling her role as family caretaker. Like many women, she felt that sewing was one way to allay some of the anxiety she felt about her place in the home and in the larger culture.

Sewing provided a refuge of traditional ideas about women in an age of dramatic change. This chapter will explore how sewing was understood to be a key aspect of women's duties and roles. Sewing was for many a routine component of a household economy, usually (but not always) cheaper than buying items ready-made. Many women of a variety of backgrounds expected to make at least some clothing for themselves and family members. Sewing represented the home, women's conventional role of caring for her family, and was associated with concepts of thrift, discipline, domestic production, even sexual morality. These values intersect with other issues of identity and cultural understanding. What can we learn from looking carefully at this routine and often invisible work? What exactly does it mean to be "thrifty" or to provide a "good home" and to whom? Meanwhile, cultural meanings are not static. This chapter will also examine the reasons why women sewed clothing for themselves and their families even as items became increasingly affordable and more women worked outside the home. As sewing became less of a basic economic function, how did it persist as a cultural behavior? Did the gendered assumptions surrounding sewing shift along with the expectations and experiences of the women and girls who were taught—or not taught—to sew?

Because sewing offers a distillation of ideas about women's role in the family and home, it also illuminates class, ethnic, and racial distinctions. This chapter will therefore examine how sewing served as a way for people to enforce ideas about their position vis-à-vis others of another class or race. Because sewing was an embodiment of gender roles, it could also serve to propagate social hierarchies. Sewing could be used to express personal and group identities, but it could also reinforce social divisions. Home dressmaking was a task shared by working- and middle-class women, black and white, native-born and immigrant. The same skills could be used for different purposes according to one's economic, cultural, and geographical circumstances. Sewing fulfilled white, middle-class ideals of domesticity and provided African Americans and working-class women a way to dress "respectably." In some ways, sewing was a unifying behavior, connecting women of different backgrounds. In other ways, it served to underscore distinctions between them and enforce social and racial hierarchies.

"WOMEN JUST SEWED"

For most of the nineteenth century and into the twentieth century, most women had few choices other than to sew at home. Factory-made men's clothing was available for purchase starting in the mid-nineteenth century, but the women's ready-to-wear industry took longer to gain a foothold. In 1890, women's styles accounted for only 25 percent of factory-made clothing.[2] According to the Middletown survey of an Indiana community in the 1920s, advertisements for fabric far outnumbered those for dresses in local newspapers until 1910.[3] As Edith Kurtz, who grew up in the Midwest in the early 1900s, put it, "Women just sewed. It was cheaper to make your own clothes, and I presume that had something to do with it, but ready-made clothes were not available."[4]

An alternative of course was to engage a dressmaker.[5] Wealthy women would almost always have their clothing custom-made by a professional. Those with less to spend might have someone make just their best dresses or pay a dressmaker to cut out a garment—often the most difficult and potentially costly part of the process—which the client would sew together at home. Gabrielle Josephine Crofton, a young woman in Illinois, had her better dresses made by a dressmaker but made her own nightdresses.[6] For many women, however, the cost of a professional dressmaker was prohibitive and they would have to choose between buying items and making them themselves. Until the ready-wear industry grew to the point where desirable clothes were available at low prices, many middle-class and most working-class women had little choice but to sew the majority of the clothing they and their families needed.

During the early twentieth century, changes in production methods, cheap immigrant labor, and other structural changes made ready-made clothing more affordable. By the 1920s, a competitive and increasingly mechanized garment industry offered a wide range of prices, and looser, less fitted styles fit well off the rack. Ready-to-wear blouses, skirts, and dresses became increasingly popular and fewer women sewed. A survey of department stores from 1911 to 1925 showed that until 1920, fabric sales kept pace with ready-made clothing, but after 1920, the ready-mades overtook fabric.[7] One businessman surveyed in the Middletown study recalled that in 1890, a fabric sale would clear ten bolts on the first day, whereas a similar sale in 1924 drew many fewer customers.[8]

During and despite this shift, many women continued to sew.[9] A series of surveys reveals the tenacity of sewing habits. One small study of families in Pennsylvania in the early 1910s found that at least half made "a few" garments at home.[10] A few years later, in 1919, a more extensive survey of farm homes found that in some regions 95 percent of households did some of their own sewing.[11] In 1926, despite the growing popularity of ready-made garments, 98 percent of rural respondents and 92 percent of urban respondents owned a sewing machine.[12] A fourth survey, by the Bureau of Home Economics (then part of the Department of Agriculture) and also reported in 1926, found that at least 80 percent of women surveyed made at least some clothing for themselves and their children. Although the women in the classic Middletown study may have bought an increasingly large proportion of their family's clothing, they continued to sew. About two-thirds of the "working class" women and three-quarters of the "business class" women spent up to six hours a week sewing and mending.[13]

The decision of whether to sew or purchase clothing was part of a complex arithmetic of time, energy, expense, and skills. Working women, the ones most likely to need to sew for economic reasons, often felt the pinch of other demands on their time and a lack of sewing education. Up to a third of the respondents to one survey bought clothing because they were "unable to make clothes at home." Moreover, in the same survey, the largest percentages of those without sewing skills were in the lowest income bracket.[14] Other women may have known how to sew but were too tired to do so. Twenty-five-year-old Lucy Cleaver, interviewed by members of the National Consumers League in 1909, worked long hours in a department store and saved money by walking to work and doing her own washing. However, "as she could not spend any further energy in sewing, she bought cheap ready-made clothes." Cleaver spent more than she could really afford on these clothes, but was "ill, anaemic [sic], nervous, and broken in health."[15]

At times, it simply wasn't worth buying fabric and spending the time to sew. Constance W. Simons, a woman who received numerous hand-me-downs from her sister, justified her purchase of a skirt:

> I went down . . . and bought a black skirt that I actually need . . . Do you think $10 much for a black silk skirt . . . with godets, plaits all, all braid . . . a little pattern enclosed [she drew a simple sketch]: I *need it so much* and could not begin to get material and have it made for that price.[16] (emphasis in original)

Likewise, Margorie Durand, who grew up in Montana during the 1920s, recalled that while her mother made the bulk of the family's wardrobe, she would order things from mail-order catalogs when the choices were cheaper or better than what her mother might make herself. Like Simons, Durand's mother sewed a great deal but recognized that it was a better use of time and money to buy the occasional item.[17] Still, other women may have had the skills and time but did not *want* to sew. For example, Florence Epstein recalled that her mother just "wasn't inclined to sew."[18]

In addition to time pressures, skills, financial calculations, and desire, whether not a woman sewed at home was also a factor of household power relations. In a family where a woman did not earn wages, whether to sew was often a question of a man's money versus a woman's time. Wendy Gamber points out that even though women were largely considered to be responsible for household consumption, they were spending "what their husbands frequently regarded as '*their* money.'"[19] Sewing was considered part of normal housework and many men could not or would not spend more in order to alleviate their partner's workload.[20] The "tipping point" at which women and their families decided to buy instead of make clothing depended on a range of factors including income level, whether a woman worked for wages, access to shops, amount of spare time, sewing skill, family dynamics, and personal taste.[21]

Judging by the proliferation of agricultural extension services, school sewing curricula, adult classes, pattern companies, and magazine articles and guidebooks, even into the 1920s, a substantial proportion of American women chose to sew. Many did so for practical reasons—a home seamstress could afford a higher quality fabric if she did the work herself or had little access to ready-made clothing—but sewing was also tightly bound to ideas of motherhood, community, domesticity, and femininity. The remainder of this chapter will examine why women sewed, while exploring the cultural resonance of the popularity of a traditional "feminine" skill.

ECONOMY

In 1901, the *New York Times* advertised a ready-made cotton percale dress for $4.88.[22] That style required about seven yards of fabric. With "fancy imported printed percale" costing about ten cents a yard, plus a five-cent pattern and some trimmings (all available from the Sears catalog), a homemade dress required less than a dollar's outlay.[23] A retrospective report by a national retailing organization recalled that "in 1910 the home dressmaker still ruled the average household for even in that period you could not buy a quality dress for less than about $30 retail while the home dressmaker could make one of equal quality for much less."[24] In 1927, a government-sponsored survey found that an overwhelming number of women who sewed did so because it was cheaper than buying ready-made clothing and nearly all of the respondents to another survey agreed that sewing was "an economy."[25]

If making a dress at home was an outright savings, it could also prove to be a better value over time. Many women argued that by sewing at home, they could afford higher quality fabrics and their garments would last longer than store-bought items. Jane Dunn, who grew up in New Jersey in the 1910s and '20s, recalled that "we all felt it was better to have one thing of high quality rather than more than one of cheap quality. By purchasing the good quality fabric and making it at home we achieved that goal."[26] Margorie Durand recalled wearing silk blouses made by her mother and said it would be a waste of time to sew clothing from inferior fabrics.[27]

In the early twentieth century, as it had been for long before then, home dress-making was usually more economical than purchasing clothing. Of course, this discounts the cost of a woman's time, but if you are not paid—or underpaid—for your time in other contexts, your time is cheap and therefore better spent than cash. Sewing to save money supported middle-class values of feminine thrift and provided a way for women to influence the household budget without earning a wage. [28] Women's magazines that offered fashion and sewing advice were quick to recognize that their mostly middle-class readers often sewed to stretch household budgets and editors portrayed economy as a virtue and not a sacrifice. If thrift was appreciated in middle-class households, it was a necessity for working-class women. They were the least able to afford dressmakers and the most likely to continue to sew once ready-mades were prevalent. For the average domestic worker earning $264 a year who read the 1902 Sears catalog, whether to order the dress or the fabric seemed a straightforward decision. [29]

Progressive-era social workers believed in this logic and often predicated their policies on the assumption that working-class women would sew much of their family's clothing. A survey published in 1920 determined that in order to maintain a "minimum standard of health and decency," a worker's wife would need to sew a significant proportion of clothing for herself and her hypothetical three children, including one apron, ten cotton dresses, one wool dress, and three cotton blouses a year. [30] Her husband's clothing would be primarily store-bought.

In fact, many working women did sew some or all of their clothing. A study by the National Consumer's League of working women in New York City, published in 1911 but undertaken two years earlier, sheds light on the difference it made for working women to be able to make at least some of their clothing. American-born Emily Clement, an unskilled envelope-machine operative earning $6 a week, made all of her clothes and some of her sister's. She was able to make a "stylishly cut and becoming" three-piece suit for $5.20, about half of what an inexpensive ready-made suit might cost. [31] Corset operative Katia Markelov earned $10 a week in good times but much less when the season was slack. She could afford to buy books and opera tickets by "making her own waists" as well as doing her own laundry. [32] A Mrs. Green, a widow who worked in a New York department store as a skilled corset fitter for the high salary of $12 a week, used her own skills to dress well at little expense. A National Consumer's League writer noted that "Mrs. Green seemed extravagantly dressed; she said, however, that she continued to have effective waists and hats by making and trimming them herself, and by purchasing materials with care at sales." [33]

As the example of Mrs. Green demonstrates, working women had to be re-sourceful in finding affordable material. Women on the Lower East Side bought bargains from peddlers or used remnants. Jewel Jimana Woods, an African

American woman supporting a disabled husband and five children in Colorado Springs in the 1920s, often received fabric from her daughter's teacher.[34] Many rural families bleached the cotton sacks that had contained animal feed or flour. By the 1940s, feed and flour companies produced the sacks with attractive patterns. Still, finding affordable sewing materials could be a challenge. A large-scale survey published by the Department of Agriculture in 1927 found that the lower the household income, the more trouble women had finding materials and patterns.[35]

Of course, if a woman's sewing skills were mediocre, all the patterns and materials in the world could still lead to frustration. Barbara Burman writes that "clothing which was known to be home-made was an ambivalent sign. Whilst it spoke of respectable thrift or neighbourly generosity, it was also an unwelcome badge of poverty."[36] A photograph from the 1910s demonstrates how observers could often discern whether clothing was home made. Her stripes do not line up; this is in part due to the folds at the waist, but it attracts attention. With no supporting context, it is not possible to judge this woman's economic status, but the photograph is testimony to the difficulties of producing a successful dress, despite the promises of the fashion pages.[37] Clothing that was obviously home made could be a source of embarrassment, as it was a clear sign of a family's economic status.

That said, many women could sew very well and were not at all self conscious about the results. In fact, much home made clothing was more attractive than what was available for sale. Marjorie Durand remembered her disappointment when she found it difficult to find dresses that fit as well as her mother's creations, and Edith Kurtz recalled a cousin who waited eagerly for her home-made hand-me-downs, which were nicer than her own mother could purchase.[38] Both women grew up in farm families and their mothers sewed out of necessity, but instead of feeling ashamed, they enjoyed their homemade clothing.

In any case, many families did not have a choice whether or not to sew. In her study of sharecroppers' wives in Texas, Rebecca Sharpless found that "numerous people recalled their mothers making virtually every stitch of the families' clothing, with the possible exception of men's dress shirts and the families' supplies of stiff denim overalls."[39] One woman in that study told the U.S. Senate Committee on Industrial Relations in 1914, "I never have got a dress readymade for myself in my life since I have been a married woman."[40] Edith Kurtz told me "I never had anything brand new." [41] Because of their economic vulnerability, black women were especially pressured to sew. Jewel Jimana Woods made the family's clothing while working full time.[42] For many women, therefore, the "choice" of whether to sew or buy was nonexistent. Clothing their families was an ongoing challenge that required significant time and effort.

MEETING STANDARDS

For many, sewing primarily served as a way to save money. Homemakers contributed to the family economy by substituting their time, effort, and skills for cash expenditures. Women who worked for wages could supplement their earnings by making their own clothing. But home seamstresses' motivations often went beyond the purely economic. Women who sewed for themselves and their families were also engaging in a process of performance, of self-representation. Home dressmaking was an important way to literally keep up appearances in the eyes of friends, neighbors, strangers and employers. As one historian put it, "Fashion was not simply about looking good. Fashion was about being good as well."[43] By making their clothing, women could try to meet community standards of fashionable and respectable appearances.

The thousands of female operatives who worked in clothing factories and sweatshops could rarely afford the garments they made. Instead, they used their skills, and often fabric remnants from the industry, to make their own clothing at night or during slow periods at work. A newspaper article described a woman's purchase of a piece of normally expensive lace for 50 cents, explaining that, "pieces of fine cloth, in sizes from half a yard to several yards, are often sold at low rates."[44] A different journalist described a young woman whose family was "in genuine poverty" but to his surprise dressed so stylishly that "one who did not know East Side girls would have said, uncharitably, that the heartless young woman was spending on clothes the money needed to buy bread for her old mother and small sisters," but the mystery was soon explained:

> The waist, thin and charmingly cool looking, she had made herself, buying the material from a Hester Street pushcart for 20 cents. Its "style" came from the really handsome neck arrangement, which she had made herself: she worked at neckwear, and the "boss" had allowed her to take the odds and ends from which she had fashioned the pretty thing. The skirt her brother-in-law, who "works at skirts," had made for her at odd times, and it cost, getting the material at wholesale, $2.50. Her hat her "chum" made at an expense of 60 cents. To the uninitiated the costume represented an outlay of $20, at least, although she had achieved it at an expense of $3.30, and was able to go abroad without proclaiming to the world the dire poverty at home. Her cleverness and the kindness of others had saved the proud old mother a severe humiliation.[45]

A working-class woman who could make high-quality garments (or who had the good fortune to be related to a skirt-maker) could pass, at least superficially, for middle-class, sparing herself and her family the embarrassment of being poorly dressed. Another example of the skills of working women is a photograph taken in New York around 1907, showing a group of women outside the building where they worked as milliners. As would be expected of professional hat-makers, their headwear is fantastic, and their clothing—matching skirts and jackets, worn with shirtwaists—is stylish as well. Dina Goldberg Gelowitz, who worked as a milliner in Boston in the early twentieth century, cared about fashion and made much of her clothing.[46] It is very likely that the women in the photograph also created their own outfits, especially because they were trained in the clothing trade.

The same art of self-presentation was important for the many women entering the growing "pink-collar" workforce at the turn of the century, but looking presentable could be expensive. In her study of department store saleswomen, Susan Porter Benson notes the "hidden cost" of being "impeccably dressed on the job."[47] She gives the example of the same Lucy Cleaver mentioned earlier who bought twenty-four poorly made shirtwaists at less than a dollar apiece for her job as a saleswoman. These would soon fall apart, but she could not pull together the additional 50 cents for better quality blouses. While a 1909 *New York Times* article urged the new "business girl" to go to "as good a tailor or dressmaker as she can afford," the reality was that women's office jobs paid only marginally more than skilled factory labor; for example, a female typist might earn $12 a week in 1911.[48] This gap had to be filled somehow and many women sewed in order to dress according to white-collar standards. Pattern makers and magazines advertised suit patterns from the turn of the century through the 1930s as appropriate for "business girls."[49] A *Ladies Home Journal* reader won a prize for her essay "How I Dressed on $100 a Year." The winner, who worked in New York City, made most of her clothes. She explained how she did the preliminary work at home and sewed the seams during visits to her parents, who owned a sewing machine.[50]

This struggle to dress appropriately was experienced acutely by African Americans. The sewing skills used on the job by women who worked as domestic servants and laundresses were employed at home not only for everyday use but also to counteract criticism and abuse.[51] Stephanie Shaw argues that African American families stressed the importance of decent dress, as they "hoped that extremely upright behavior would ward off dangerous attention and counteract the negative stereotypes of African Americans that were common throughout white America."[52] E. Azalia Hackley, an African American singer and activist, wrote *The Colored Girl Beautiful*, a booklet aimed at African American women desiring professional work. In it, she admonished readers that dress was part of "race pride," noting:

On the streets and as the street cars pass our homes, colored people should give the best pictures possible of themselves, if they can not of the houses in which they live. We are a poor people but we can be quiet, clean, becomingly and fittingly dressed. We must stifle the desire to be conspicuous unless it is to be conspicuous by quietness.[53]

Winifred Byrd | Read transcript Hackley suggested that her readers stick to classic designs and not follow the latest fashions, in part because "few colored women can afford to keep the pace of styles."[54] She did not write specifically of sewing, but her acknowledgement of practical as well as political decisions in dress was accurate; many African American women had to sew to make ends meet. Those who could not sew literally paid the consequences. Alice Owens Caufield and her sister, who lost their mother in 1912, strained their financial resources to buy inexpensive dresses until they had sewing classes in high school and were able to make their own clothes.[55] Jewel Jimana Woods made nearly all of her family's clothing in the 1910s and '20s, especially after her ailing husband could no longer work.[56] Woods, who was trained as a teacher but worked as a custodian, re-used tissue paper patterns (at 35 cents, they were considered expensive) and re-made second-hand clothing. In the eyes of her daughter, Winifred Byrd, Woods succeeded in dressing her family well. Byrd remembered the matching dresses her mother made for her and her sister and claimed that she never minded wearing home-made clothing as a child.[57] Byrd's memories may be shaped by time and affection, but they may also demonstrate how some children understood the financial realities their parents faced.

FARM CULTURE

While many middle-class women made a calculated decision whether to sew or not, and urban working women could buy cheap clothing if they could not manage to sew, women who lived in isolated areas, regardless of their economic status, had fewer options. Women and girls who lived on farms consistently sewed more than urban women. Rural women's sewing was based in part on traditional gender roles, which may have run deeper in less urban areas. Many rural women worked full-time on the farm itself and rarely went to work for wages. Perhaps their household labor was more immediately visible as work, but they also had less access to ready-made clothing, making their home dressmaking that much more vital to the family economy.

Rural women often had to plan ahead and buy material on rare visits to town. Mabel Price of Oliver County, North Dakota recalled:

When you went to town you planned for a week and went for two days. We stayed overnight because Mom's cousins were there. We went with a horse and buggy. If Papa was along, we took the wagon, otherwise we took the horse and buggy. We would walk the streets, and my folks got groceries and some clothes, stuff we needed, always had to have clothes.[58]

Price was a child in the 1900s and the situation was the same more than twenty years later. Edna Zimmerman, born around 1922, recalled that when her mother took a load of wheat into town after the harvest, "she'd buy herself material to sew dresses over the winter, and the groceries, like sugar and flour."[59] Margorie Durand recalled that there were few dresses available in Warden, Montana during the 1920s, and said that instead of buying clothing, all the local women sewed. Her mother made dresses, aprons, children's things, and household items such as towels.

Rural women were eager patrons of the mail-order houses. Montgomery Ward started its catalog in the 1870s and Sears, Roebuck debuted in 1893, but catalog shopping boomed after the implementation of Rural Free Delivery in 1896, when package delivery became financially sustainable.[60] Montgomery Ward, Sears, Roebuck and smaller companies sold fabric and other sewing supplies, including sewing machines, through the mail. Of course, shoppers missed the tactile quality of shopping for fabrics, but the catalogs accommodated customers by offering samples. For a penny, Sears, Roebuck shoppers could order as many swatches as they wanted—an especially helpful service given that the catalog images were black and white.[61] The major catalogs also carried ready-made clothing, the selection of which increased over the decades in proportion to its prevalence in stores. For women in isolated rural areas, these catalogs were one of the few ways they could obtain ready-made dresses or sewing materials.

Women who were raised in rural areas remember shopping from catalogs. Marion Goodman grew up during the late 1910s and early 1920s on a forest station where her father was the ranger. With the nearest town fifty miles away, Mrs. Goodman's mother had little choice but to sew. She would order all of her supplies from Montgomery Ward and her husband would travel to the post office in town once a week. Margaret Durand's mother was not nearly as isolated, but when she wanted something ready-made, such as men's overalls, she might order it from Sears, Roebuck and other catalogs when on sale.[62]

Another source of fabric for rural women was sacks in which flour and animal feed were packaged. Lu Ann Jones addresses the history of using sack material in her study of Southern farm women. She writes that women used sacks for clothing by the late nineteenth century, but it was during the 1920s that sack material became "an emblem of poverty, a testament to ingenuity, and a badge of pride."[63] Before companies started to make their bags with attractive prints, in approximately 1940, women worked hard to remove company logos. A woman from North Dakota recalled that her mother was good at bleaching the bags but thought "some people had Pillsbury, probably, on their seat."[64] Marion Goodman's mother bleached flour sacks, which Goodman used to make towels for her grandmother's Christmas gifts.[65] As Jones points out, however, "For a woman to have access to a lot of 'free' bags required a certain degree of affluence" since having many sacks meant you could afford a lot of flour or had a large flock of chickens.[66] Other women used bags that were directly linked to their hard work in the fields. Alice Caufield recalled how African American sharecroppers

> bleached the cotton sacks, what you put cotton in. They would bleach them and sleep on them. You know it comes about this wide [three feet] and they'd sew it up each side, so if you're going to make a sheet, you just unrip one side and hem the ends. And I know they have made sheets out of it and they have used it for tickings to fill pillows.[67]

There was an extensive infrastructure aimed at teaching rural women to sew. A series of federal acts, including the Hatch Act of 1887, organized federal funds for land-grant institutions. The original intent of creating land-grant colleges was to offer practical as well as more academic studies to the working class. The fact that home economics was regularly part of their curricula demonstrates how rural culture recognized the value of women's domestic labor.[68] The Smith-Lever Act of 1914 made these programs more accessible by creating cooperative extension services to provide education to rural populations. The text of the act stated that the federal government and the states would organize and fund "useful and practical information on subjects related to agriculture and home economics." Such initiatives suited Progressive ideas of professionalizing home work and improving family welfare through rationality and science. Women were included from the start. For example, one of the bill's namesakes, Senator Asbury Francis Lever of South Carolina, specified that lawmakers had not hitherto appreciated rural women's contributions and that this bill was a way to rectify that neglect.[69]

Course offerings at rural educational institutions reflected these pragmatic ideas. The Iowa State College of Agriculture and Mechanic Arts recommended that "if the student expects to live in the country, she may fit herself more fully for her life there by taking some agricultural subjects or by enrolling as a student for a combination course in home economics and agriculture."[70] Students could take a college-level course that required them to spend a third of their time studying "technical" subjects such as sewing and laundry. If they did not qualify for the college course, women could also take a two-year program in which

> ... much time is given to sewing and its related subjects. Students learn to draft patterns, to make garments and to dress appropriately at moderate cost. In the two years, each student makes a complete set of underwear, two cooking dresses, a shirt waist, a wool skirt, a lingerie waist, an unlined silk and a tailored linen dress. She also renovates and alters an old dress.[71]

The Alabama Polytechnic Institute, later renamed Auburn University, offered similar courses. The dressmaking classes were held in the agricultural building, a sign of how sewing was ingrained in rural culture. Photographs from the 1920s show students sewing at machines and modeling dresses they had made. Their dresses are stylish and fit well for the straight shapes of the 1920s.

Some of the students in these courses likely expected to use their skills to run a household, but many went on to become state-employed home demonstration agents. One photograph of Auburn students is in fact labeled "Students at API preparing for Home Demonstration Work by studying methods in teaching clothing and millinery." To provide the "useful and practical information" specified in the Smith-Lever Act, college-educated male and female extension agents worked with communities and families, providing instruction as well as social activities such as clubs and picnics. The agents sought to increase farm productivity and improve home life by teaching a range of skills, including how to remove stumps from fields, fight pests, raise chickens, pickle vegetables, improve nutrition, and make clothing. In Alabama, female agents were designated as "foods and nutrition" or "clothing" experts and designed their curricula at subject-matter conferences. Judging from their annual reports, the sewing goals were quite sophisticated, including creating fabric "permanent patterns" fitted to an individual that could be used again and again "to cut other dresses which can then be made up without fitting."[72]

The agents who taught sewing ran meetings at which women and girls helped each other make dresses. One agent described a whirlwind of a day:

> At one meeting I had 25 girls and they all wanted a pattern, all of them except two wanted the dress cut. Fortunately 4 ladies came to help me. By taking the older girls and giving them the directions for cutting the dress pattern from the individual measurements, then cutting the dress, I was able to cut 25 patterns and 22 dresses in 3 hours.[73]

Another agent described a "rally" featuring a fashion show exhibiting dresses and hats made by members of different clubs, and exhibits of extension service work included dressmaking.

While extension clubs were social events, the sewing education was more than entertainment. For the poorest families—often African American—help with making clothing made a real difference. The southern extension service was segregated and African American agents dealt with the effects of racism and poverty. One supervisor of African Americans reported:

> On account of financial depression, there was very little money handled by rural people who need the help of community workers. In some instances, while there was food, which had been raised on the farm, there was no money with which to buy the necessary winter clothing. In many instances the children were able to remain in school because the agent instructed the mother in collecting, ripping, dying and making over old garments.[74]

The training provided by the extension services led to noticeable changes. Agents' reports included improvements in sanitation, reductions in numbers of underweight children, and increased quantities of home-canned food—changes that affected the health and overall quality of life of rural families. One report that counted the dollar value of canned food revealed that like the financial savings of home sewing, canning was another way to squeeze more value out of home production. The agent reported that in 1923, women in Alabama preserved at least $258,233 worth of fruit, vegetables, and meats.[75] The act of promoting these skills and giving them an actual dollar amount reinforced the value—cultural as well as economic—of women's domestic work.

GOOD WIVES

Extension programs focused on the pragmatic advantages of sewing. However, home extension programs were more than practical—they were also ideological. In her study of home demonstration work in the south, Lynne Anderson Rieff argues that "agents continually urged women to improve and perfect housekeeping techniques rather than teaching them quick ways to perform household duties so they might engage in non-domestic activities."[76] In other words, the home demonstration agents' agenda was to focus on the value of domestic skills, not to train women to leave the home. But women already knew that sewing had deep connections to abstract ideas of what women should do. In addition to saving money, providing for a family, and meeting community standards of dress, sewing was tied up with ideas of class identity, domestic security, and feminine morality.

Among these more ideological understandings of sewing was its relation to being a good wife. While the definition of "good wife" changed according to the social ethos of the day, the ability to run a household has remained a central theme in American conceptions of family harmony. In the idealized (white, middle-class) Victorian family, the breadwinner husband made key decisions and was supported by his homemaker wife who considered sewing to be part of her duties. This ideology of "true womanhood" was echoed in domestic science courses in the early twentieth century.[77] The Garland School of Homemaking in Boston was devoted to this scheme. A course in ethics was also a study in gender and class ideology. Students were instructed that the father was to be the head of household, whereas the mother was its "heart." The same course taught that if a woman earned money, it diminished the dignity of the man in her household.[78]

In keeping with this theme, Garland students were taught to sew. They made decorative items like hemstitched tablecloths and garments as complicated as a fitted shirtwaist, even when someone of their social class could have purchased such things ready- or dressmaker-made. Sewing skills were assumed to be important, regardless of whether or for what purpose the student might use them. Garland students were taught that it was inappropriate for white, middle- and upper-class women to earn wages. They nevertheless learned forms of work that were acceptable for their class and laden with ideas about what a woman should be able to produce.

The education offered at the Garland School was, however, becoming obsolete. At least one Garland student (or her daughter) sarcastically called the school the "Garland School of Matrimonial Bliss."[79] New education and employment possibilities, together with lower birthrates, expanded views of a woman's role in the home. Women comprised 40 percent of college students in 1910 and nearly 50 percent by 1920.[80] Working-class women, both white and black, had fewer opportunities for education but took evening classes in topics like economics and literature through organizations such as the Women's Trade Union League or the YWCA. Those who took domestic science courses were encouraged to see homemaking as a profession, complete with scientific justifications for kitchen design and childrearing.[81]

Nancy Cott writes that during the 1920s, marriage came to be seen as "a specialized site for emotional intimacy, personal and sexual expression, and nurture among husband, wife, and a small number of children."[82] These changes affected how women—at least those in the middle class—perceived and performed household work. Instead of being seen as a woman's duty, or a way to enforce respectability, or rendered optional (for those who could afford it) by the growing ready-to-wear industry, sewing was portrayed less often as a useful form of household labor than as a way to nurture a family and encourage sexual attraction.

The Woman's Institute of Domestic Arts and Sciences, a correspondence school for sewing and cooking, reflected this changing understanding of a desirable home and marriage in its advertisements. One full-page ad in 1922 told the story of a subscriber who resuscitated her marriage by learning to sew. Before taking the course, she wore dowdy old dresses or "purchased some cheap, ill-fitting dress at the store." She and her husband argued about money, he no longer found her attractive, and their marriage was suffering, but help was on the way:

> One day I heard of a woman just like myself who had learned to make pretty, becoming clothes at home, through the Woman's Institute . . . I realized with startling clearness that here might be the solution to my own clothes problem—that if I could really learn to make my own clothes it would be easy to get the pretty things I had been needing so badly.

When the narrator wore her spiffy new outfits, her husband became attracted to her once more. She claimed, "I don't care what the poets say—no man is going to love a woman with the same old fervor of the sweetheart days unless she keeps herself attractive." [83]

Enterprises such as the Woman's Institute and the magazines in which it advertised recognized changes in women's lives. They could see that women, especially those in the middle class, had more access to education, family planning, and paid work. They also came under more pressure to look young, stylish, and sexually appealing, but most family finances were still controlled by men. The Woman's Institute therefore touched on insecurities and desires that emerged as demands on domesticity waned. Such advertisements appealed to readers for whom sewing was not a household fixture but a way to fulfill desires for less money.

CARING MOTHERS

Despite smaller families, or perhaps because of them, sewing was linked with motherhood. Maternalist ideology became more important as the material base for traditional behavior declined—when someone had the opportunity to buy a child's outfit, it became more meaningful to make it at home. This connection between caring for children and making at least some of their clothing persisted whether ready-made children's clothing was available or not. Poor women had little choice but to sew for their children, and wealthier women felt making baby clothes demonstrated their love and devotion. Schoolgirls of all backgrounds were taught to make doll clothes, and home economics textbooks argued that learning to sew was crucial to taking care of a family. One text defined household arts, including sewing, as "the scientific study of all matters and means which will contribute to the happiest, healthiest, and most efficient family life."[84] One how-to guide emphasized the link between sewing and motherhood:

> As a matter both of sentiment and economy, many mothers prefer to make baby's little things themselves. It is only natural that the interested expectant mother should be able to express much individuality and daintiness not present in little ready-made garments.[85]

Even as interest in sewing waned in the 1920s, women continued to sew for their children. In 1922, a small survey of married graduates of college home economics courses revealed that a high percentage of respondents made practically all of their children's clothing. The survey analysts acknowledged that theirs was a select group but hoped that the idea that college-educated women might be expected to sew less than those without access to higher education would be offset by their experience in home-economics courses. A "large majority" claimed to make "most of the clothes for all of the children, except the older boys." They admitted they "sewed for their children more than for themselves because 'children's clothes are easier to make' and 'can be made from used materials to advantage.'"[86]

However, some women felt they were better mothers if they spent their time earning a living or playing with their children rather than sewing for them. One woman wrote to the *New York Times* to explain that she bought clothing so that she could "find time to play with my baby once in a while, instead of frantically imploring, 'Oh, please, please go away until I finish stitching this sleeve.'"[87] A survey of 300 Georgia homemakers undertaken in the late 1920s indicated that ready-to-wear children's clothing was catching up with home-made: 65 percent of the respondents bought children's rompers and 55 percent bought little girls' dresses.[88] (Those same women made 83 percent of their children's coats. This apparent discrepancy might be explained, however, when we realize that women often cut down and remade an adult's coat for a child.) Pattern makers and publishers fought mothers' reluctance to sew by offering more appealing children's designs and declaring that "when a romper suit for a wee lad or lassie who is the pride of the household is the point in question, sewing most certainly cannot assume a foreboding nature."[89] This insistence on the superiority of homemade clothing assumed free time and implied that sewing was a pleasurable way to nurture children. In this light, sewing was not work but a gift of love.

These ideas about children's clothing held fast as many women who could afford to buy ready-made or have clothing made by a professional still chose to sew for their family. The Bureau of Home Economics survey revealed that women in the highest income bracket sometimes made *more* items for children than women in the lowest bracket.[90] After all, with the income to pay someone else to do the laundry, cooking, cleaning, and child care, wealthy women had plenty of time to sew if they cared to. In her letters to family and friends, Joanna Maria du Pont Dimmick often mentioned sewing for her young daughter. In a note to her sister-in-law, she discussed making underwear for the girl, and another letter indicates that the two women often exchanged sewing patterns for children's outfits. The two women were members of an affluent family and Dimmick does not mention making things for herself, yet both she and her sister-in-law were active in sewing for their children.[91] These women had little need to earn or save money, but they chose to undertake labor that had meaning for them as mothers.

Many women, of course, did not have the luxury of deciding to sew for their children; they simply could not afford any other options. Poor women with many children bore the largest burden. Sharpless acknowledges that among the many jobs of Texas farmers' wives, "keeping large, growing families of children clothed may have been the most difficult part of women's sewing duties."[92]

Whether or not a mother felt making an outfit for her child was a way to express her love, she was aware that others formed their opinions of a woman by looking at her children. Sometimes, this pressure came from outside institutions. Spelman College, for example, demanded adherence to a strict dress code until the 1920s with rules about acceptable colors, skirt widths and lengths, collar height, and decoration. The idea was to enforce a virtuous sobriety by requiring "simple, suitable, and healthful clothing," but the rules also served to announce the professionalism and respectability of the African American pupils.[93] Given the notion that African American women were sexually available, modesty in dress was paramount. Some students may have made their own clothing and other families bought school clothing at a store, but no doubt many mothers worked hard to make suitable outfits for their daughters, knowing that the results would be judged by teachers and administrators and would reflect upon their home.

The pressure to dress in a certain way could also come from within a family. Some Middletown girls threatened to leave school if they lacked the right outfits. One working-class mother told the Lynds, "Most of my time goes into sewing for my daughter. She's sixteen and I do want her to keep on until she graduates from high school and she wants to too, but she won't go unless she has what she considers proper clothes."[94] The definition of *proper* was a source of contention as the younger generation gravitated toward new styles and tested the boundaries of what their mothers considered acceptable. Other girls rejected their mothers' efforts altogether, believing that cheap store-bought clothing was superior to anything home-made.[95] Still, many petulant teenagers took advantage of their mothers' skills and vulnerabilities, aware that their mother's sewing was a tool for keeping up appearances.

HELPFUL NEIGHBORS AND CITIZENS

Making clothing for children, even when they could afford not to, was a way in which women used sewing to perform traditional gender roles. However, some people did not have children to sew for, or they wanted to extend the reach of their dressmaking. These women could sustain traditional ideas of femininity by sewing for charity. Individual women and women's aid societies made practical things like clothing, blankets, and diapers to give directly to others or fancier items like embroidered pillowcases to sell at fundraising fairs.

Women from the upper or middle classes had a history of belonging to social and philanthropic sewing groups. Frances Trollope, visiting the United States in the 1820s, recounted how wealthy women in Philadelphia formed a charitable sewing circle; they would sell articles at a fair and then donate the proceeds to a charity.[96] During the Civil War, women on both sides of the conflict made uniforms, bandages, and quilts for soldiers. This behavior persisted during the late nineteenth century; for example, in a note to her sister-in-law Dimmick mentioned that she had finished an "afghan" [sic] but that "the society has ordered another, so I will have enough work to last me some time."[97] The Cambridge Sewing Club in Cambridge, Massachusetts noted in its constitution that each member be responsible for at least one garment per year to be donated to the Cambridge Visiting Nurses Association.[98] In 1915, they amended the club's constitution to require "that each member be obliged to make during the year 1 woman's nightgown, 1 child's nightgown and as many diapers as possible."[99]

Charitable sewing began early. A home economics text asked readers, "Do you belong to a sewing club or society? Perhaps you can form a sewing club at your school or in your town as the girls of Pleasant Valley did." These fictional girls apparently "make garments for the little children who come during the summer to the Fresh Air Home near their town."[100] A novel about college girls included this kind of project: the young women sewed clothing for dolls that were then given to a settlement house. At one point, the characters talk about the work that went into the dolls:

"Well," sighed Georgie, "I'm hungry, but I suppose I might as well go in and dress that doll for the College Settlement Association. The show's to-night." "Mine's done," said Priscilla; "and Patty wouldn't take one. Did you see Bonnie Connaught sitting on the back seat in biology this morning, hemming her doll's petticoat straight through the lecture?" "Really!" laughed Patty. "It's a good thing Professor Hitchcock's nearsighted."[101]

Charitable sewing became militarized once again during the First World War. The Red Cross and other organizations oversaw the efforts of thousands of women who sewed and knit articles for soldiers. Ellen S.V. Motter's April 1918 letter to her daughter conveys the passion these women put into their war work:

> Last night was my surgical dressings class, & we meet two evenings now,—& are glad to do it—as the need is so great. My Unit work this week is to make pillow cases, & I'll have at another sweater, but how pitifully little that is when one longs so to do with all one's powers . . . [102]

Motter also wrote of making pajamas and of her frustration when the military stopped accepting bandages made by volunteers. Even children contributed to the war effort. Edith Kurtz, born in 1904, recalled knitting washcloths for soldiers while her mother and other local women made more complicated items.[103]

Charitable sewing, like many philanthropic efforts, came with its own ideas of class behavior and prerogative. The dolls in *Patty Goes to College* were sent to New York City settlement houses with the intent that "East Side mothers could use them as models for the clothing of their own children."[104] The fictional story reflects the idea held by many in the middle class that immigrant women needed help with sewing. In a study of Italian and Jewish immigrants, Kathie Friedman-Kasada cites a settlement sewing instructor's comments on the Italian women with whom she interacted:

> In the matter of clothing the women were equally ignorant and equally teachable. The mothers were sincere in protesting that they would be glad to make cheap, simple garments for themselves and their children if they only knew how. In these cases they were supplied with a pattern and enough material to for one garment and given one or more lessons in cutting, fitting and fashioning it.[105]

The settlement worker accepted the immigrant women's comments at face value because she assumed they would need help, but Friedman-Kasada argues that such assumptions failed to recognize that many immigrants already knew how to sew. She suggests instead that the immigrants understood the idea that the Americans perceived sewing to be part of American motherhood. They used the same language as the magazines and pattern advertisements—they wanted "cheap simple garments for themselves and their children"—to get free materials, free patterns, material, and assistance. In the end, both sides walked away with something they needed. Charity sewing was not only for the intended beneficiaries but also served to reinforce middle-class ideas of their social role.

CONCLUSION

Charlotte Louise Jewell Jencks studied at the Pratt Institute in Brooklyn and was certified to teach sewing and cooking as a home economics teacher. When Jencks ran her own household, she sometimes hired a young woman to do some housework. More than once, her helpers lacked sewing skills and were unable to do even basic mending.[106] Their families had been unable to teach them and they had not learned the skills in school, probably because they dropped out in order to work for a living.

To a woman like Jencks, who was invested in sewing both personally and professionally, not being able to sew was more than an inconvenience—it was a disgrace. For a woman of her generation and background, home sewing was an important feminine domain. It represented maternal responsibility, financial caution, feminine attractiveness, social connections, and household respectability. Sewing was in a sense a distillation of American ideas about what women should do with their time and for their families. However, there is more to this story. Sewing was work, but it was also fun. Sewing helped women to be thrifty wives, but it also gave them some control of household finances. It was a way to dress according to the rules and also a tool for making new rules. The following chapter will look at the many ways in which women and girls used sewing to confront ideas about how they should dress and act.

NOTES

1. Mrs. H.S., letter to the Editor, *Woman's Home Companion* (May 1934): 134.

2. Strasser, *Never Done*, 134. This would soon change: between 1890 and 1914, the value of factory-made women's clothing grew from $68,000,000 to almost a half a billion

dollars. Victor S. Clark, *History of Manufactures in the United States* (New York: McGraw-Hill Book Co., for Carnegie Institution of Washington, 1929, volume 2), 224. Another option may have been a used-clothing market. In her study of eighteenth-century French saleswomen, Jennifer Jones notes that there was a thriving market in secondhand clothing, and it is probable that such goods were popular in eighteenth- and nineteenth-century America as well. See Jones, "*Coquettes* and *Grisettes*: Women Buying and Selling in Ancien-Régime Paris," in Victoria de Grazia, ed., *The Sex of Things*, 25–53.

3. Robert S. Lynd and Helen Merrell Lynd, *Middletown: A Study in Contemporary American Culture* (New York: Harcourt, Brace and Co., 1929).

4. Edith Kurtz, interview by author, tape recording, Oberlin, Ohio, 25 May 2001.

5. For a fascinating look at dressmakers, see Wendy Gamber, *The Female Economy: The Millinery and Dressmaking Trades, 1860–1930* (Urbana: University of Illinois Press, 1997).

6. Gabrielle Josephine Crofton, Diary,1894, Crofton/Shubrick Papers, Hagley Library.

7. "Sewing at Home Decreases as 'Ready-Mades' Gain Favor - but Survey by Bureau of Home Economics Discloses Rural Women Still Ply the Needle," *New York Times*, 18 December 1927, sec. 10, p.10.

8. Lynd and Lynd, *Middletown*, 165.

9. Barbara Burman notes that the exact extent of home sewing is difficult to determine. For example, sales figures for fabric do not distinguish between fabric produced for home use versus industrial use, and consumer expenditure statistics list "clothing" as one category.

10. J.B. Leeds, *The Household Budget, With A Special Inquiry Into the Amount and Value of Household Work*, Ph.D. diss., Columbia University, 1917, quoted in Ruth O'Brien and Maude Campbell, *Present Trends in Home Sewing*, Miscellaneous Publication No. 4 (Washington, DC: United States Department of Agriculture, September 1927), 2.

11. F.E. Ward, *The Farm Woman's Problems*, Circular 148 (Washington, DC: United States Department of Agriculture, 1920), cited in O'Brien and Campbell, "Present Trends In Home Sewing," 2.

12. Mabel Hastie and Geraldine Gorton, "What Shall We Teach Regarding Clothing and Laundry Problems?" *Journal of Home Economics* 18 (March 1926): 127–133, 129. Hastie and Gorton sent their survey to 2,989 city families and 1,450 rural families in Delaware, Pennsylvania, Nebraska, New York, and Texas. They do not specify the response rate.

13. Lynd and Lynd, *Middletown*, 165. Women were classified according to their husbands' professions.

14. Katherine Cranor, "Homemade Versus Ready-Made Clothing," *Journal of Home Economics* 12 (May 1920): 230–233, 230 and O'Brien and Campbell, 13.

15. Sue Ainslie Clark and Edith Wyatt, *Making Both Ends Meet: The Income and Outlay of New York Working Girls* (New York: MacMillan Co., 1911), 7.

16. Constance W. Simons to Elise Simons du Pont, 18 May 1895, box 17, Francis Gurney du Pont Papers.

17. Marjorie Durand, interview with author, tape recording, telephone interview, 12 April 2001.

18. Florence Epstein, interview by author, tape recording, telephone interview, 2 May 2001.

19. Gamber, *The Female Economy*, 120, emphasis in original.

20. Elaine Abelson argues that middle-class women "had virtually no control over money. A woman's allowance or pocket money was generally a gift bestowed, not something to which she was entitled." See Abelson, *When Ladies Go A-Thieving: Middle-Class Shoplifters in the Victorian Department Store* (New York: Oxford University Press, 1989), 166. Abelson discusses an earlier period but many of the same issues would have persisted into the twentieth century.

21. Severa shows how during the late 1800s most people used a combination of homemade and mass-produced clothing. The shift to buying *many* items came during the 1910s and 1920s.

22. Scott Derks, ed. *The Value of a Dollar: Prices and Incomes in the United States, 1860–1989* (Lakeville, CT: Grey House Publishing, 1999), 59.

23. Sears, Roebuck & Co., *Catalog No. 111* (Chicago: Sears, Roebuck & Co., 1902), 869.

24. Tobe, "Women's Apparel," in *Twenty-Five Years of Retailing, 1911–1936* (New York: National Retail Dry Goods Association, 1936), 154.

25. O'Brien and Campbell, "Present Trends in Home Sewing," 9, and Clara Brown, "Open Forum: Are We Justified in Teaching Clothing Construction?" *Journal of Home Economics* 15 (February 1923): 88–90, 90

26. Note from Jane Dunn as follow-up to telephone interview, 4 May 2001.

27. Durand, interview.

28. Household guides urged thriftiness as an admirable trait. An early guide by Lydia Marie Child entitled *The American Frugal Housewife (Dedicated to those who are not ashamed of economy)* warned against profligacy in the household (Boston: Carter, Hendee, and Co., 1833, reprint by Applewood Books).

29. Derks, *The Value of a Dollar*, 53.

30. United States Department of Labor, Bureau of Labor Statistics, *Minimum Quantity Budget Necessary to Maintain a Worker's Family of Five at a Level of Health and Decency* (Washington DC: Government Printing Office, 1920), 20.

31. Sue Ainslie Clark and Edith Wyatt, *Making Both Ends Meet*, 88, and advertisement for Stern Brothers, *New York Times*, 8 December 1912, sec. 1, p. 14.

32. Clark and Wyatt, *Making Both Ends Meet*, 104.

33. Clark and Wyatt, *Making Both Ends Meet*, 18.

34. Winifred Byrd, interview by author, tape recording, Plainfield, New Jersey, 24 May 2001.

35. O'Brien and Campbell, *Present Trends in Home Sewing*, 10.

36. Burman, *The Culture of Sewing*, 37.

37. McBurney Family Photographs, 1873–1913, folder 4, Joseph Downs Collection of Manuscripts and Printed Ephemera, Winterthur Museum, Garden and Library. For more on studying clothing in photographs see Joan L. Severa, *Dressed for the*

Photographer: Ordinary Americans and Fashion, 1840–1900 (Kent, Ohio: The Kent State University Press, 1995). This dress would have been more successful if made with a solid color fabric or more subtle print.

38. Durand and Kurtz, interviews.

39. Rebecca Sharpless, *Fertile Ground, Narrow Choices: Women on Texas Cotton Farms, 1900–1940* (Chapel Hill, University of North Carolina Press, 1999), 98.

40. Beulah Steward, testimony, in U.S. Congress, *Report by the Commission on Industrial Relations*, 64th Cong., 1st sess., Senate Document 415 (1916) 9 and 10, p. 9041, quoted in Sharpless, *Fertile Ground, Narrow Choices*, 98.

41. Kurtz, interview.

42. Byrd, interview.

43. Joselit, *A Perfect Fit*, 5.

44. "Thursday in Hester Street," *New York Daily Tribune*, 15 September 1889, 7.

45. "East Side Fashions," *New York Tribune Illustrated Supplement*, 26 August 1900, 13. "Waist" is shorthand for a shirtwaist, or blouse. This young woman may have been particularly talented, but figures like Clara Lemlich often noted how garment workers made their own clothing on factory down time.

46. Jackie Day and Benjamin Gordon, personal correspondence with the author. Dina Goldberg Gelowitz was my paternal grandmother's half-sister.

47. Susan Porter Benson, *Counter Cultures: Saleswomen, Managers, and Customers in American Department Stores, 1890–1940* (Urbana, IL: University of Illinois Press, 1986), 194.

48. Mary Mortimer Maxwell, "How Should a Business Girl Dress?" *New York Times*, 28 February 1909, sec. 6, p. 9, and Derks, *The Value of a Dollar*, 98.

49. Mary Katherine Howard, "Tailor-Made Suits for Summer," *Women's Home Companion* (May 1900), 36 and "Nine to Five and Five to Nine, A *Companion*-Butterick Triad for the Business Girl," *Woman's Home Companion* (January 1937), 43.

50. Mary Haniman, "How I dressed on $100 a Year," *Ladies' Home Journal* (October 1911), 102, quoted in Connolly, "The Transformation of Home Sewing," 159. Connolly argues however that as standards of dress rose and ready-made clothing dropped in price in the 1920s, office workers were increasingly likely to buy their clothing, 281–2.

51. The nursemaid and ladies' maid courses offered to African American students at the Brooklyn YMCA included sewing. "Young Women's Christian Association of Brooklyn—Lexington Avenue Branch," *The Colored American Magazine* (February 1906): 99–101.

52. Stephanie J. Shaw, *What a Woman Ought to Be and to Do: Black Professional Women Workers During the Jim Crow Era* (Chicago: University of Chicago Press, 1996), 15.

53. E. Azalia Hackley, *The Colored Girl Beautiful* (Kansas City: The Burnton Publishing Company, 1916), 75.

54. Hackley, *The Colored Girl Beautiful*, 72.

55. Sharpless, *Fertile Ground, Narrow Choices*, 96.

56. Byrd, interview. Jewel Jimana Woods was Mrs. Byrd's mother.

57. Byrd, interview.

58. Sagness, *Clothes Lines, Party Lines, and Hemlines*, 32. The book lists Mrs. Price as being 90 years old; if she was 90 at time of publication, she would be recalling a childhood in the 1900s.

59. Sagness, *Clothes Lines, Party Lines, and Hemlines*, 25. Zimmerman would have been a child in the 1920s.

60. In *Dressed for the Photographer* Joan Severa argues that changing postal services and catalog shopping put many rural stores out of business, 454–55.

61. For example see the "Department of Colored Dress Goods" in the 1902 Sears, Roebuck *Catalog #111*, 830.

62. Durand, interview.

63. Lu Ann Jones, *Mama Learned Us To Work*, 172.

64. Arlene Sagness, ed., *Clothes Lines, Party Lines, and Hemlines* (Fargo: North Dakota Extension Homemakers Council, 1989), 79.

65. Marian Goodman, interview with author, tape recording, Wallingford, CT, May 9, 2001.

66. Jones, *Mama Learned Us to Work*, 174.

67. Sharpless, *Fertile Ground, Narrow Choices: Women on Texas Cotton Farms, 1900–1940* (Chapel Hill, University of North Carolina Press, 1999), 82. It is not clear whether sharecroppers had to purchase these bags.

68. National Association of State Universities and Land Grant Colleges, *The Land-Grant Tradition* (Washington, DC: NASULGC, 1995), unpaginated website, http://www.nasulgc.org/publications/land_grant/land.htm.

69. Lynne Anderson Rieff, "'Rousing the People of the Land': Home Demonstration Work in the Deep South, 1914–1950," Ph.D. Dissertation, Auburn University, 1995, 50.

70. "Education in Home Economics," *Official Publication of Iowa State College of Agriculture and Mechanic Arts* 16 (25 July 1917): 5.

71. "Education in Home Economics," 31.

72. "Report of Committee Work," circa 1923, 4. Alabama Cooperative Extension Service, Auburn University Archives.

73. Unpublished report, Alabama Polytechnic Institute, "Cooperative Extension Work in Agriculture and Home Economics, State of Alabama," 1923, 93. Alabama Cooperative Extension Service, Auburn University Archives.

74. State Home Demonstration Agent, 1921 Annual Report, Extension files, Auburn University Archives, 1, cited in Mary Amanda Waalkes, "Working in the Shadow of Racism and Poverty: Alabama's Black Home Demonstration Agents, 1915–1939," Ph.D. Dissertation, University of Colorado at Boulder,1998,1.

75. "Cooperative Extension Work in Agriculture and Home Economics, State of Alabama," 1923, 152. That figure was for thirty-one counties and did not include statistics from an additional four counties.

76. Lynne Anderson Rieff, "'Rousing the People of the Land'", 206–207.

77. The phrase "the cult of true womanhood" has become entrenched in women's and gender history; see Welter, "The Cult of True Womanhood, 1820–1860," *American Quarterly* 18 (1966): 151–174.

78. Elizabeth Chafee Gamble, Class Notes, ca. 1910, Elizabeth Chafee Gamble Papers, Schlesinger Library, Radcliffe Institute for Advanced Study.

79. See notes by Sheila Gamble Cook in Elizabeth Chafee Gamble Papers, folder 1, Schlesinger Library, Radcliffe Institute for Advanced Study.

80. Nancy F. Cott, *The Grounding of Modern Feminism* (New Haven: Yale University Press, 1987), 40.

81. For more on the professionalization of the home economics profession see Joan L. Sullivan, "In Pursuit of Legitimacy: Home Economists and the Hoover Apron in World War I," *Dress* 26 (1999): 31–46, 33.

82. Cott, *The Grounding of Modern Feminism*, 156.

83. Advertisement for The Woman's Institute of Domestic Arts and Sciences, *Woman's Home Companion*, January 1922,

84. Anna M. Cooley, *Domestic Art in Woman's Education (for the use of those studying the method of teaching domestic art and its place in the school curriculum)* (New York: Charles Scribners' Sons, 1911), 9.

85. *Home Sewing Helps: Ideas and Instructions That Make Possible the Development of Many Lovely Garments and Articles of Use in the Home* (Scranton, PA: Woman's Institute of Domestic Arts & Sciences, Inc., in association with the International Educational Publishing Company, 1925), 7.

86. Brown, "Open Forum," 89. The surveyors wrote to 200 women graduates of five schools. Approximately 67 women responded, of whom 85 percent of had children. Therefore, out of about 56 women, about 20 made all of their children's clothes.

87. Mrs. Freddie P. Hoose, "Women and Spare Time," letter to the editor, *New York Times*, 4 January 1928, 24. Hoose was reacting to a sarcastic article that questioned what women did with all the time they gained by buying clothing.

88. Cora M. Winchell, *Home Economics for Public School Administrators* (New York: Teacher's College, Columbia University Bureau of Publications, 1931), 133.

89. Awilda Fellows, "Rompers in Fascinating Variety," *Inspiration* (March 1923): 5.

90. O'Brien and Campbell, "Present Trends in Home Sewing," 7. For example, 35.3 percent of women in households earning less than $1,000 made children's rompers, compared to 36 percent of women in households with $5,000 or more.

91. Joanna Maria du Pont Dimmick (Minnie) to Elise Simons du Pont, n.d., box 14, Francis Gurney du Pont Papers, Hagley Museum and Library. The undated letter was marked "after 1880" by an archivist.

92. Sharpless, *Fertile Ground, Narrow Choices*, 99.

93. *Twelfth Annual Circular and Catalog of Spelman Seminary for Women and Girls*, 1892–93, 29–30, *Thirtieth Annual Circular of Spelman Seminary for Women and Girls*, 1910–1911, 14, and *Catalog of Spelman College*, 1929–30, 55, quoted in Shaw, *What a Woman Ought to Be and to Do*, 89.

94. Lynd and Lynd, *Middletown*, 163–4.

95. See Barbara Schreier, *Becoming American Women: Clothing and the Jewish Immigrant Experience, 1880–1920* (Chicago: Chicago Historical Society, 1994), 68.

96. Frances Trollope, *Domestic Manners of the Americans*, ed. Donald Smalley (New York: Vintage books, 1960), 281–82, cited in Susan Strasser, *Never Done: A History of American Housework* (New York: Pantheon Books, 1982), 133.

97. Joanna Maria du Pont Dimmick to Elise Simons Du Pont, 23 January "after 1880," box 14, Francis Gurney du Pont Papers.

98. Constance Hall to "Hatty," 1 January 1960, file 1, Cambridge Sewing Club Papers, Schlesinger Library, Radcliffe Institute for Advanced Study.

99. Records, *Cambridge Sewing Club Papers 1910-*, file 2 of 2, Radcliffe Institute for Advanced Study, Schlesinger Library.

100. Helen Kinne & Anna M. Cooley, *Clothing and Health: An Elementary Textbook of Home Making* (New York: The MacMillan Company, 1916), 4.

101. Jean Webster, *When Patty Went to College* (New York: Grosset & Dunlap, 1903), 50–51.

102. Ellen S.V. Motter to Margaret Motter, 11 April 1918, box 23, Margaret Motter Miller Papers, Winterthur Museum, Garden and Library.

103. Kurtz, interview . . .

104. Jean Webster, *When Patty Went to College*, 51.

105. Olivia Dunbar, "Teaching the Immigrant Woman," 1913, cited in Kathie Friedman-Kasada, *Memories of Migration: Gender, Ethnicity, and Work in the Lives of Jewish and Italian Women in New York, 1870–1924* (Albany: State University of New York Press: 1996),113.

106. Patricia Gordon, interview by author, tape recording, Wallingford, Connecticut, 9 May 2001. Charlotte Louise Jewell Jencks was her mother.

2. "BOUNDLESS POSSIBILITIES"

In 1922, a magazine article urged readers to order a pattern for a "popular, picturesque dress for the girl of sixteen." The dress could be made in a variety of fabrics, with different shaped collars, and with or without sleeves.[1] The article claimed this style had "boundless possibilities," a reference to the flexibility of the design but also a reflection of a particular understanding of home dressmaking at that time.

A sixteen-year-old might have sewn that particular dress for a range of reasons: she might not have had the cash to buy a more expensive ready-made dress, it might have assigned in her home economics class, she might have wanted to wear something unlike or similar to her friends' outfits, or she might have simply enjoyed sewing. Regardless of her specific motive, she was participating in a long tradition of women's home sewing that brought with it many practical and symbolic meanings. Although sewing could support traditional gender ideology, it did not always or automatically do so. Sewing is a skill upon which reasons and goals are imposed by the user. If some women used sewing to support conservative ideas about their domestic and social role, others wielded needle and thread to challenge such ideas. Moreover, one individual could pursue multiple agendas with one project. This chapter explores these challenges by women from a variety of ethnicities, regions, and socioeconomic positions.

For many women, sewing served as a creative outlet and a tool for self-definition. A teenager could make one dress as proof of an appropriately domestic education and another—using the same pattern—to shock her mother. Sewing could also provide a way for women to earn a living or at least make some supplemental money, a crucial skill in an economy that offered few options to women, especially those who were rural, poor, and not white. We have seen that sewing could be used to enforce class and ethnic hierarchies, but it was also a way to express ethnic and racial identity. Sewing also provided opportunities to enjoy other women's company, encouraged individual style and taste, and offered a source of pride. Home sewing thus moved beyond its functional role as housework to become a means of self-expression, independence, and pleasure. In many respects, it was a way to transform traditional roles and understandings of women's domestic labor.

MORE THAN PIN MONEY

The most common motivation behind home dressmaking was economy. Sewing at home was usually cheaper than buying ready-made clothing, even though most families bought as well as sewed their clothing in some combination. By making garments at home, a woman fulfilled certain expectations about her role in the family as nurturer and producer. Sewing was part of housework and satisfied notions of virtuous thrift.

The flip side of household thrift was the leverage women gained over household financial dynamics by sewing at home. Essentially, sewing was a subtle yet effective way to challenge traditional gender strictures regarding wages and household expenditures. As a way to *save* money, home dressmaking played a major economic role in a household. It fit in with raising chickens and selling eggs, saving money by canning homegrown vegetables, or bargaining with the grocer. Women who did not earn wages or who earned less than husbands, fathers, and sons were still economic agents in a household. Sewing skills gave women the ability to reduce cash expenditures whether they earned money themselves or not. Even the federal government was aware that sewing could affect domestic power relations, concluding a survey by noting:

> As long as the woman at home has no direct source of income and her chief duty is in caring for the home and its occupants, she will, no doubt, consider that making at least a part of the clothing for the family is a wise way of 'stretching' the family income.[2]

For many women, however, the benefits of sewing went beyond these practical concerns. Women who were not professional dressmakers could still earn some money sewing for others who did not have the time, skills, or resources to make their own clothes. Many women who did not work for wages on a regular basis were able to supplement their income by sewing for others. For example, as a member of a middle-class southern family in the late nineteenth century, there were few socially acceptable ways for Margaret Drummond to earn a living, but Drummond, who never married, depended on the income she received for cleaning, sewing, and quilting for friends and family.[3] Other women ran informal dressmaking businesses from their home: Beulah Steward made dresses for local customers during the 1910s until creditors seized her sewing machine and eliminated her income of up to $2 a day.[4]

The Woman's Institute published stories sent in by women suffering "financial reverses" who turned to sewing to earn extra money or support themselves entirely. Mrs. John Williams of Wilson, North Carolina, claimed to have supported her family by sewing for neighbors after her husband's business failed, and the widowed Agnes Gordon of Detroit maintained five children doing the same. If true, the testimonials are excellent examples of how women used sewing as an alternative or supplement to wage work. If invented as advertising, they show what the institute believed readers would find compelling. There was also a perky insistence that these skills were a route to independence—graduates never seemed to work for someone else or take in industrial work but instead sewed for neighbors or owned their own businesses. Such stories tacitly acknowledged that women could manage without a male breadwinner. Home sewing was still "work" but instead of unpaid drudgery, it was presented as a respectable and interesting way of earning a living. After all, the testimonials were in an article entitled "Women Served and Made Happier."[5]

This sort of informal business should be differentiated from piecework, for which women worked at home assembling garments for an industrial producer. As housework, home sewing was indeed part of the gender-specific domestic maintenance that Eileen Boris argues supported exploitative industrial homework.[6] Like piecework, an informal dressmaking business would probably provide a woman with a low and inconsistent income, but it could at least protect her from unscrupulous managers who were known to find nonexistent mistakes and deny a seamstress her pay. It was also an option in rural areas where there was no piecework to be found. While imperfect, a cottage sewing industry was a way for women to earn some money outside of formal wage work and it allowed mothers to be at home with children.

PLEASURE IN SEWING

The "boundless possibilities" associated with sewing go far beyond economics. Sewing could also challenge understandings of domestic labor by turning work into pleasure. Sewing was often a source of creativity, pride, and accomplishment. Because it was such a part of women's everyday lives, some may not have taken it seriously as a form of personal expression. Others simply saw it as a chore, but some were very aware of the pleasure they derived from sewing.

In her journals that also served as newsletters to friends, Lilla Bell Viles-Wyman often described the clothing she made for herself and her friend Lon. A young woman studying dance in New York in the 1890s who supported herself as a music teacher and performer, Viles-Wyman was aware of the skill and artistry that went into sewing:

Oh! Such a warm day! Dressmaking without—without anything I need—no patterns, no tape measure. Cut my skirt partly by guess & partly by measurement taken with a string of my black dress - cut the waist by the "guess" pattern that I made my practicing waist by - Lon thought it so pretty, concluded, without anything to go by, I better "guess again" by it.[7]

Viles-Wyman's dress was apparently a great success. A few entries later she wrote, "Monday night I wore my new gown . . . They all liked it very much . . ."[8] She received commissions as well. A subsequent entry reads "Lon is very much taken with my 'guess' patterns and tried on my waist, & Thursday I'm going to her house to cut her a blue percale by my pattern."[9]

An acute observer of fashion, Viles-Wyman commented on styles she admired in shop windows and operated on the assumption that her friends were also capable of replicating the commercial designs. Shirtwaists, for example, required very specific detail. She alerted her friend, "Lovely Lady! When you make your shirt waist to have it 'real swell' it must have yoke back & front 8211; a breast pocket & cuffs that turn back. I price them at Atkins $2.75–$3.50, $4 and $4.50 for cotton ones."[10] Years later, others did the same. Jane Dunn would go shopping with her mother and aunt. Her aunt would admire something in a store window and say, "I can make that!" Dunn's mother often had to sew for economic reasons, but she also took pride in her skills.[11]

Lilla Bell Viles-Wyman took pride in her ability to make desirable dresses for herself and others, taking the time to make sketches of her ideas and pin samples of fabrics into her journals. Several decades later, Ethel Whiting, a middle-class woman in California who sewed for her college-bound daughter during the 1920s expressed similar feelings:

"Fortunately sewing is my bent (if I have one)! People need to express themselves and sewing expresses *me* . . . It was fun to whiz along on my new (second hand) sewing machine from eight-thirty in the morning until five o'clock each day—with only a cracker and a glass of sherry for lunch."[12]

Whiting could have presumably bought at least some clothing, but she found pleasure in the process of choosing fabric and making the garments. She wrote about the fun of finding "wonderful remnants of the best material" and "putting my ingenuity to work."

This sense of pleasure and pride in sewing started early. Harriet Lange Hayne made a dress for her eighth grade graduation from P.S. 25 in Brooklyn in June 1920. The white cotton dress was quite stylish for its time and was made with tiny stitches and sophisticated seams. Decades later, Hayne donated the dress to a museum with the following note:

> The girls in my 8th Grade class were required to make their own graduation dresses. We had had a class in sewing and I remember learning the various stitches and how to turn a French seam. I recall buying the pattern and the material, cutting the fabric, and the many evenings spent sewing while I sat around the dining room table with my parents and brothers. I was fortunate to win the prize for the best made dress: a gold thimble.[13]

The dress was so important to Hayne that she recalled making it—and being rewarded for her work—when she was ninety-one.

Contests organized by magazines, state fairs, industry, and schools to promote sewing often placed a high value on creativity. Many competitions rewarded neat work such as Hayne's dress, but others went further and asked contestants to submit original designs for garments. The winners of the 1922 *Woman's Home Companion* contest for the best "Wearable Dress" won praise and saw their ideas made into commercial patterns and sold by the magazine. The first place winner was Miss Marion W. Bea of Brooklyn. Bea was commended for her design's "variety; its adaptability to changing styles; its economy; its simplicity of construction; and its becomingness." Contestants sent in "hundreds and hundreds of designs," many as sketches but also as miniature models and full-blown dresses. [14]

A few years later, the *New York Times* sponsored a nationwide contest for schoolgirls in 1928 and 15,000 girls submitted dresses. The girls could pick from nine basic designs and were judged according to standards suggested by the United States Department of Agriculture.[15] The U.S.D.A was concerned about dwindling interest in sewing by the late 1920s, but these contests served more than one purpose. In addition to promoting sales or domestic skills, sewing competitions encouraged and rewarded women and girls for their creativity and talent. The editors of the "Wearable Dress" contest noted, "It's a pity we couldn't show some of the other dresses, for they had, many of them, real originality" and they listed a number of "honorable mentions" in addition to the first- and second-place winners. True, it served the magazine to engage readers, but the fact that the editors valued creativity as well as straightforward sewing skills speaks volumes about sewing as a source of pleasure and pride.

It is easy to see how wealthy and middle-class women who did not need to sew for survival might see sewing as a hobby, but working-class women also sewed for pleasure. Rebecca Sharpless argues that for poor women, sewing was often one of the few ways they could bring some beauty into their lives. She writes, "Many women actually enjoyed sewing, to a point; it was an exercise in creativity, which they rarely had other opportunities to express."[16] For example, Mexican women in Texas enjoyed crocheting decorative pieces for their homes. One woman recalled, "Even poor women could buy thread at three cents a ball, and she and her relatives decorated plain sheets when they could not afford other goods, adding crocheted borders to their sheets because they had no bedspreads."[17] Recent immigrants also used their skills to make fabric valances and other decorations that could brighten a crowded tenement apartment.[18]

Some forms of needlework were more pleasurable than others. Marjorie Durand recalled her mother taking rare breaks from running a farm household to do "fancy work" such as crochet or tatting, noting that the household sewing "needed to be done" but fancywork was more relaxing.[19] Myrtle Calvert Dodd recalled how her mother quilted so much that the house was not always as clean as expected; sometimes when Dodd and her siblings came home their mother would ask them to finish the housework "because she'd be sewing or quilting."[20] Quilting could also have deep personal meaning. After her husband died, Jewel Jimana Woods made four quilts out of his suits and gave one to each child.[21] These forms of sewing were clearly an escape from everyday chores. By producing colorful quilts, tatted lace, or embroidered pillowcases, women could dress up their modest homes with objects that had personal meaning.[22]

Sewing and related arts were also a way for women to form a sense of community. The Jacob A. Riis Neighborhood Settlement offered numerous clubs for adults and children, including separate Mother's Clubs for Italian and Irish members.[23] At least part of the clubs' activities was to sew items that were sold in conjunction with the girls' sewing clubs. Florence Epstein's Italian neighbor, who made piecework buttonholes for a living, would help Epstein with her own buttonholes when she was a girl.[24]

Magazine writers encouraged community sewing. The *Delineator* counted 25,000 girls in its Jenny Wren Dressmaker's clubs by 1908.[25] The *Woman's Home Companion* urged readers to "pool your sewing to save money and lighten work" and offered a series of free leaflets on "The How-To's of Community Sew-ing."[26] Forming a "sewing cooperative" could save members money by buying materials in bulk and sharing patterns. It would also be fun: "Leaving out the delightful social possibilities," asked the author, "doesn't it seem efficient for each woman to concentrate on the part of the work that she best likes doing?"[27]

Overall, while the majority of women sewed in order to save money, many of them also enjoyed the process and its results. The authors of the Bureau of Home Economics survey admitted that they regretted not asking women whether they *liked* to sew. However, they noted, "This reason was volunteered by many women and indicates that not all are sewing entirely because of eco-nomic reasons."[28] Those anonymous respondents went out of their way to re-mind the survey takers that they took pleasure in what many viewed as a purely practical task.

"CLOTHES THAT ARE *MINE*"

By sewing their own clothing women could make choices and develop designs that suited their tastes, afford higher quality fabrics, and fit garments to indi-vidual bodies. This interest in individuality appears repeatedly in magazines, diaries, and interviews and was beautifully expressed by Rachel Middlebrook, a gleeful Women's Institute graduate, when she claimed sewing gave her "the ability to express my own personality in clothes that are *mine* and not to be duplicated."

Middlebrook's ebullience served the Women's Institute well. Institutions that depended on home dressmakers were eager to tout the pleasurable dimen-sions of sewing. Middlebrook raved about the confidence one could gain by learning to sew and claimed that after making a "One-Hour Dress" (which she admits took her a day), "I was ready for any attempt . . . At last I could declare, in awed happiness, 'I can make anything!'"[29] A fabric industry leader countered concerns that women were buying all of their clothes with two examples of women who enjoyed sewing. "Miss A." worked in a department store and said she sewed in part to have things that were "different." "Miss B.," a chemical engineer, told him, "I simply won't have anything just like some other person's and I will not pay the prices that one must pay to get fine materials in dresses of real individuality."[30]

While self-serving, this emphasis on creativity began before industries be-came concerned about their clientele's fading interest. From the start, the pattern industry was aware of the possibilities for variety and personal expression inherent in home dressmaking. Many patterns were designed to offer variety. For example, a simple blouse pattern would often come with extra pieces so that the consumer could choose a particular collar or sleeve detail that suited her needs and tastes. Patterns were advertised with these options. A typical Butterick pattern for a "Ladies' Shirt-Waist or Shirt" was "to be made with straight or turn-up cuffs and with a standing or turn-down collar."[31] The picture showed one version of the blouse, while a smaller image demonstrated another combination of collar and cuffs. In the 1890s, the fashion editor of the *Ladies' Home Companion* responded to a reader's letter by encouraging personal adaptations of commercial patterns:

> You make the mistake of most home dressmakers in thinking that you just follow patterns exactly. Designs are given from issue to issue to suggest. If the pattern calls for ten yards around the bottom and you have material enough for but six, merely reduce each breadth proportionately and cut the skirt to fit your materials.[32]

Magazines and pattern companies promoted interpretations of pattern designs. An article in a 1915 *Woman's Home Companion* entitled "Four Ways of Wearing One Skirt" showed four decidedly different outfits obtained using the same skirt pattern by varying details, fabric, and trim. Not only did the author acknowledge that such cleverness was a way to save money, she encouraged the idea that sewing was aesthetically satisfying, telling the reader to "select the development that pleases you."[33]

The emphasis on the creative joy of sewing only increased during the 1910s and 1920s as manufacturers and retailers realized they were fighting an uphill battle with ready-made clothing. Industries with an interest in home sewing stressed the fact that by making her own clothing at home and shunning what they portrayed as generic ready-made garments, a woman could dress with more individuality. Several magazines that promoted sewing also sold patterns and were therefore eager to see readers choose to sew. One article gushed about the freedom accorded by the latest styles of the twenties:

> You are permitted to do as you please. The styles we have with us this spring are an open solicitation. To go in for round necks and square necks, V and straight-across necks. And a hundred and one other variations in curves and angles, widths and breadths and dimensions generally.[34]

An internal Butterick document written in 1929 conceded, with some bitterness, that ready-to wear clothing had its appeal and associated it with another mass-produced product: "It has been made possible for the woman with a flapper figure to clothe herself quickly, conveniently, and inexpensively in a 'Ford' outfit." However, the writer was convinced that off-the-rack clothing would never satisfy a truly discerning customer, insisting that "if she desires something individual, something that has not been taken off of a rack, and acquired at a price which is probably known to her social intimates, she uses piece goods and a pattern."[35]

Edna Maine Spooner's wedding dress, made in 1916 according to a Butterick pattern, offers an excellent example of how women adapted commercial designs. The pattern envelope explained that the style could be made with a "Slightly Raised Waistline: consisting of a Waist, In High or Lower Round Neck, with Elbow or Shorter Sleeves: and an Attached Tucked Straight Skirt, with or without the shirrings." Spooner chose the high-neck option, but gave her dress wrist-length sleeves, decorated the skirt with ribbons instead of tucks, and included gathered sleeves, a satin sash, and a detachable train—none of which were suggested by Butterick. She used the pattern for guidance but was confident enough to branch out on her own to create the dress she wanted. That she saved the pattern along with the dress and a family member donated the dress, pattern, and photograph to a university collection is an indication of the pleasure and pride she took in making the dress herself.[36]

Personal taste and a sense of adventure in styling were popular reasons for sewing at home, but other women had more practical reasons for creating particular styles. If their body was different than the commercial norm—if they were, for example, petite, Rubensesque, tall, pregnant, or had physical limitations— many women found that sewing was the easiest way to suit their shape. Butterick's 1911 guidebook offered a chapter on "The Best Method of Altering Patterns" with directions for adapting the designs for women with "long or short waisted figures," "extra large or small bust," "round-shouldered or over-erect figures," etc.[37] Other advice warned that "commercial patterns are cut according to model measurements, but as very few women have model figures, the patterns require alteration to meet individual needs."[38] Since many ready-to-wear clothes were made according to those same "model measurements" (how little has changed!), they required work and possible expense to alter. Perhaps the reality of their body shapes drove nearly 65 percent of women in the Home Economics Bureau survey to claim they made clothing because "homemade garments more nearly met individual needs."[39]

MAKING OVER

Another way sewing could be used to serve individual needs was to renovate older garments. "Making over" clothing had a variety of connotations, ranging from simply changing details to taking a garment apart and using the fabric to make an entirely new item. This was not always a pleasurable activity and was often more work than making a new garment, but making something over was also a test of creative and technical skills that allowed women to re-use fabrics to their advantage. Women might update the trim or sleeves on a dress, re-cut a worn-out adult's coat for a child or use material from an out-of-date dress to fashion a new skirt.

Remodeling hand-me-downs was a common way for families to stretch a clothing budget, but this practice was hardly limited to the poorest house-holds. Nine out of ten letters to the long-running "What To Wear and How To Make It" column of the *Ladies' Home Journal* concerned such projects. [40] Dinah Sturgis, editor of the column during the 1880s and '90s, once instruc-ted a "Mother" in "Springfield" to cut up her silk dress to make a new waist. "Mother" was most likely from a relatively affluent family, since few working women would have a dress of such desirable fabric.[41] Blanche Ellis took fabric from an "old brown dress" and "made it into a petticoat." Another entry reads, "been making over my red dress."[42] Years later, a young Mount Holyoke stu-dent received a note from her mother asking, "Can you use, or would you like to have my velvet coat? Otherwise, since I have the fur one I thought I might have the coat made into a peplum waist for the velvet skirt."[43] Her mother could afford to pay someone to do the work, but she still wanted to re-use the valu-able velvet.

Making over garments was even more of a challenge than sewing from new materials. Marjorie Durand recalled that "to re-make things is extremely diffi-cult."[44] One sewing guidebook agreed:

> There is no doubt about the fact that it takes more brain power to produce a success-ful make-over than it does to make a lovely gown from sumptuous new material, for the pieces of material to be made over have certain set limits beyond which we may not go, while new material stretches out yard upon yard to lure the scissors.[45]

In making over a garment the home seamstress was limited in the amount, shape, condition, and type of fabric with which she had to work. One had to pick apart seams, press the pieces, and figure out how to combine odd shapes and different fabrics. An article describing the 1910 Paris fashions took into ac-count that many readers would be renovating older dresses and focused on styles that combined different textures so readers could make them out of remnants:

> Many of the new French frocks which I saw were indeed beautiful pictures, but they offered but little to the woman of average means, who wanted to study their good points with the idea of using them in renovating her own gowns . . . . The fetching little dress illustrated in picture 2 combines chiffon and serge in a most effective way. This dress also has many ideas which will be useful to the woman who is making over her last year's frock.[46]

A great deal of effort could be poured into a reworked garment, with disappointing results. Margaret Motter Miller received a letter from her mother describing a dress she'd worked on for her:

> Well, I got your parcel post box off yesterday, & hope it reaches you safely with its darned contents. Now that's literal as well as figurative, for I put such lots of sewing on those things, & yet it doesn't show a bit or seem in the least worth it. The blue silk is still an utter mess, & look out where you put on the old pink not to stick your blessed arms through those straps I've got across the front, & so tear it all out again.[47]

Others had more success with remodeling projects. Lilla Viles-Wyman commented, "I have an idea for making over duck skirts that have shrunk in the laundering" and updated her dresses to suit the latest fashions by changing details such as sleeves. She wrote, "I staid [sic] at home & shifted a ruffle on my white lawn dress waist. Last year it was a 'hip ruffle' this year it is 'transferred' into a bertha ruffle."[48] Edith Kurtz had an entire wardrobe of made-over garments when she went to college in the 1920s. Kurtz recalled of her mother "she was quite skillful at making things over to make me feel that they were something new and different."[49] Winifred Byrd recalled making herself a two-piece dress for her ninth-grade graduation. She knew that the other girls would be well dressed, but she could not afford anything new, so she used some turquoise taffeta from a donated dress and combined it with a black velvet top and remembered being very pleased with the result.[50]

CHALLENGING AND ASSERTING RESPECTABILITY

The freedom to make choices about how to make up a garment, renovate an old dress, or suit particular bodies went beyond creativity and practicality. This flexibility gave women a means of defining their own standards of modest or fashionable or appropriate dress. A description of an 1886 Butterick pattern noted that a woman could determine the dress's particular use by choosing the fabric and other details. It explained, "For evening and day wear the costume is equally handsome and appropriate, the materials and color selected for its development determining its suitability to any occasion."[51]

The understanding and implications of "suitable" clothing cannot be over-emphasized. When the Spelman dress code required that skirts not "be too short or too narrow, and necks to be high enough to avoid any appearance of immodesty," it was reiterating what the African American students already knew: the style of their garments was interpreted as a sign of their character.[52] Photographs from the late nineteenth century show Spelman students wearing those decades' *de rigueur* corseted, high-necked, long-sleeved, and bustled dresses.[53] The women pictured may not have made all of their clothes, but it is likely that they made at least some elements of their pictured outfits. By choosing factors such as collars, sleeves, skirt dimensions, and trim, home dressmakers took control of a small but important element of how they were perceived.

In the interest of sales and reputation, no commercial pattern company would suggest immodest styles, but there was a range of what people thought of as acceptable coverage at any time. In 1900, whether to make short or long sleeves or a high collar versus a lower one was a decision with real consequences. In 1908 some New York City schoolgirls were told they could no longer wear "waists with short sleeves."[54] A few years later, Margaret Motter Miller's father, a strict man in general, wrote to tell her how much he disapproved of lower necklines:

> Do you remember a girl by the name of Hoke, who was confirmed with your class, last Easter? She died on Thursday, I think on her way to school, of congestion of the lungs. I speak of it as a warning against the silly and dangerous fashion of having the neck and chest exposed as much in winter as in summer. [55]

Dr. Miller couched his concern in terms of health, but judging by his other letters, he most likely thought lower necklines to be immodest as well. He was surely horrified only a few years later when post-World War I fashions allowed for shorter hemlines and magazine articles claimed sleeves were entirely optional. People took details such as collar height or skirt length seriously, so the ability to choose costume details mattered.

The choice of fabric was also an issue. Softer fabrics would drape differently, revealing more of a woman's shape and movement than a stiffer weave. The "peek-a-boo" shirtwaists outlawed by Horace Mann High School in 1908 were most likely shocking because of their net or lace inserts; hardly revealing by today's standards, they still attracted enough attention to be banned by school authorities and noted in the *New York Times*.[56] By changing elements of a garment, women negotiated a degree of space within codes of dress and self-presentation.

MASKING—OR HIGHLIGHTING—ETHNIC AND CLASS DISTINCTIONS

Women adapted styles to fit their definition of modesty but also made decisions about their appearance that related to their social class. As demonstrated in the previous chapter, garment-industry operatives used their work skills to create attractive outfits, essentially masking their poverty. Photographs show that while they struggled to clothe themselves on low wages, many wage-earning women managed to dress well.

For some of these women, however, it was not enough to pass for someone who did not have to work hard for a living. Many wanted to stand out as fashionable dressers. A writer for the *Yiddishes Tageblatt* argued that not only were working women stylish, they were trendsetters:

> The very latest style of hat, or cloak, or gown, is just as likely to be worn on Grand Street as on Fifth Avenue. The great middle class does not put on the newest styles until they have been thoroughly exploited by Madam Millionaire of Fifth Avenue and Miss Operator of Essex Street.[57]

The versions worn by factory operators were surely made of cheaper material and most likely were too flashy for many middle-class observers. Kathy Peiss points out that many working women chose especially ornate fashions, sometimes displaying "aristocratic pretensions," although

> working women's identification with the rich seems to have been more playful and mediated than direct and calculated, as much as commentary on the rigors of working-class life as a plan for the future. Significantly, women did not imitate *haute couture* directly, but adapted and transformed such fashion in creating their own style.[58]

Nan Enstad writes of the same flamboyance that working women were challenging the dominant meaning of "ladyhood," creating their own distinctive style that implicitly denied that labor made them masculine, degraded, or alien."[59] Style was a way to assert that you deserved notice. Sixteen- year-old

Sadie Frowne, a garment worker, claimed that "a girl who does not dress well is stuck in a corner, even if she is pretty." [60] Plainly dressed Sara Smolinsky, the ambitious working-class protagonist of *Bread Givers*, is scolded by her sister who tells her, "You don't dress like a person."[61] Glamour and fashion helped women claim identity and importance in a society that viewed wage earning women as unfeminine.

These "flashy" young women were criticized by some in the middle class who believed a sober appearance was more in keeping with upward mobility. Indeed, when *Bread Givers'* Sara achieves her goal of attending college, she notices the "plain beautifulness" of the other students' clothing in comparison to the "cheap fancy style" of the Lower East Side.[62] What those observers missed, however, was that money and time spent on fashion was a response to a life of work and financial constraint. In an article explaining the shirtwaist strike of 1909, Clara Lemlich argued, "We're human, all of us girls, and we're young. We like new hats as well as any other young women. Why shouldn't we?"[63] The same sewing skills that allowed these women to earn a living, dress appropriately for their jobs, dress like an "American," or hide their family's economic troubles also gave them a tool to express their own sense of beauty and glamour.

While some women sewed in order to assert differences, others did so to demonstrate that they fit in. As demonstrated in the Spelman College example, African American women often sewed in order to conform to—or surpass—standards that the more affluent believed to be beyond their economic and moral capabilities. This was an uphill battle. For example, an 1899 article in the *New York Times* described a study by W. E. B. Du Bois of the living conditions of African American families. The study claimed, among many other things, that rural African Americans dressed poorly relative to their urban counterparts. It also noted that only a few rural households were in possession of sewing machines, and those machines "were not yet paid for." Du Bois was interested in documenting problems with the goal of "racial uplift," but the mainstream white press took his observations of poverty and included the line "Much Depravity is Found" in the headline.[64]

In this environment, dressing well was a political act. Textile scholar Patricia Hunt writes, "Adoption of current fashions in their dress was one way in which some African American women both asserted their affluence and assimilated into mainstream American society."[65] Kathleen Adams, a teacher who grew up in a middle-class household, recalled the fashionable Sunday morning scene on Atlanta's Auburn Avenue with the churchgoers dressed in quality fabrics and stylish designs.[66] Many photographs of African Americans show them wearing the same styles as touted in the women's magazines aimed at a middle-class white audience. In one image, Leah Pitts of Jones County, Georgia wears a shirtwaist and long skirt trimmed with ribbon; most likely she made both pieces as she enjoyed a reputation as a seamstress despite her blindness. Another photograph, taken at about the same time, shows the members of the Cairo, Georgia Mothers' Club sitting on a porch. The women are all dressed in stylish dresses or shirtwaists and skirts; as community-oriented clubwomen, they would have been heavily invested in dressing well. Home sewing helped these women match or even surpass white standards of propriety.

However, not all African Americans conformed to white fashions. Many made cloths with which to cover their hair in a distinct ethnic style. As Hunt explains, many African American women, out of economic necessity or choice, "participated in aesthetic and artistic expression that had nothing to do with following the latest fashion. Their artistry is particularly evident in their headcloths."[67] The kerchiefs were often made of bright and patterned fabric. A photograph of a woman from Thomas County, Georgia shows her wearing a paisley headcloth.[68] These kerchiefs were practical. They served the utilitarian purpose of keeping hair neat and protecting skin from the hot sun, they were less expensive than formal hats, and they could be worn during agricultural and domestic labor. In addition to their practical uses, headcloths were decorative links to African and slave practices. Making and wearing headcloths was a way for women to use sewing skills to accommodate practical needs while dressing according to their own style.

CONCLUSION

During the late nineteenth century, most women sewed out of necessity and custom, but as other options competed with home sewing, the reasons why women sewed became more complex. Family dynamics, free time, sewing skills, cultural priorities, rural isolation, and community pressures all affected who chose to sew clothing at home. First and foremost was economics: sewing was almost always cheaper than buying clothing. Yet home dressmaking was also a source of personal pride, a symbol of motherly love and wifely duty, and a way to have greater control over physical appearances. Sewing was a sea of contradictions and understandings of women's work and roles. The same skills that aimed to create an ideal housekeeper, wife, and mother also promised sexual attraction and artistic satisfaction, masked class difference, and allowed for personal interpretations of modesty and style.

As a form of labor that adapted easily to changing traditions, sewing was unlike much wage work. Women had a great deal of control over the process. Home dressmakers enjoyed a choice of materials, designs, and methods. To a certain extent, they could control the amount of time they spent on a particular job and when they did the work. They struggled to match varying degrees of skill to demanding styles, tastes, and outside pressure. However, many home dressmakers were rewarded for their efforts with significant cash savings, pleasure in the process itself, approbation from family and neighbors who associated sewing with appropriate domestic priorities, and a product that allowed a degree of self-expression. As the authors of the Bureau of Home Economics study noted:

> A fact which should not be overlooked is that many women admitted they sewed at home because they enjoyed it. One of the best avenues and often the only one which women have for expressing and developing their creative ability is in making their own clothing or that of their family. No doubt women of the future will continue to exercise this ability because they find it a joy and satisfaction.[69]

While understood as a staple of domestic labor, home sewing could also provide an outlet for personal tastes and pleasures. Moreover, it could serve as a tool for challenging some of the prejudices against women who were so often judged by their appearance. In this way, women could take a skill that for many represented limitation and hard work and make it a tool for expressing individuality and opening doors.

It took time and effort to sew well enough to use it as this kind of tool. Sewing was a lifetime skill that was often learned early and girls learned practical skills along with their accompanying cultural connotations. Girls were therefore taught not only how to sew, but why—and that "why" depended greatly upon who they were and the lives they would supposedly lead as adults. The following chapter will explore the multiple dimensions of sewing education and its cultural ramifications.

NOTES

1. "The Bouffant Frock, the popular, picturesque dress for the girl of sixteen," *Woman's Home Companion* (January 1923): 64.

2. O'Brien and Campbell, "Present Trends in Home Sewing," 15.

3. Laurel Horton, *Mary Black's Family Quilts: Memory and Meaning in Everyday Life* (Columbia: University of South Carolina Press, 2005), 88.

4. Sharpless, *Fertile Ground, Narrow Choices*, 98.

5. "Women Served and Made Happier," *Inspiration* (February 1926): 11.

6. Eileen Boris, *Home To Work: Motherhood and the Politics of Industrial Home-work in the United States* (Cambridge: Cambridge University Press, 1994), 2.

7. Lilla Bell Viles-Wyman, book three, 5 June 1893, Lilla Bell Viles-Wyman Diaries, Schlesinger Library, Radcliffe Institute for Advanced Study.

8. Viles-Wyman, book three, inside back cover, Lilla Bell Viles-Wyman Diaries.

9. Viles-Wyman, book three, 6 June 1993, Lilla Bell Viles-Wyman Diaries.

10. Viles-Wyman, "Fashion Supplement" at the end of unpaginated diary of 24 August-16 September 1893, Lilla Bell Viles-Wyman Diaries.

11. Dunn, interview.

12. "The Diary of Ethel Robertson Whiting," *Private Pages: Diaries of American Women 1830s-1970*, ed. Penelope Franklin (New York: Ballantine Books, 1986), 409–448, 424–5.

13. Harriet Lange Hayne, dress of cotton voile trimmed with lace and punched embroidery, 1920, and note on accession card, 91.214.1, gift of Harriet Lange Hayne, Costume and Textile Collection, Museum of the City of New York.

14. "Here are the Prize-Winners, The best designs from the Wearable Dress Contest - with *Companion* patterns," *Woman's Home Companion* (January 1922): 69.

15. "Prizes are Awarded to Girl Dressmakers," *New York Times*, 29 December 1928, 2.

16. Sharpless, *Fertile Ground, Narrow Choices*, 96.

17. Sharpless, *Fertile Ground, Narrow Choices*, 102.

18. See Lizbeth A. Cohen, "Embellishing a Life of Labor: An Interpretation of the Material Culture of American Working-Class Homes, 1885–1915," *Journal of American Culture* 3 (1980): 752–775. Middle-class observers often criticized these decorations, however, as unhygienic clutter.

19. Durand, interview.

20. Sharpless, *Fertile Ground, Narrow Choices*, 100.

21. Byrd, interview.

22. Quilting has been studied extensively. See for example Jonathan Holstein, *The Pieced Quilt: And American Design Tradition* (New York: Galahad, 1973), Patsy and Myron Orlofsky, *Quilts in America* (New York: McGraw-Hill, 1974), Roderick Kiracofe, *The American Quilt: A History of Cloth and Comfort* (New York: Clarkson Potter Publishers, 1993), and Laurel Horton, *Mary Black's Family Quilts: Memory and Meaning in Everyday Life* (Columbia: University of South Carolina Press, 2005). See also the publication *Uncoverings*, published by the American Quilt Society.

23. "Community Workers Report," December 1919, 1–2, box 15, folder 3, Jacob A. Riis Neighborhood Settlement Records, Manuscripts and Archives Division, Humanities and Social Sciences Library, New York Public Library.

24. Epstein, interview.

25. "How to Conduct Tableaux: Hints for a May Party for the Jenny Wren Club," *Delineator* (May 1908): 887–8. For more on the Jenny Wren clubs see Chapter Three.

26. Isabel De Nyse Conover, "Community Sewing," *Woman's Home Companion* (October 1923): 68.

27. Conover, "Community Sewing."

28. O'Brien and Campbell, "Present Trends in Home Sewing," 9.

29. Rachel Middlebrook, "A Fairy Tale's Practical Sequel," *Inspiration* (March 1926): 13.

30. "How Business Will Aid Yardage Sales, Director of Costume Group Cites Wide Interest in Home Sewing," *New York Times*, 25 December 1927, sec. 2 p. 14.

31. "Fashions for July, 1895," *Delineator* (July 1895): 35.

32. Dinah Sturgis, "The Letter-Box" section of "What To Wear and How to Make It," *Ladies' Home Companion*, (May 1895): 8–9, 9.

33. Grace Margaret Gould, "Four Ways of Wearing One Skirt," *Woman's Home Companion* (February 1915): 51.

34. Isabel De Nyse Conover, "To Pick and Choose From; waistlines up and waist lines down, skirts that are long and skirts abbreviated," *Woman's Home Companion* (March 1923): 59.

35. G.A. Ruppell, *The Story of Butterick*, unpublished typescript, Butterick Company Archives, 1929, sec. 3, p.19. "Piece goods" was a common term for fabric and trimmings.

36. Dress of cream silk, silk net and satin ribbon, 1916, University of Rhode Island Historic Textile and Costume Collection, gift of Edna Maine Spooner, and Butterick Pattern 8691 for a "Dress for Misses or Small Women," ca. 1916, Betty Williams Pattern Archive, University of Rhode Island Special Collections.

37. *The Dressmaker* (New York: Butterick Publishing Co., 1911), 65–67

38. Catherine Griebel, "The Permanent Pattern," *Rutgers University College of Agriculture Extension Service*, Extension Bulletin #58 (July 1926): 1.

39. O'Brien and Campbell, "Present Trends in Home Sewing," 9.

40. Dinah Sturgis, "What to Wear and How to Make It," *Ladies' Home Companion* (September 1893): 8–9.

41. Dinah Sturgis, "The Letter Box" section of "What To Wear and How To Make It," *Ladies' Home Companion* (October 1893): 8.

42. Blanche Ellis, Diary, 1889–1890, entries of 8 May and 3 January 1890.

43. Ellen S.V. Motter to Margaret Motter, 18 January 1918, folder 2, box 23, Margaret Motter Miller Papers. A peplum forms a small ruffle around the hips.

44. Durand, interview.

45. *Home Sewing Helps: Ideas and Instructions That Make Possible the Development of Many Lovely Garments and Articles of Use in the Home* (Scranton, PA: Woman's Institute of Domestic Arts & Sciences, Inc., through the International Educational Publishing Company, 1925), 20.

46. Grace Margaret Gould, "Gowns and Hats of the Smart French Girl," *Woman's Home Companion* (November 1910): 90.

47. Ellen S.V. Motter to Margaret Motter, 18 January 1918, folder 2, box 23, Margaret Motter Miller Papers.

48. Viles-Wyman, unpaginated "Fashion Supplement" at end of diary dated 24 August-16 September 1893 and diary entitled "The Log, An account of travel, adventure and Fashion," entry of 18 July 1893, Lilla Bell Viles-Wyman Diaries. A bertha was a wide, often ruffled collar.

49. Kurtz, interview.

50. Byrd, interview.

51. Description of Misses' Costume No. 1199, in "Seasonable Styles, Prevailing and Incoming Fashions," *Delineator*, November 1886, 313–350, 353.

52. Shaw, 89. Color was also an issue: Nan Enstad describes how working women often chose brighter hues and more combinations of colors than the more soberly attired middle-class, and that some dismayed reformers encouraged them to tone down their outfits for the sake of "ladylike" dressing.

53. Photographs of Spelman College students in Patricia K. Hunt, "Clothing as an Expression of History: The Dress of African American Women in Georgia, 1880–1915," *Georgia Historical Quarterly* 76 (Summer 1992): 458–471, 466–7.

54. "Horace Mann Girls Must Eschew Frills: Peek-a-Boo Waists, False Puffs, High Heels, and Jewelry Blacklisted," *New York Times*, 2 May 1908, 5.

55. Dr. Murray Galt Motter to Margaret Motter Miller, 12 December 1915, folder 1, box 23, Margaret Motter Miller Papers.

56. "Horace Mann Girls Must Eschew Frills."

57. "The Observer," *Yiddishes Tageblatt*, 13 January 1902, quoted in Enstad, *Ladies of Labor, Girls of Adventure*, 78.

58. Peiss, *Cheap Amusements*, 65.

59. Enstad, *Ladies of Labor, Girls of Adventure*, 78.

60. Peiss, *Cheap Amusements*, 64.

61. Anzia Yezierska, *Bread Givers* (New York: Persea Books, 2003, 3rd edition), 185.

62. Yezierska, *Bread Givers*, 212.

63. "Leader Tells Why 40,000 Girls Struck," *New York Evening Journal*, 26 November 1909, 3, quoted in Enstad, *Ladies of Labor, Girls of Adventure*, 146.

64. "Negro Life in the South; A Study of the Residents of the Georgia 'Black Belt.' Much Depravity is Found Whisky, Tobacco, and Snuff Used to Excess—The People in the Towns Better than in the Count." *New York Times*, 17 July 1899, 3.

65. Hunt, "Clothing as an Expression of History," 463–4.

66. Kathleen Adams, interview, cited in Tera W. Hunter, *To 'Joy My Freedom*, 153.

67. Hunt, "Clothing as an Expression of History," 464.

68. Hunt, "Clothing as an Expression of History," 465.

69. O'Brien and Campbell, "Present Trends in Home Sewing," 15.

3. "WHEN MOTHER LETS US SEW"

Girls, Sewing, and Femininity

The first line of a sewing textbook from the 1890s reads, "Girls: You have now become old enough to prepare for woman's duties; one of these is the art of sewing, which we will take up as simply as possible. By following the given instructions carefully, you will become able to dress your dolls, assist your mothers in mending, make garments, fancy articles, etc."[1] A decade later, a girls' sewing club near Boston made dolls' clothes to raise funds for charity.[2] The *Colored American Magazine* praised sewing classes for African American teens, and Jewish and Italian immigrant girls took sewing classes at a settlement house on the Lower East Side. There was a great deal of variety in both ideology and practice regarding girls' sewing education. Despite economic and social changes, however, girls from all backgrounds were encouraged to sew.

The specific reasons why girls were taught to sew and the settings in which that education took place depended on their social class, ethnicity or race, and geographical location. Girls, teenagers, and adult women of a variety of backgrounds often used sewing skills for different reasons. Most sewed chiefly in the home, but others worked in the garment industry as machine operators and piece workers, while others ran their own dressmaking establishments. But most girls would sew for themselves and their families at some point in their lives. Some educators, sensitive to or prejudiced by differences in race, class, and region, tailored their curricula to particular populations and their supposed futures. As a result, some girls received a very practical education in sewing, whereas others learned more decorative skills that may or may not have been applicable to their daily lives. Some were channeled into vocational training that prepared them for work in industry or domestic service while others learned to run a middle-class household. A close look at how girls were taught to sew can therefore act as a microscope for understanding the cultural meanings of home sewing.

In addition to looking closely at how class, region and race shaped girls' sewing, this chapter will address the relationship between girls' sewing and changing conceptions of gender during the late nineteenth and early twentieth centuries. *How, why,* and *what* were girls taught to sew at a time when growing numbers of American women worked outside the home and clothing was increasingly available for sale? Moreover, what could girls actually sew and how did they feel about it? As sewing skills became less crucial to running a household, they gained in symbolic importance as a means of teaching cultural and gender ideology. Sewing embodied a set of values such as discipline, creativity, thrift, and domesticity considered critical for preparing girls for adulthood. How did girls respond? Did they emulate their mothers? Did they resent the emphasis placed on domestic work? Did they enjoy sewing as a creative or social outlet? Altogether, how did girls respond to the cultural as well as the pragmatic dimensions of sewing?

LEARNING AT HOME

The obvious starting point for sewing education was the home. Most adult women already knew how to sew and they often taught their daughters basic skills. Mary Ellen Coleman Knapp, born in 1904 in St. Louis, was taught to sew by her mother and made doll clothes out of scraps from her mother's sewing projects.[3] Jane Dunn, who was born in 1913 and grew up in New Jersey, also learned to sew by making doll clothes at home. Mrs. Dunn recalled making simple dresses by folding over a piece of cloth, cutting a drawstring neck and armholes, and sewing one seam down the side.[4] Marion Goodman helped her mother by sewing on buttons and snaps.[5] It was much more unusual for a girl to learn to sew from her father. Florence Epstein's mother did not enjoy sewing, so her father, a Jewish immigrant from near Bialystock, taught her to use a treadle Singer machine in the early 1920s. Epstein shared memories of her father patiently pinning her skirt hems while she stood on the dining room table.[6]

Publishers understood that many girls were taught to sew at home and provided books and dolls for young girls. One appealing book for young girls, *Easy Steps in Sewing, For Big and Little Girls, or Mary Frances Among the Thimble People*, taught basic hand sewing techniques through a story about a lonely little girl who spent summers with her grandmother. [7] Much to her delight, Mary Frances finds that the tools in her grandmother's sewing basket are alive and teach her to sew for her doll. The book ingeniously contains miniature tissue-paper patterns for each project. In addition to teaching skills and inculcating a desire to sew, the "thimble people" taught lessons about proper attitude: Mary Frances is taught to work diligently, have patience, obey her grandmother, clean up after herself, and express maternal feelings for her doll as she dresses it.

Toy manufacturers also jumped on the sewing bandwagon. Bradley's Tru-Life Paper Dolls encouraged girls to design and make tiny dresses. The box contained three girl dolls, patterns, colored "fashion plates," cardboard "buttons," and paper "cloth" in several designs, including gingham check. The instructions claimed:

> [The dolls] provide a new and interesting means of industrial occupation embodied in the most pleasing pastime known to childhood. They teach the child how to make dresses in just the same manner as its own little dresses are made, and assist her to cultivate subconsciously a really educational discrimination in the selection of material, color schemes and styles. . . . Any child will find delight in producing, as the results of its own efforts, pretty dresses for her paper dolls—dresses made in the style she prefers, cut out to fit perfectly, and which look just like the product of a real dressmaker. The patterns are all miniature reproductions of modern styles, each being a facsimile in every detail of a present-day fashionable design.[8]

Paper dolls were hardly a new concept—children had been cutting out figures and outfits since paper became cheap enough to be "wasted." Now, however, this toy was considered educational, as a writer for the *Delineator* noted: "How many mothers, I wonder, realize the possibilities of the paper doll as a factor in home training. Very few, I imagine, and yet scarcely any other plaything can be made to interest through all the years of childhood and early youth." Like the Bradley doll set promoted a decade later, the author believed that paper dolls were a valuable means of teaching children real skills: "Children carried on [sic] in this kind of play cannot help but grow to be competent, artistic housekeepers."[9]

SCHOOLS, RACE, AND CLASS

Despite such endeavors, some girls did not learn to sew at home. Their mothers may have worked outside the home full time, may not have known how to sew themselves, or may have disliked sewing. Although Helen Schwimmer could sew by hand, her mother feared Helen would break the sewing machine and did not teach her to use it until she was fourteen.[10] Other children, such as Alice Owen Caufield and her sister, did not have a mother to teach them. For the Caufields and many other girls, public schools were a main site of sewing education.

In 1891, the Boston primary schools organized an exhibit which included aprons made in classes; the pamphlet describing the exhibit explained that schools taught sewing because, like reading and writing, it was "general preparation for the duties of life."[11] Sewing had been taught in the Boston school system since at least 1820. In 1835, the city's school board had resolved that young girls would learn sewing skills at least one hour each school day. In 1854, the board asserted that "no girl could be considered properly educated who could not sew." By the end of the nineteenth century, Boston schools were requiring girls to learn sewing for two hours a week in the fourth, fifth and sixth grades and in some situations, into high school.

The New York City public schools followed a similar pattern. In 1896, an exhibit compared the work of schoolchildren from New York, Philadelphia, Rochester, New Haven, and Baltimore with samples of work from European and Japanese schools. Charles Bulkley Hubble, president of the New York City board of education, declared at the exhibit's opening, "We have reached the point where we deem manual training, inclusive of sewing, as a most important factor in the school curriculum. The needle in the hands of a woman is like the plough in the hands of a man."[12] Hubble attributed what he saw as "the present movement in favor of teaching sewing in American public schools" to the group that organized the show, the New York Association of Sewing Schools; that such an organization even existed is evidence of the general attitude regarding children's sewing.[13]

The African American community also considered sewing education to be useful and necessary. African American women faced few job options, limited resources, and severe prejudice; sewing could offer them work skills and access to domestic respectability. Historian Stephanie Shaw argues that middle-class African American families often urged their daughters to learn to sew as an acceptable backup to other plans. According to Shaw, "Domestic ability, especially hatmaking, baking, and sewing, prepared these women to earn an income without leaving their homes if they were unable to obtain work in the professions."[14] Employment as an independent dressmaker was far much preferable to domestic service. Besides, argues Shaw, even if African American girls did not work outside the home as adults, homemaking skills helped reinforce their efforts on behalf of "racial uplift."

In a 1905 article in *The Colored American Magazine*, Margaret Murray Washington praised practical training and sewing in particular. She discussed African American students in "the secondary and higher schools of the race"—many of whom were enrolled in industrial training courses—and claimed that female graduates were in a position to uplift the race:

> If one should take the time to go into the homes of these women, whether single or married he would find a broadening of the family circle, tasty furnishings, order, cleanliness, softer and nicer manners of the younger children, a stricter idea of social duties and obligations in the home.[15]

In addition to helping women care for their families or to earn money sewing for paying customers, sewing skills were directly translatable into teaching careers, one of the more desirable of the narrow occupational options available to African American women at the time. Washington described one graduate who helped her family by teaching school and working as a dressmaker in the summers. She concluded by arguing that "teachers of the arts of dressmaking, millinery and weaving are in demand, and the time will come when our public schools will need women who can both think and act. These two things were never intended to be separated."[16]

Vocational training in sewing was offered to working-class girls of all racial and ethnic backgrounds. The thinking was that girls needed to learn to sew in an industrial or domestic service setting as well as in their own households. A journalist for the *New York Times* offered a third reason for teaching working-class girls to sew—a solid background in sewing would keep them from taking men's jobs:

> The accusation that women are invading masculine domain in seeking to earn a living cannot be lightly considered, for it is a patent fact that some of woman's own peculiar provinces are superficially treated, and in some instances quite neglected . . . Dressmaking should be just as much the part of a liberal education for a girl as manual training is for a boy . . . if a girl can't mend her dress neatly, she is not fit to take upon herself the care of her own children later in life. In these days of ephemeral fortunes, what young women is sure, though she marry a millionaire, that her circumstances will always allow her to pay for the sewing of a family?[17]

According to this writer, an education in sewing ensured that working-class girls would be fit to run a household and so would no longer threaten the job prospects of more deserving men.

Sewing instruction could thus reveal ingrained ideas about class and race. Different groups of girls were taught to sew in varying ways was because authorities—school boards, textbook publishers, contest organizers, etc.—felt that African American or working-class Jewish or Native American or rural girls needed to sew for different reasons. Such beliefs were not inherently a sign of racism or prejudice; they often reflected economic and social realities that shaped girls' lives. Many working-class immigrant girls did in fact need to earn a living, and rural girls would likely run a farm household. Still, these assumptions became problematic when they limited girls' options and used past experience and present reality to determine their futures.

I have already argued that many African Americans believed sewing was an important skill for women. As problematic as vocational training may have been, many African Americans sought to provide sewing lessons for their children, but the limited education available to most African Americans was echoed in the access to, and scope of, sewing training. Some children learned in someone else's home—a photograph of a woman surrounded by ten children and adolescents on a porch is captioned "Mrs. Louisa Maben and Her Sewing School."[18] This kind of arrangement may have been common, since a survey undertaken in 1923 found that

> courses in home making in the public schools for colored children are limited in number. In a few large cities home-economics courses are offered in the high schools, but expense of equipment and maintenance have usually barred it from the elementary schools and have limited its development in high schools.[19]

One African American institution that encouraged sewing education was the Hampton Institute. Opened in 1868 in Virginia, the Hampton Institute offered vocational and academic training to African Americans and Native Americans. Hampton also ran the Hampton Summer Normal, the first summer school for teachers from African American schools in the South who, according to an article in the *Colored American Magazine,* came to the program "for inspiration and help in this work of uplifting the race."[20] Like many articles in the same publication, the author praised vocational training. She wrote that the teachers recognized that most of their students would work as farmers, and, "always thinking how best to serve those for whom they labor, many rural teachers elected the course in sewing, so that they might introduce it in their schools."[21] A posed photograph of a dressmaking class at the Hampton Institute was part of a photography exhibit on the "contemporary life of the American

Negro" at the Paris Exposition of 1900.[22] The same exhibit included dramatic "before" and "after" images of squalid living conditions changed into tidy homes by virtue of a Hampton education. These posed photographs are problematic in their allegiance to vocational training to the exclusion of other social changes, but they offer a good sample of skills thought to be "uplifting."

At least some African American women who were taught sewing and other household tasks used these skills to earn a living and viewed their training as beneficial. Melnea Cass graduated from a Catholic boarding school for "underprivileged girls" (mostly Native American and African American) in 1914. In addition to a full academic course load, she and her classmates studied domestic science. Cass recalls:

> We had time when we did domestic work, when we learned how to keep the house and all that, because mostly colored girls at that time were hired out as domestics. So they taught us that too. So you really could do that, too, if you wanted to wait-the-table, cook. We had cooking classes. And all sorts of things that made you learn how to do things in a house, if you were going out to work in a house. It was very good, because most of us did go out and work in the house; we who couldn't go on to college, you know.[23]

Cass recognized that she and her classmates would need to earn a living and that the job opportunities available to them were severely limited. Not all African American girls had as broad an education as Cass, however. The idea that sewing was a way to provide uplift for African Americans and therefore a necessary subject in schools could backfire if practical skills took priority over more academic training. Moreover, the decision of white administrators and educators to emphasize practical training over academics reveals their bias toward African American as workers who should work for whites or as people inherently unable to provide for themselves.

Elizabeth Holt, a white home economist, was convinced that African American families needed domestic skills in order to improve their alleged unsavory habits. Instead of acknowledging chronic discrimination and violence as factors affecting African American homes, she wrote that "the original racial instincts of the negroes, and the poverty in which they have lived from the time that the support of the wealthy slave-owners was withdrawn, have caused the home life of the present-day negro to be utterly lacking in system, cleanliness, and comfort."[24] Holt, who wrote about the African American public schools in Georgia, claimed that sewing and other housekeeping classes were instrumental in improving living conditions, but she was also concerned about preparing African American children for the workforce, claiming that domestic training "may enable them to render efficient service in the lines of work that they must necessarily

follow in this section of the country under present conditions." [25] To someone like Holt, training in sewing, cooking, and laundry would make African
American girls better laundresses and domestic servants. This goal is made
clear when she explains that graduates of the "industrial program" will receive
certificates—and that "the names of those receiving the certificates are kept on
record, and so far as possible their future records as house-servants will be in-
quired into."[26] While Holt later concedes that "if on the other hand they do not
go into service, we propose to qualify them for keeping better homes of their
own," her emphasis is on using vocational training to create workers.

Holt was walking a fine line between condescension and pragmatism. Sewing skills were useful in African American homes, just as they were in white
homes. Indeed, given the economic differences, home sewing might have been
relatively *more* helpful to African American women. Besides, as Cass's experience demonstrates, because of the need for African American women to work,
many girls found such training helpful in finding a job. The problem was that
instead of complementing other schooling, sewing and other vocational training often took precedence over academic training. Holt claims that

> this industrial education is not being forced upon the negro. In fact it was first intro-
> duced into the white schools, and there the negro leaders in the educational life of
> the community, seeing the great advantage that it would be to their people, asked
> that they also might have it. In order to forestall any denial of their request by the
> Board of Education for financial reasons, they voluntarily offered to reduce the
> 'book-learning' of the schools in order to use some of the regular grade teachers in
> the new Industrial Department.[27]

At least some African American school administrators went along with the
plan, agreeing—at least in the article—with the idea that sewing and related
classes were beneficial for students. One principal is quoted as saying:

> Since sewing and cooking have been introduced into our school the teachers of the
> school, together with the friends, both white and colored, have remarked that the
> pupils are neater and cleaner in their personal appearance and more orderly in their
> conduct. A number of their employers have testified that they are more helpful to
> them now than they were before the work was introduced. The children themselves
> are so interested that they are willing to work before and after the regular school
> hours.[28]

In 1912, girls in African American grammar schools in Georgia spent about
five hours a week in cooking, four in sewing, and three in laundry. This is more
time devoted to such training than other comparable school systems allowed in

their schedules. According to the same article, many of these schools only went through the seventh grade. While sewing and housekeeping lessons were surely very handy in the home, opened doors for employment, and offered girls and women means for personal expression, was it worth slighting other subjects? Did African American girls learn sewing at the expense of other skills that could have provided more chances for social and economic mobility?

Native American girls were also offered sewing education, but with a very different agenda. Girls at government-run boarding schools were trained to sew, often with the presumption that they would return to reservations and that their training would help them run a "proper household" and care for others who had not been "Americanized." Government-run boarding schools for Indian children have come under intense criticism. The schools forced children to wear Western clothing and speak English and discouraged the practice of Native religions. Overall, they distanced students from their own cultures.[29] While some children were sent to schools by their parents, one Puyallup woman told an interviewer, "Five generations of Puyallup children were rounded up and taken off to government schools."[30] The schools used domestic training for girls—cooking, laundry, and cleaning as well as sewing—ostensibly to educate and train children for work and some schools did place students in domestic service jobs. However, these skills were also a way to imbue children with Western culture, and at least one scholar argues that domestic education for Indian girls was proof of an "underlying federal agenda" intended to indoctrinate "Indian girls in subservience and submission to authority."[31]

Like schools teaching white or African American girls, one reason the schools taught sewing to Native American girls was to improve home life. In the Native American context, this often took the form of encouraging the abandonment of traditional habits. Reformers intent on changing Native American communities argued that girls who were trained to keep a home in the Anglo-American style would "make their homes better, and more permanent, besides preventing much gadding about and gossip, by keeping young mothers at home and industrially employed." Jane Simonsen, in her study of attempts to "domesticate" Native American women, writes that "implicit in this condemnation of gossip and transience is the suggestion that isolating women in their homes would keep them from speaking out in tribal councils, preserving rituals and stories, and maintaining kinship ties."[32]

So, while the African American girls were taught to sew at least in part so they could work as domestic servants, Native American girls were specifically sent home as acculturating agents. This plan was clear in a booklet published by the Office of Indian Affairs in 1911. Entitled *Some Things that Girls Should Know How to Do, and Hence Should Learn How to Do When in School*, the booklet explained that

the pupil will not go out to work but will return home after finishing the day or res-
ervation boarding school course. It would be well to give actual practice in the
homes of some of the people with the assistance of the field matron. There are many
old and helpless Indians on reservations who would not resent being assisted in this
way. The girl would receive actual experience under difficulties which confront the
average Indian and which distress the educated student upon his return from a different mode of life in the boarding school.[33]

It is not the content—the lesson plans and class projects are the same as in
texts that assume a middle-class, white student 8211; but the context of sewing
instruction for Native girls that is specific to this Americanization agenda. An
Office of Indian Affairs lesson plan noted that the instructor should teach students how to use a modern stove by emphasizing its "advantage over [a] fire of
sticks."[34] The same booklet said that before teaching students how to make or
choose home furnishings, she should investigate "home conditions" and "tact-
fully suggest improvements."[35] In sewing classes, girls were taught to make Western
clothing such as shirtwaists and aprons. The extensive sewing curricula outlined
in the Office of Indian Affairs publications, therefore, can be read either as a
well-intentioned educational program or as a means of coerced acculturation.

Segregated school systems facilitated the process of teaching sewing to African American and Native American girls with a distinct economic and social
agenda. While it is harder to find evidence that working-class girls of European
ethnicities were treated differently, sewing courses aimed at training future
workers can provide some insight into whether, and how, working-class white
girls were taught differently than their middle-class counterparts.

Some public schools implemented vocational programs in the late nineteenth century as a response to a perceived decline in family cohesion and virtue.
One scholar of urban education notes that administrators questioned whether
poor mothers, especially immigrants, "knew or were concerned about inculcating the principles of moral family building in their daughters."[36] Middle-class
school officials believed providing for a family was women's primary duty and
administrators in industrial cities were clear in their belief that sewing lessons
would help ameliorate social conditions. Young factory operatives in Fall River,
Massachusetts, were among the first to have sewing classes in 1875 because
they had no time to learn such skills at home. The New Bedford superintendent
of schools argued that it was the lack of sewing skills that caused what he saw to
be the "unthrift and ragged shiftlessness of many homes."[37] Sewing lessons for
working-class girls therefore went beyond basic skills to become a means of
improving homes and characters.

Special courses for working-class girls were sometimes noted in the press. In
1896, a *New York Times* article claimed "How to Make Dresses Inadequately

Taught in New York" and argued that such a condition kept "many women from learning a woman's work."[38] The author asserted that this lack of gender-appropriate training meant that women were invading the male sphere of work:

> Thousands of young women, on leaving school, rush to office, workshop, typewriting and factory work, who cannot sew a button properly, much less mend decently, and very much less make a garment, though they might have to dress in rags because they did not know how to do these things.[39]

The author hardly distinguishes between industrial and home sewing, at one point implying that at the very least, sewing in an industrial setting is more appropriate for women than for men. He (or possibly she) claimed to have "investigated the possibility of securing instruction for young women who wish to give up factory and shop work for the more homelike occupation of making clothes" and that this switch was justified because "the amount saved in the dressmaking bills of a family more than makes up for the amount earned by one of this class."[40] He proposed a publicly-funded dressmaking school that would attract girls who were turned off by the prospect of the poorly paid drudgery of apprenticeship yet could not afford the classes offered at the Y.W.C.A. and elsewhere. His logic was flawed 8211; he assumed a school setting was preferable to an apprenticeship and he did not account for the family that already sewed its own clothing and still needed the daughter or wife's income. The implication, however, was that "the intermediate and very poor classes" required dressmaking education to earn an income and to provide clothing for themselves and their families and that with proper and inexpensive training, they would be able to do so without threatening the livelihoods of men.

Such a school was created about sixteen years later when the Manhattan Trade School for Girls was formed for "the girl pupils of the public schools, who are not able to stay in school after they are fourteen because they are obliged to earn their own living." The students were "taught not only how to make attractive garments for themselves, but a trade by which they can support themselves" through a year-long course in millinery, dressmaking, or machine operation.[41] The timing of the course was planned so that after graduation in July, the girls would have some vacation time before the garment season began in the fall.

Students at the Manhattan Trade School for Girls bought their own materials and made garments for themselves, which provided incentive as well as hands-on training. Girls in the machine operating class could make as many garments as possible in the time allowed, thereby training them for the speed (and speed-ups) of the factory setting. The dressmaking students, on the other hand, were taught to make fewer but finer quality items. The school was racially integrated and the article took pains to note that "a young colored girl was working yesterday on a deep rose-colored frock and one of the prettiest pieces of underwear in the better-class underwear department was made by another colored girl."[42]

Two years later, another school was planned, this time by the garment industry itself. Apparently, the lack of sufficiently trained operatives was threatening the future of the trade and so with the cooperation of the mayor, the Dress and Waist Manufacturers' Association intended to form an institution to train workers. Whether this plan worked is unclear, but the demand for such institutions sheds light on at least two things: first, sewing instruction in most New York City schools was *not* oriented toward a professional or industrial setting and second, specialized sewing instruction was in the interest of employers and at least some students.

Vocational training is a fascinating way to understand race and class politics as experienced by girls, but not all schools were oriented toward wage work. Most schools, in fact, provided a more general, home-oriented curriculum, in which home economics teachers emphasized girls' future domestic needs in their teaching. Moreover, girls who went on to work in the sewing industries would also need to use their skills at home. One textbook writer, who was also the director of sewing in the New York public school system, recognized the tension between training for homemaking and for wage earning. In the end, she felt that the general curriculum should prioritize domestic issues. In the introduction to a basic sewing textbook, she explained:

> In the last few years trade and vocational schools have been established where the courses in domestic art received in the elementary schools may be supplemented by a training which will fit the girl to be a successful wage-earner, and consequently elevate her above the body of unskilled workers.
>
> The most important factor, however, in our public-school work is the training for efficiency in the family and in home life. Lessons are taught in domestic economy which will enable the pupils in later life to solve the question of wise and judicious expenditure.[43]

Focusing on skills for home use hardly eliminated class concerns. Some teachers were very aware of the economic background of their students and at times worked to accommodate the girls' particular needs. In the late 1920s, a home economist published an article in the *Journal of Home Economics* describing the layette project she directed in her junior high class. She explained that the girls, from a poor community in Denver, often had partial or complete responsibility for younger children in their homes. She therefore sought to teach them a range of skills. The girls made a layette set and learned about feeding, bathing, and other elements of baby care. As part of the project, the girls raised money with bake sales, learned to comparison shop, and did research on childcare. In the end, Wilson claimed that

> as a result of this project the girls' purpose in making the layette . . . some needy family helped them to learn many things concerning child care. They obtained an elementary knowledge of the clothing, care, feeding of babies and learned where information on child care may be obtained. . . . they used skills they had acquired in clothing and food work and obtained in addition to knowledge of how to care for a baby. There was much more interest in making the garments and book because an atmosphere of helpfulness for others was created. Some of the ideals and attitudes the girls developed were: the spirit of helpfulness, unselfishness, industry, and cooperation. [44]

In this classroom, the goal was to teach working-class girls to apply their sewing skills to their immediate and presumed future family duties.

Another teacher described a survey she undertook of her students in 1928. The subjects were "working girls" at the Milwaukee Vocational School, aged fourteen to eighteen, who lived at home and went to school part time. She helped them realize that on average, they spent a full half of their own earnings on clothing and she taught them how to make a budget. Eighty percent of the girls reported that they sewed at least part of their own wardrobes, so the assumption was that they already knew at least the basics.[45] In the Milwaukee class, the focus was on making a budget, not on learning how to sew, but the message that sewing one's clothing was usually cheaper than buying was evident. Moreover, when the girls realized that clothing costs used up such a large portion of their earnings they were driven to ask such questions as "What would I do if I were living away from home?" and "How could I meet other expenses when my clothing bill alone exceeds my pay check?"[46] The author noted with approval that "girls apparently avoid the habit of charging or buying on the installment plan," at least when they shopped with their mothers, as 87 percent said they did. The teacher was obviously aware that attention to the cost of homemade versus store bought clothing and wariness of credit are issues that most working-class girls would continue to face as they got older. In these two cases, the particular needs of working-class girls were addressed in their home economics classrooms without condescension.

While these educators were aware of the particular needs of their students, most home economics textbooks assumed a white, middle-class student who would marry, have children, and keep house. One article opened with the reminder that "90 per cent of our girls will be in their own homes within a few years" and asked "what shall we teach them that will aid them the most when these tasks fall upon their unaccustomed shoulders?"[47] In their discussion of finances, text authors incorporated sewing into the larger context of a woman's role as nurturer, budget director, consumer, and producer. Some authors addressed the potential for earning a living through sewing, either independently or in an industrial setting, but they were more likely to focus on how home sewing squeezed more money from family budgets. One textbook told readers, "Girls must begin to learn how to spend wisely, for they will very soon have the responsibility of being spenders. If you make some of your clothing, you will help to reduce the cost."[48]

Sewing textbooks focused on a standard series of stitches, suggesting projects that became increasingly more sophisticated. Girls were taught to recognize different types of fabric, to assemble and care for sewing tools, to sew simple seams, mend and darn, and to make buttonholes and tricky details like gussets. Some books taught pattern making or how to use commercial patterns, and some assumed that girls would use sewing machines in school or at home.

In addition to their technical content, many of these texts reflected the same values that drove schools to teach sewing in the first place: the authors felt that girls *ought* to sew. The books are clear that sewing was a woman's duty and girls would need to know such skills when they ran a household. Sewing courses and textbooks also contained more subtle details that informed girls' understanding of their role as girls and women in American culture. Books emphasized the need to be neat, organized, and tidy. They often had girls make doll clothes as practice garments, reinforcing the idea that their central role was as mothers and nurturers. Girls made towels and curtains not only because they were simple projects but also because they were a way to learn how to establish a reputable household. Girls were assumed to have a natural desire to be fashionable or stylish and a need to appear "respectable."

The attitudes prevalent in the textbooks also changed with the times. Books from the 1890s and early 1900s tended to emphasize women's roles in the household. One book from 1908, which may have been intended for home or school use, sympathized that little girl mothers have almost as much trouble as grown-up mothers about their children's clothes" and promised to "show you how to have your dollies beautifully dressed without troubling big people or costing much money." [49] A text published in 1911 urged that students should be set to work making practical items as soon as possible, since "these girls are to become home-makers. They can not be overtrained in the subject in so short a time."[50]

By the 1910s, authors began to expound on Progressive-era ideas of bringing science and hygiene into the home. For example, a book published in 1916 entitled *Clothing and Health: An Elementary Textbook of Home Making* is revealing. The authors, well-established home economists, explain that clothing was related to health and well-being and therefore the domain of the woman of the house, telling readers, "Our clothes are important for they help to keep us well."[51] Sewing was a way to be organized, clean, and resourceful, but it was also to be fun. *Clothing and Health* and other texts referred to the pleasure girls could find in making their dresses, the money they could save, and the help they would provide their families. There was little doubt that "sewing is an art which all girls should learn."[52]

SETTLEMENT HOUSES, SCOUTING, AND CLUBS

While schools are a logical place to study how, what and why girls were taught to sew, other institutions played a large role as well. For example, settlement houses frequently offered sewing classes and clubs for girls. In 1915, the Jacob Riis House in New York City offered seventeen sewing classes weekly, apparently for young women, in addition to the five weekly sewing clubs for adult women.[53] By the 1920s, if not earlier, the sewing courses were taught by students at the Pratt Institute in Brooklyn, which offered teacher certification in home economics. The Jacob Riis House was located on the Lower East Side, a neighborhood famous for its Jewish and Italian residents, and the clubs at the settlement house reflected this population. The settlement house offered a range of services, from legal help and English classes to social clubs and dances. It may also have served as a vehicle for acculturation. An undated report, most likely from the 1920s, reflected this role in teaching cultural norms. The author wrote:

> We offer our children clubs and classes. We offer them play and story hours, and game-rooms. We know that from all this they gain a little in the techniques of cooking or sewing, embroidery or knitting, a little in the training of manners and customs, a little in the building of mind and character, and a great deal of individual and group enjoyment.[54]

This and other settlements offered adult women's sewing clubs as well. By teaching children and their parents sewing skills along with "manners and customs," institutions such as the Jacob Riis House helped reinforce the idea that sewing was part of being an American woman.

Many girls learned to sew as members of clubs and associations. The Girl Scouts of the U.S.A., founded in 1912 by Juliette Low, offered a range of civic, domestic, and outdoor skills to girls. The Girl Scouts are a fascinating source of information on just how and what American girls were taught about women's roles in the early twentieth century. Overall, it seems that they were offered a wide range of images of femininity. Scouts were encouraged to develop career skills. An early handbook reads, "Really well-educated women can make a good income by taking up translating, dispensing to a doctor or in a hospital, as stock-brokers, house decorators, or agents, managers of laundries, accountants, archi-tects."[55] The same book, however, also indicates that girls are distinctly different than boys and should develop those traits that are innately womanly. Early on in the guide, under the heading "Be Feminine," Low wrote:

> None of us like women who ape men . . . Girls will do no good by trying to imitate boys. You will only be a poor imitation. It is better to be a real girl such as no boy can possibly be. Everybody loves a girl who is sweet and tender and who can gently sooth those who are weary or in pain. Some girls like to do scouting, but scouting for girls is not the same kind of scouting as for boys. The chief difference is in the courses of instruction. For the boys it teaches MANLINESS, but for the girls it all tends to WOMANLINESS and enables girls the better to help in the great battle of life.[56]

The Girl Scout Law stipulated that scouts be pure and dutiful, follow orders, be courteous, cheerful, and thrifty, all of which could be construed as classic pillars of traditional femininity. One way in which girl scouts could learn to be womanly was through homemaking skills. The guidebook has a section on "Housewifery" which reads, "Every Girl Scout is as much a 'hussif' as she is a girl. She is sure to have to 'keep house' some day, and whatever house she finds herself in, it is certain that that place is the better for her being there."[57] The section on needlework focused mainly on mending and included a photograph of girls sewing, one with a foot-powered sewing machine. The text described sewing as a way of making torn things "all right and serviceable" as well as mak-ing "useful presents" and "articles for their hospitals."[58] A later edition of the ubiquitous Scout handbook, published in 1920, also praised domestic skills; the "Home Maker" section equated homemaking with patriotism. The author wrote, "Every Girl Scout knows that good homes make a country great and good; so every woman wants to understand home-making."[59]

The Girl Scouts published a magazine called *American Girl* that ran arti-cles on a variety of subjects, such as camp skills and international scouting. One regular column covered sewing and clothing and included instructions on how to look "smart" as well as how to make garments. One article from 1928 described how an adult woman wanted to sew but did not know how, having never learned as a girl. She related how she felt when she saw a dress she ad-mired and was informed that a girl made it. The author exclaims that she would love "to be the clever girl who can make it herself—a new party dress, for instance, when a party comes up unexpectedly that you just have to have a new dress for, or lots of simple summer dresses that you can make for very little and that do cost a lot when you have to buy them." She went on to depict a particular dress:

> You can make for yourself if you have a tape measure and a pair of scissors and a little patience. It doesn't even require a paper pattern. And once having succeeded with this, you may be emboldened to try something more difficult. Who knows but that before the end of the summer, you'll be making all sorts of charming frocks for yourself, and perhaps for your little sister too![60]

The article then described the cost of the required material and the steps for making the dress. As far as its sewing content was concerned, *American Girl* was very similar to adult women's magazines of the time.

The Girl Scouts are an excellent example of how sewing was a means of teaching values to girls. Scouts were encouraged to clothe themselves and were assured that by doing so they were being frugal, clever, fashionable, and nurturing, all traits that were valued by adults. Home sewing instruction was both a means and an end. On one level, the sewing was a useful and entertaining skill for many girls, but it was also a way to behave like their mothers and other role models.

In addition to these many public or voluntary efforts, there was money to be made teaching girls to sew. While the role of business in encouraging sewing is examined in more detail in a later chapter, two important examples of for-profit ventures demonstrate that companies eagerly sought the girls' market. The first is the Singer Sewing Machine Company, which embraced sewing education on several fronts. Singer supplied schools with machines and included photographs of Singer-equipped classrooms in its instructional manuals. One manual, published in 1914, noted:

> The great aim in education is to equip the scholar for his or her future career. One of the surest means to this end, in a girl's education, is to teach her how to use a sewing machine . . . A girl who has been properly trained in the use of a Singer Machine is not only able to save herself and family much money and time, but is equipped to earn her living, should she be require [sic] to do so, in one of the great sewing industries.[61]

The same manual included photographs of girls and young women using Singers at the Manhattan Trade School for Girls and the Domestic Science Department of Woodward High School in Cincinnati. Singer offered free sewing classes at affiliated sewing shops, linked its classes to Girl Scout sewing badges, and marketed its products directly to girls. Singer advertisements suggested that by sewing their own clothing, girls would have more clothes than they might otherwise be able to afford but also emphasized that sewing was fun. One such ad offered the testimonial of a happy customer who gushed:

> Already I have five of the prettiest dresses I ever had—more than I ever dreamed of having this season . . . And the materials for all of them have cost just about as much as the price of that one ready made dress I had chosen . . . . It has been the most fun—choosing the patterns and materials and then planning everything.[62]

Testimonials are advertising and may or may not come from real customers. What *is* reliable is how Singer wanted to be perceived.

As a constituency that did not have much expendable income, girls may not appear to be the best audience to target. Singer worked around that problem by appealing to parents' practicality. The above ad explained that the girl in question asked for a Singer as a gift when she could not afford the ready-made clothing she wanted. Moreover, the fact that girls had limited cash was a built-in incentive to sew. Add to that mix the concept that sewing was fun and creative and Singer had a constituency that might remain loyal to the brand in their adult life.

A second example of business involvement in girls' sewing is an extensive club network organized by Butterick. In the autumn of 1906, after the *Delineator* ran an article describing a sewing club organized by one child's grandmother, the magazine was deluged with requests for help setting up similar clubs. The result was the Jenny Wren Doll's Dressmaker Clubs, named after a girl who sewed doll clothing in Dickens' *Our Mutual Friend*. Girls were to organize in groups of 6 to 12 with help from an adult "directress" and were expected to establish a set of rules, charge modest dues to help pay for materials, and elect officers. When they sent in a list of members to the *Delineator*, the girls received an official club charter, membership pins, and free patterns for doll clothes. Girls responded eagerly: in approximately one year there were more than 30,000 members in clubs throughout the U.S., its territories, and foreign countries.[63] The *Delineator* ran regular articles describing their work and offering project suggestions. "Junior" club members were instructed to focus on doll clothing, whereas "seniors" sewed for themselves. All members were encouraged to sew items to sell at a fair (organized by members and patient parents) and donate the proceeds to charity.

The Jenny Wren club network was ingenious brand development. Butterick would surely garner future customers as the Jenny Wren girls matured and graduated from doll clothes to dressing themselves and their own families. The articles describing the original Jenny Wren club casually mentioned Butterick products:

> The money in the treasury would pay for the patterns they should need for the dolls' clothes, for patterns were most necessary. Even Jenny Wren, who was the very cleverest dolls' dressmaker that ever was, had to use patterns. Only there were no Butterick patterns in her day, so she had to shape them herself, and they cost her poor, crooked little back many aching hours. The club that had named itself after her was very much better off; for nowadays one could buy for very little money, the very smartest of patterns, made expressly for dolls.[64]

In addition to being a novel business model, the Jenny Wren network was means of social modeling. The clubs echoed the standard set-up followed by adult clubs. By electing officers, charging dues, keeping minutes, and sewing in the interest of charity, they were emulating middle-class club women's procedures and goals. For example, the Allston club donated items they made such as sheets and diapers, as well as the cash proceeds of their fairs, to the Boston Floating Hospital. Butterick was nurturing not only its customer base but also the social structures that that base valued. By encouraging girls to sew, the company, the organizations that accepted the girls' charitable efforts, and the families who supported the clubs transferred values to the next generation.

KNOW HOW TO . . .

If the apparatus of sewing education can be considered to be a cultural artifact, full of meanings about a particular era's gender, class, and racial roles, then the courses, textbooks, dolls, and magazines created for girls reflect cultural *expectations*. We also need to analyze what girls were actually capable of sewing. Understanding what they thought about all of this sewing is yet another matter. It is possible to ascertain at least some "reader response" or "real life" aspects of girls sewing through sources such as workbooks, club minutes, and dresses. They can help us understand how girls felt about sewing and what they were capable of making. Interviews also help us gain insight into (adult memories of) girls' thoughts on sewing.

A textbook can tell us what and how well a girl was expected to learn to sew in school. For example, girls were consistently taught basic stitches and techniques such as buttonholes, gathering, and hemming. After teaching these elements of hand sewing and depending on budgets and the students' ages, some schools also taught girls to use sewing machines. Textbooks taught a progression of projects, often starting with aprons and moving to full-size dresses. The timing of this progression was variable. One book, published in 1893, outlined an ideal schedule that included six years of sewing, starting in kindergarten. In the first year, girls were expected to be able to make aprons and underwear; by the third, they might make a dress for themselves.[65] Older girls could work faster, especially when using a machine. An article by a high school teacher written in 1919 acknowledged that "the amount of sewing that should be accomplished in the first year of high school is always an open question." For a class meeting five hours a week, she required thirteen garments including undergarments, a "kimono" dressing gown, and two blouses in the first semester.[66]

Some textbooks in archival collections have the one-time users' names inscribed inside, so it is possible to determine that real girls used them. Otherwise, it is hard to tell which books were used and impossible to judge whether they are realistic guides to what girls could make. Other sources, however, provide direct links to real people. A number of workbooks made by school-aged girls and a set of lesson plans drawn up by a high-school sewing teacher provide clues to what girls were actually taught and what they made.

Stella Blayly and Gertie Blair put together workbooks of their sewing lessons. The books are not dated but are estimated by an archivist to be from between 1880 and 1900. There is nothing to indicate that the two girls were at the same school, but both follow a similar pattern that reflects the lesson plans in sewing textbooks. There is something magical about these workbooks. They are a testament to the work and concentration of some little girl. To the modern observer, the level of workmanship is extraordinary. Each page has a particular lesson with some text plus a fabric sample attached with rusting pins. The girls' lessons included basic stitches, hemming, patching, making buttonholes, and gathering fabric into a cuff or waistband. Stella's work is better than Gertie's—her stitches are tiny and her gathering sample is stunning, with tight even stitching. Judging from her handwriting and endearing misspellings, Gertie may have been younger than Stella, which makes her accomplishments all the more impressive.[67]

Older students made workbooks as well. Several were made by a woman named Lucy Pierce, who studied at the University of Rhode Island and planned to become a teacher. She put together a detailed set of notebooks, two dated 1914. One is entitled "Plain Sewing" and includes how to use a sewing machine, directions for making an apron, how to hem items, and pieces of fabric. Some of the notebooks include envelopes with fabric samples labeled "Teacher's Models." Pierce later taught at the Technical High School in Providence. Her effectiveness as a teacher is evident in a notebook created by Maude Perrin Streeter, dated 1921 and entitled "Domestic Arts Dressmaking with Lucy Pierce." Streeter included lists of skills and samples of her sewing and embroidery stitches.[68] These notebooks indicate what was taught in domestic arts and sewing classes, and what students were capable of doing. Judging by the quality of work in Pierce's and Streeter's notebooks, they were capable of a great deal, from understanding textile manufacture and designing patterns to invisibly mending holes, and constructing sophisticated garments. Moreover, the level of organization evident in Pierce's teaching notebooks indicates how seriously she took her work.

The range of difficulty and variety of projects in home economics classes is also evident in women's recollections of what they made. Edith Kurtz, who had sewing in eighth grade in Michigan around 1918, does not recall doing much more than mending.[69] Meanwhile, Florence Epstein's Rochester, New York, sewing teacher required the girls to make middy blouses to wear for their eighth grade graduation in the mid-1920s.[70] Many girls were required to make their own eighth-grade graduation dresses. Making one's own dress was a practical way to demonstrate skills learned in school. It was also a way to clothe girls in a relatively uniform way without demanding much expense on the part of their families.

Because children's clothing often wore out or was handed down many times, it rarely survived for historical analysis. The exception is clothing worn for special occasions such as these graduation dresses, several of which are in the collection of the Museum of the City of New York. Marie W. Fletcher made her graduation dress in 1914 of white batiste trimmed with lace, tucks, and embroidery.[70bis] Fletcher was taught sewing in elementary school from the third grade through the eighth, and made this dress at P.S. 22 in Flushing, Queens, when she was twelve and thirteen years old. Another dress, made of white cotton voile with net around the neck and with short puff sleeves, was made by fourteen-year-old Anna Frankle for her graduation in 1918.[71] Anna's sister Helen made her own dress for her graduation in 1926. Years later, Helen and Anna noted, "It was customary for each girl to spend a year making her graduation dress in the eighth grade."[72] Whatever their feelings about these projects as girls, these women kept their dresses for years and eventually donated them to a museum.

Many girls made dresses and other garments outside of the classroom. Helen Schwimmer made a dress when she was fourteen using her mother's sewing machine. After she made her middy blouse in school, Florence Epstein made curtains for the kitchen. She also made something for her mother at least once and at one time, made scarves for her brother (and then for at least a dozen of his friends). Mostly, however, she made clothing for herself.[73]

Another way of understanding what girls were capable of sewing is to look at sources from the clubs they formed or joined. Some girls may have belonged to informal clubs in their neighborhoods. Helen Schwimmer remembered a group she belonged to as a young girl in Toledo, Ohio, saying, "We used to have a little sewing club, even with the boys."[74] She recalled sitting in a circle on the porch with other children from the neighborhood. They were able to buy small but desirable dolls (with china heads no less) for very little money and she would make clothing and hats for the dolls while the children sat and waited for her to finish.

Other clubs, such as the Jenny Wren clubs discussed earlier, were more formally organized. A group of girls in Allston, Massachusetts a suburb of Boston), organized their own Jenny Wren club in 1908. When the club formed the members ranged in age from eleven to fourteen, most being twelve and thirteen. The club kept charming and meticulous records. Entries for three meetings in 1908 include what the girls were making:

> October 1, 1908
> The President is to make a handkerchief case. Ruth, an apron, Pauline a pin case, Beatrice a sachet, Ida a sofa pillow and Constance dusters.

> October 8, 1908
> Ruth's apron is almost done.

> October 22, 1908
> Pauline has dressed a pretty doll and made a sachet. Emilie is making a handkerchief, Ruth another apron, while Muriel has finished her handkerchief case. Ida has made good headway on her sofa pillow . . . Everyone but Bea had sewing, but as she was provided with some by Dorothy we all had some and we sewed about an hour. Refreshments were served and the meeting adjourned at 6.00 being wound up with a game of Post Office.[75]

Following the suggestions from Butterick, the Allston Jenny Wrens held an annual fair at which they sold their products and donated the proceeds to a children's hospital in Boston. In addition to showing what they could make, their records indicate that these girls used sewing as the basis for sociability and charity, a pattern that echoed the activities of thousands of middle-class women.

The Girl Scouts provide another way to understand the expectations and realities regarding girls' proficiency in sewing. Early on in the organization's history, there were three levels of scouts, and to be a "First Class" scout, girls had to make a skirt or blouse by themselves. The scouts also offered sewing badges and as of 1920, there were two, "Needlewoman" and "Dressmaker". According to sales records, these were among the most popular. Between 1913 and 1938, the national suppliers sold 177,935 of the two categories combined. In comparison, the suppliers sold 156,256 "Cook" badges, 31,398 "Swimmer" badges, and 26,301 "Naturalist" badges over the same time period.[76] Judging from this evidence, we can presume that tens of thousands of Girl Scouts were able to perform at least the basic skills required for the badges. Some may have learned to sew as part of their scout activities and others probably knew how to sew when they joined the organization. In fact, when Marion Goodman joined the Campfire Girls, a different organization than the Girl Scouts but with a similar structure, she chose to do other projects because she already knew how to sew.[77] The badges may have been popular in part because many girls already knew how to sew when they joined the scouts, but the popularity of the badges shows that sewing skills were widespread.

Contests provide another peek into the expectations of adults regarding girls' sewing skills. The state meeting of the Nebraska Girls' Domestic Science Association ran a sewing contest for girls. The 1909 guidelines listed several categories, including:

- A sewing apron, entirely hand made, no machine work.
- A "Domestic Science" apron; machine made, may have some hand work.
- Work apron (with sleeves, and buttoned in the back) including hand and machine work on the garment.
- Washable sofa-pillow cover with top and back sewed together on three sides.
- Plain wash shirt waist.[78]

Prospective contestants were further reminded that "even stitches, strong sewing, and neat finish are of greater importance than expensive trimmings. When aprons and waists are finished there should be no raw nor unfinished seams, no basting threads, and no gathers which have not been stroked . . ."[79] A less stringent "Style Show" was organized by the Girl Scouts of Waterbury, Connecticut, in 1926. Forty-one girls wore dresses they had made before representatives of the Waterbury Institute of Arts and Crafts, who judged them "not only on the sewing but on becomingness of the material, the color and the style."[80] The seven winners—none of whom can be older than twelve or so—wear attractive, if simple, dresses, and one wears a hat she made as well. Such contests were popular and the State Fair in Nebraska continues to hold sewing contests today.[81]

"HOW I HATE SEWING!"

Girls sewed at home, in clubs, and at school. Their mothers and teachers had varying attitudes toward sewing and their experiences varied according to class and race, but if we are seeing to understand the range of cultural meanings of sewing, we also have to try to see what sewing meant to the girls themselves. Did girls *like* to sew? Why or why not? And what did it mean to them?

Surely, many enjoyed the process or at least its results. Florence Epstein told me that she sewed because it allowed her to have pretty things, and recalled specific outfits with pride, including a wool suit she made as a teenager. She said, "You could pick up a piece of material for almost nothing, very little money, and that meant that I could make myself a dress anytime I wanted a new dress. I didn't have to worry about having the money to go out and buy one. I could just make one."[82]

Even girls who liked to sew did not want to do so all the time. The Jenny Wren club in Allston, Massachusetts, was ostensibly formed with the goal of sewing, but it is clear that the girls often preferred to socialize. Minutes from early meetings indicate that the needlework was often abandoned rather quickly:

> February 6, 1908
> There was no business discussed and the sewing was began [sic] as soon as the preceding weeks [sic] report was read. Small cakes and candy were served while the members were sewing and when it was dark curtains were pulled down and ghost stories were told by candle-light.

What makes the above passage especially revealing is that whoever took the minutes wrote the words "at last" right before it was dark" and then, apparently embarrassed by her eagerness to get on with the fun, struck them out. Another record echoed this sentiment:

> February 20, 1908
> All had there sewing [sic]. Refreshments were served. Miss Woodbury then left. As we did not seem to want to sew then a little business was talked and it was decided that we would have a fare [sic] to make more money. There was a long discussion over what we should have, but we finally decided. The meeting was adjourned at 6 o'clock. All had a very merry time.[83]

This ambivalence toward sewing persisted as the club members grew older. The minutes from a club meeting in 1913 document that the majority of members agreed they should sew instead of playing card games at meetings and they proceeded to play more cards once there was "no further business" to discuss.

Sewing can be quite challenging, especially for young fingers or when teachers and parents set high standards of neatness and workmanship. Given the quality of work in girls' sample books, the frustration level most likely ran quite high. Helen Schwimmer, who sewed extensively and with much pleasure throughout her life, spoke vehemently of the frustration she felt as a child. Her mother had very strong opinions about how things should be made and Mrs. Schwimmer has "memories of ripping out all of the time . . . At that time it used to kill me as a child. And my mother would never tell me just to leave it go. It had to be done right."[84]

While these examples show that many girls preferred to play games or disliked spending hours working on one item, others flat-out disliked sewing. For them, the task ranged from a boring job that kept them from other things they enjoyed to an extraordinarily frustrating chore forced upon them by their mothers or teachers. In a diary entry for August 7, 1915, thirteen-year-old Marion Taylor wrote "I had to sew a lot this morning. Mother says if I don't finish that negligee, before we go to the beach I'll have to do it there! I don't take any interest in my clothes at all and it makes mother so mad."[85] Marion's attitude toward sewing did not change; when she was seventeen, she wrote:

In sewing I was making a pair of drawers—they were in two pieces and I hadn't the slightest idea how they went together and when I went to join the pieces together, I found that the ruffles, instead of being around the legs, ran up the middle of the front and back! My teacher thinks that I'm an inspired idiot. I've spent four periods, ripping those ruffles out. I spend most of my time in sewing ripping things out. How I hate sewing. It nearly drives me wild.[86]

Shortly thereafter she noted:

Mother won't let me read. I have to sew. I simply hate to sew, and I don't accomplish anything. I am so lazy. I don't like to move around, I hate housework. I just like to read and write. It's awful. Oh dear. Why am I so awful. Why wasn't I a man. I suppose I would be a poor sort of man, too.[87]

Marion obviously associated sewing with other domestic labor and with "women's work," which she thought she might have avoided had she been a man. For her, sewing was stultifying. She would much rather read or write in her copious journals, which her mother apparently considered "the epitome of all that is foolish, impractical and idle."[88] Marion's mother seems to have had conservative ideas about marriage and women's roles. She apparently told her daughter that when a woman marries, she must submerge her personality."[89] She also struggled financially after her husband left her, and it is possible that she considered sewing not only something women ought to do but a necessary means of saving money.

Teenagers were not the only ones expressing doubts about the virtues of sewing. Some home economists were also skeptical about the need for sewing in women's lives. Greta Gray, a home economics teacher in Laramie, Wyoming, expressed concern that girls' options were limited by their education. She recognized that many young women would leave school early to work, and therefore supported vocational training, but she expressed concern that many students were getting *too much* training in home economics, and feared that girls' education would be skewed in favor of homemaking skills. She wrote that home economics

> seems to make matrimony the sole aim of girls. If they take vocational home economics work they cannot in most cases take any other vocational work, their only way of earning a living will be by housekeeping, they will not always freely choose marriage, for marriage will be the only course open to them.[90]

Instead, she argued, girls who want homemaking training should receive it, but others should be given a wider variety of options. Gray, who we might assume to be more traditional in her outlook because of her rural setting, nonetheless argued that "woman has given, and has received, by stepping out from the home."[91]

Another teacher doubted the assumption that sewing was the best course of action for her students. By the 1920s, when more women worked outside the home and purchased clothing instead of making it, home economics teachers began to acknowledge that sewing was not always the best use of a woman's time. One educator outlined an assignment she had arranged for her students in which they compared the prices of ready-made clothing to garments they could make, designing a system for calculating the cost of home-made garments to include the woman's labor. The students came up with a "price of labor per hour" reached by dividing the cost of materials by the number of hours spent making the item, and concluded that it does indeed pay to sew at home, but only if there is no other work which pays more.[92] Texts and educators therefore echoed changing attitudes about sewing, which in turn reflected changes in women's roles.

CONCLUSION

This chapter has explored the multiple meanings of teaching girls of diverse class, ethnic, and racial backgrounds to sew. It covers the decades in which adult women chose, increasingly, to buy clothing instead of making it at home. The ability or desire to purchase clothing varied according to income level, cultural values and access to ready-made items but reflected a general trend away from home production. Still, while some home economists acknowledged this diminishing need for sewing skills, girls were consistently encouraged or required to sew in school, in clubs, through contests, and at home.

In 1911, a home economist began a textbook by claiming, "The permanency of Domestic Art as a feature in the education of women is assured. It is so vital an expression of her nature that any curriculum which does not include training for the home sphere ignores the very center about which her life revolves."[93] By the mid-twenties, however, when sales of ready-made clothing had overtaken sales of fabric, teachers were beginning to express doubt over the centrality of homemaking skills in girls' education. One article acknowledged, "In this age of ready-made clothing and commercial laundries, home economics teachers are confronted with the question as to what place the construction of clothing and laundry work should have in the school curriculum."[94]

The authors of this article analyzed the responses to a survey undertaken by the American Home Economics Association, which demonstrated the widening gap between the sewing habits of rural versus urban women. For example, about 85 percent of the rural respondents made house dresses, compared to about 15 percent of urban women.[95] This led to the authors' questioning whether rural and urban girls should even be taught the same curriculum. However, they could not necessarily follow their instinct, since according to the same survey, 95 percent of rural and 92 percent of urban women still thought girls should be taught to sew.[96]

The realities of women's lives, therefore, did not always translate into how they thought their daughters should be educated. Women who rarely sewed themselves still wanted their daughters to learn. This persistent interest in girls' sewing is evidence that sewing was symbolic as well as practical. Sewing represented a set of ideas about women and their roles. It evoked ideas of discipline, thrift, motherly love, beauty, and production. At the same time, varying methods and intensities of sewing education reflected ideas about race and class, as educators decided that different groups needed different skills for particular reasons. As sewing became less a critical practical skill, it remained an important and persistent means of transmitting cultural values to girls and young women.

NOTES

1. Olive C. Hapgood, *School Needlework: A Course of Study in Sewing Designed For Use In Schools* (Boston: Ginn & Company, 1893), Teacher's Edition, 1.

2. Jenny Wren Club of Allston, Massachusetts records, Schlesinger Library, Radcliffe Institute for Advanced Study.

3. Mary Knapp (subject's daughter-in-law), conversation with author, New York, New York, 27 March 2001. According to Mary Knapp, Coleman Knapp's mother was not an especially warm person, and sewing may have been one of their few joint activities.

4. Dunn, interview.

5. Goodman, interview.

6. Epstein, interview. Despite the number of men who worked in the garment trades, there is little evidence that these men sewed at home or taught family members sewing skills. Sewing was acceptable as a way to earn wages, and men in the garment industry regularly earned more than women, but it was not male leisure or domestic work.

7. Jane Eayre Fryer, *Easy Steps in Sewing, For Big and Little Girls, or Mary Frances Among the Thimble People*, illustrated by Jane Allen Boyer (Philadelphia: Universal Book and Bible House, 1913). The copy at the Winterthur Library had obviously been used as several of the patterns had been cut out. The book was apparently one of a series—there are also housekeeping, cooking and a first-aid books with a similar pretext.

8. *Bradley's Tru-Life Paper Dolls* (Springfield, Massachusetts: Milton Bradley Company, 1914, 1916), page 2 of instruction booklet, Joseph Downs Collection of Manuscripts and Printed Ephemera, Winterthur Museum, Garden and Library.

9. Olive Hyde Foster, "The Evolution of a Paper Doll," *Delineator* (October 1906): 625–27, 625.

10. Helen Schwimmer, interview by author, tape recording, Oberlin, Ohio, 25 May 2001.

11. *A Conference on Manual Training* (Boston: New England Conference Education Workers, 1891), 160–161.

12. "An Exhibition of Sewing: Progress in the Training of American and Foreign Children Contrasted," *New York Times*, 24 March 1897, 2.

13. "The Sewing Exhibition," 7.

14. Stephanie J. Shaw, *What a Woman Ought to Be and to Do: Black Professional Women Workers during the Jim Crow Era* (Chicago: University of Chicago Press, 1996), 27.

15. Margaret Murray Washington, "The Advancement of Colored Women," *The Colored American Magazine* (April 1905): 183–189, 185. Washington was married to Booker T. Washington and like him argued for practical training as the best way to improve the economic prospects of African Americans. Others argued that focusing

on industrial training shortchanged other forms of education and reinforced the idea that African Americans were only suited to be laborers.

16. Washington, "The Advancement of Colored Women," 188.

17. "Dress Making Schools: How to Make Dresses Inadequately Taught in New York - Free Instruction An Urgent Need - Conditions Which Prevent Many Women From Learning a Woman's work - Fashionable Establishments," *New York Times*, 23 February 1896, 27.

18. Thomas Oscar Fuller, "Mrs. Louisa Maben and Her Sewing School," 1910, New York Public Library Digital Library, Digital Record ID #1240254.

19. *A Study of Home-Economics Education in Office* (1923, reprint NY: Negro Universities Press, 1969), 10, quoted in Connolly, 337.

20. Emily A. Harper, "The Hampton Summer Normal," *The Colored American Magazine* (October 1902): 403–411, 403.

21. Harper, "The Hampton Summer Normal," 408.

22. The Museum of Modern Art, New York, *The Hampton Album, 44 Photographs by Frances B. Johnston from an album of Hampton Institute* (New York: Doubleday & Co., 1966).

23. Interview with Melnea A. Cass, in *The Black Women Oral History Project*, Ruth Edmonds Hill, ed., vol. 2 (Westport, CT: Meckler, 1991), 269–414, 290.

24. Elizabeth G. Holt, "Negro Industrial Training in the Public Schools of Augusta, GA," *The Journal of Home Economics* 4 (October 1912): 315–323, 315.

25. Holt, "Negro Industrial Training in the Public Schools of Augusta, GA," 315.

26. Holt, "Negro Industrial Training in the Public Schools of Augusta, GA," 316–17.

27. Holt, "Negro Industrial Training in the Public Schools of Augusta, GA," 315.

28. Holt, "Negro Industrial Training in the Public Schools of Augusta, GA," 322.

29. One scholar who has written about Indian schools is K. Tisianina Lomawaima; see her article "Domesticity in the Federal Indian Schools: The Power of Authority over Mind and Body," *American Ethnologist* 20 (1993): 227–240. See also Devon A. Mihesuah, *Cultivating the Rosebuds: The Education of Women at the Cherokee Female Seminary, 1851–1909* (Urbana: University of Illinois Press, 1993).

30. Ramona Bennett, "The Puyallup Tribe Rose from the Ashes," in Jane Katz, ed., *Messengers of the Wind: Native American Women Tell Their Life Stories* (New York: Ballantine Books, 1995), 153.

31. Lomawaima, "Domesticity in the Federal Indian Schools," 229.

32. Jane E. Simonsen, *Making Home Work: Domesticity and Native American Assimilation in the American West, 1860–1919* (Chapel Hill: University of North Carolina Press, 2006), 88–9.

33. Office of Indian Affairs, *Some Things that Girls Should Know How to Do, and Hence Should Learn How to Do When in School* (Washington, DC: Government Printing Office, 1911), 5.

34. Office of Indian Affairs, *Outline Lessons in Housekeeping, including Cooking, Laundering, Dairying, and Nursing* (Washington, DC: Government Printing Office, 1911), 8.

35. Office of Indian Affairs, *Outline Lessons in Housekeeping*, 11.

36. Marvin Lazerson, *Origins of the Urban School* (Cambridge, Mass.: Harvard University Press, 1971), 104.

37. Sylvia Chase Lintner, "A Social History of Fall River," Ph.D diss., Radcliffe College, 1945, 295, and New Bedford, *School Report*, 1882, 86–91, cited in Lazerson, 106.

38. "Dress Making Schools," *The New York Times*, 23 February 1896, 27.

39. "Dress Making Schools."

40. "Dress Making Schools."

41. "Trade Course for Public School Girls," *The New York Times*, 28 July 1912, section 4, 5.

42. "Trade Course for Public School Girls," 5.

43. Anne L. Jessup, ed. *The Sewing Book, Containing Complete Instructions in Sewing and Simple Garment-Making for Children in the Primary and Grammar Grades* (New York: The Butterick Publishing Co., 1913), unpaginated introduction.

44. Edith B. Watson, "A Layette Project," *Journal of Home Economics* 20 (November 1928): 803–805, 804.

45. Hattie E. Anderson, "Making a Clothing Budget for Working Girls," *Journal of Home Economics*, 20 (May 1928): 315–320, 316.

46. Anderson, "Making a Clothing Budget for Working Girls," 318.

47. Nancy G. Gladish, "Household Arts and the High School Girl," *Journal of Home Economics* 11 (November 1919): 488–497, 488.

48. Helen Kinne & Anna M. Cooley, *Clothing and Health: An Elementary Textbook of Home Making* (New York: The MacMillan Company, 1916), 230.

49. Mary H. Morgan, *How To Dress A Doll* (Philadelphia: Henry Altemus Company, 1908), 3.

50. Gertrude T. Johnson, *Domestic Science, A Text in Cooking and Syllabus in Sewing, prepared for use in the Kansas City Elementary Schools, Yet eminently fitted for home work* (Kansas City, MO: The Burton Publishing Co., 1911), 142.

51. Kinne & Cooley, *Clothing and Health*, 3.

52. Kinne & Cooley, *Clothing and Health*, 3–4.

53. "Activities, 1914–1915," fundraising card, box 17, folder 3, Jacob A. Riis Neighborhood Settlement Records, Manuscripts Collection, New York Public Library.

54. Mrs. Hambridge, "Girls' Work Report," undated (in folder with other documents from the 1920s), 3–4, box 16, folder 7, Jacob A. Riis Neighborhood Settlement Records, Manuscripts and Archives Division, New York Public Library.

55. Juliette Low, *How Girls Can Help Their Country: Handbook for Girl Scouts* (1913, Washington, DC: Girl Scouts of the USA, reprinted 1972), 114.

56. Low, *How Girls Can Help Their Country*, 12. Interestingly, while Low was intent on maintaining gender distinctions, she sought to address class divisions. The Girl Scout Law included the line "A Girl Scout is a Friend to All, and a Sister to every Other Girl Scout no Matter to what Social Class she May Belong," 5.

57. Low, *How Girls Can Help Their Country*, 77.

58. Low, *How Girls Can Help Their Country*, 78–80.

59. *Scouting for Girls: Official Handbook of the Girl Scouts* (New York: published by The Girl Scouts, Inc., 1920), 106. This talk of homemaking as patriotism and of scouting as "helping the country" is evocative of the concept of "Republican Motherhood" as explored by Linda Kerber in *Women of the Republic: Intellect and Ideology in Revolutionary America* (Chapel Hill: University of North Carolina Press) and other historians.

60. Helen Perry Curtis, "Anyone Can Make It," *American Girl* (July 1928): 17–18, 17.

61. *A Manual of Family Sewing Machines* (New York: Singer Sewing Machine Company, 1914), unpaginated preface, Singer Sewing Machine Co. records.

62. Advertisement for Singer Sewing Machine Co., *American Girl* (April 1929): 2.

63. "The Jenny Wren Club of the *Delineator*, Hints and Bylaws, Hints to Dolls' Dressmakers" (Butterick Publishing Co., no date), Schlesinger Library, Jenny Wren Club of Allston, MA records.

64. The Dolls' Dressmaker, "The Story of a Jenny Wren Club," *Delineator* (November 1906): 816–820, 817.

65. Hapgood, *School Needlework*.

66. Gladish, "Household Arts and the High School Girl," 491.

67. Workbooks by Gertie Blair and Stella Blayly in the Joseph Downs Collection of Manuscripts and Printed Ephemera, Winterthur Museum, Garden and Library.

68. Notebooks by Lucy Pierce and Louise Vaughn in the collection of the University of Rhodes Island Textile Studies department.

69. Kurtz, interview.

70. Epstein, interview.

70bis. Girl's Dress, white batiste with lace, 1914, 72.17.3, gift of Mrs. Marie W. Fletcher, Costume and Textile Collection, Museum of the City of New York.

71. Girl's dress, white cotton with ruffles, 1918, 59.178.1, gift of the Misses Anna S. & Helen Frankle, Costume and Textile Collection, Museum of the City of New York.

72. Girl's dress, 1918, 59.178.1. For text see accession card.

73. Epstein, interview.

74. Schwimmer, interview.

75. "Property of the Jenny Wren Club, Reports and Records, 1908, Book I," box 1, Jenny Wren Club of Allston, Massachusetts records.

76. All badge figures are from Mary Degenhardt and Judith Kirsch, *Girl Scout Collector's Guide: 75 Years of Uniforms, Insignia, Publications & Keepsakes* (Leonard, IL: Wallace-Homestead Book Co., 1987). The "Needlewoman" badge was re-named "Dressmaker" in 1920 when a new "Needlewoman" badge was introduced.

77. Goodman, interview.

78. "Something About Sewing for Nebraska Girls," Series II, Bulletin No. 10, published by the Department of Public Instruction, Lincoln Nebraska, July 1909, 3.

79. "Something About Sewing for Nebraska Girls," 3.

80. Agnes M. Scheir, "Presenting A Style Show—Girl-Scout-Made," *American Girl* (November 1926), 31.

81. Jenny Kenyon, conversation with author, November 2000.

82. Epstein, interview.

83. "Property of the Jenny Wren Club, Reports and Records, 1908, Book I," entries for 6 and 20 February 1908, box 1, Jenny Wren Club of Allston, Massachusetts records.

84. Schwimmer, interview.

85. "The Diary of Marion Taylor," in Penelope Franklin, ed., *Private Pages: Diaries of American Women 1830s-1970s* (New York: Ballantine books, 1986), 2–62, 17. Franklin notes that names have been changed.

86. "The Diary of Marion Taylor," 48.

87. "The Diary of Marion Taylor," 51.

88. "The Diary of Marion Taylor," 4.

89. "The Diary of Marion Taylor," 51.

90. Greta Gray, "Vocational Training for Girls," *The Journal of Home Economics* 11 (November 1919): 493–497, 495.

91. Gray, "Vocational Training for Girls," 496.

92. Louise Phillips Glanton, "Does it Pay to Sew at Home?" *Journal of Home Economics* 15 (May 1923): 277–279.

93. Anna M. Cooley, *Domestic Art in Woman's Education (for the use of those studying the method of teaching domestic art and its place in the school curriculum)* (New York: Charles Scribners's Sons, 1911), vii.

94. Hastie and Gorton, "What Shall We Teach Regarding Clothing and Laundry Problems?" 127.

95. Hastie and Gorton, "What Shall We Teach Regarding Clothing and Laundry Problems?" 130.

96. Hastie and Gorton, "What Shall We Teach Regarding Clothing and Laundry Problems?" 131.

4. COMMODIFYING "DOMESTIC VIRTUES"

Business and Home Sewing

In 1926, an organization of fabric wholesalers met in New York to discuss what they perceived to be a troubling decline in sales. They announced that at the root of their difficulties was "a lack of knowledge of sewing and the art of dressmaking by young women, who were given over to enjoying themselves and neglecting the domestic virtues of their mothers and grandmothers."[1] Their concerns about losing customers were legitimate. By the twenties, the number of women sewing at home had decreased, since more women were working outside the home and ready-made clothing was inexpensive and attractive. However, those social and economic realities were not nearly as important to the retailers as the idea that business was suffering because women were abandoning their traditional roles.

This chapter examines the relationship between businesses and home sewing. Throughout the nineteenth century and into the twentieth, most middle- and working- class American women assumed that they would do at least some sewing for their families. While businesses competed with each other for a share of the market, they did not have to justify sewing to their customers. After the First World War, however, as more women worked outside the home or spent their time in other pursuits and ready-made clothing was more available than ever, fewer women needed or wanted to sew. Sewing-goods manufacturers and retailers found that they now needed to convince women to return to their sewing machines.

Businesses devised a variety of strategies to revitalize sewing. A unifying theme was that sewing not only saved money or expressed personal style, but was also a way to be appropriately feminine. Sewing was portrayed as a way to be a good mother and an attractive (yet frugal) wife. The cultural values attached to sewing, among them thrift, discipline, maternal love and feminine beauty, were cultivated by businesses to encourage demand for their goods. Incessantly used to sell products, traditional femininity and maternalism became commodified. It was in the interest of business and profits to promote sewing and the gendered ideas that accompany it, and so "domestic virtue" became a consumer good.

The home sewing industry turned to the feminine nature of sewing as a way to entice customers back to the piece goods department, but it was primarily interested in profit, not ideology. Advertising executives and others involved in marketing decisions were capable of considering multiple gender constructions. Companies also proved to be relatively sensitive to class and race issues as, perhaps out of necessity, they explored alternative markets for their products. The traditional imagery used to promote sewing was therefore porous and flexible and in the long run, businesses were more wedded to their financial interests than to any particular cultural ideology.

This chapter will first outline how various players in the home sewing industry promoted their products at a time when sewing was assumed to be part of everyday life. It will then explore how some of those strategies changed once businesses could no longer take home sewing for granted. These firms adapted their sales practices to a changing environment, taking into account shifting notions of class, race, and gender. Through the promotion of sewing-related goods and services, companies connected women's consumption to domestic labor and attached social values to household production.

SEWING AND THE U.S. ECONOMY

Home sewing, while in many ways a private activity done in the home largely for one's self or family, has nonetheless been an important factor in the public setting of the American economy. Home dressmakers welcomed developments in technology and purchased vast quantities of fabric, sewing machines, and paper patterns. They subscribed to magazines that endorsed sewing, took sewing classes, and bought all kinds of "notions" such as needles, buttons, and trimmings. The *New York Times* claimed in 1926 that "home sewing is probably the largest private industry in the country. Wholesale and retail merchants in the tens of thousands exist to supply its needs."[2]

That observation was made when home sewing had already begun to decline in popularity. During the late nineteenth century and the beginning of the twentieth, when home sewing was in full swing, related businesses used a variety of methods and arguments to sell their goods. Firms promoted the quality and/or cost of fabric, new pattern designs, and the efficiency and ease of sewing machines. Sewing goods and services were certainly associated with women and women's work, and the advertisements and promotions reflect this understanding of cultural roles. However, the sewing industry had not commodified gender values to the extent it would in later years when it was in a state of panic over the decline of home sewing.

Take a look at a magazine or newspaper from the early twentieth century and you will find copious advertisements for fabrics, sewing machines, and related goods alongside promotions for ready-made clothing. These advertisements hawked free samples, claimed to have the most variety and/or best quality of stock, and assured consumers that their prices beat the competition. This high volume of advertising for sewing-related products is evidence of the demand for such goods and of the competition for consumers among producers. Home dressmaking supported a variety of businesses, from manufacturers and retailers to educators and publishers. To clothe themselves and their families, consumers bought fabric or "dress goods," notions, tissue paper patterns, dressmaking guides, sewing machines, sewing lessons, and magazines. According to their income level and where they lived, women could buy these items from department and specialty stores, small-town general stores, mail order catalogues, and pushcarts. Altogether, the home dressmaking industry was an amalgam of very different types of firms, business practices, and ideologies. It represented a significant portion of the economy, especially in major urban areas such as New York City.

TEXTILES

One industry central to the home dressmaking trade was textile manufacturing and sales. Some materials were imported, but factories mainly based in New England and in the South employed hundreds of thousands of workers and produced more than a billion and a half dollars worth of products in 1909. By 1919, U.S. textile mills churned out more than three hundred million square yards of cotton gingham alone.[3] Much of this fabric was intended for use by the garment industry, but it was also sold by the yard in catalogs, at department and specialty stores, and by peddlers. A vast variety of fabrics were available—cotton, linen, wool, silk, and by 1910, artificial silk, later known as rayon—in a range of patterns, textures, colors, and prices. Fabric and related sewing goods were considered normal household expenditures. Many wealthier customers who hired a dressmaker to do the work would still purchase their own fabric, and middle- and working-class women who did the bulk of their family's sewing bought fabric regularly. Textile purchases made up a significant portion of women's expenses, and textile producers and retailers were sizeable players in the economy at large.

Textile companies used straightforward tactics to sell their goods. Sears, Roebuck pushed the quality, affordability, and in some cases, the exclusivity of their fabrics. Catalog shoppers were exhorted to examine the "beautiful new styles" and offered vague explanations as to "how we make our prices so low."[4] Those prices ranged from wools and silk and wool blends for 25 cents a yard, less expensive cottons as low as 5 cents a yard, and silks at 29 to 39 cents a yard. One of the most expensive fabrics in that same catalog was an imported French silk and wool blend for $1.48 a yard.[5]

Aside from price, women chose fabric according to its appropriateness for a particular type of garment and its visual and tactile appeal. Magazine advertisements focused on the colors, textures, and prints available that season and readers could send for samples as they planned their wardrobes. Manufacturers sometimes promoted the technological modernity of their goods. One artificial silk by the name of "Himalaya Cloth" was supposedly

> developed after years of experiment in response to the demand for a fabric which would be as beautiful as the real Rough Silks, yet would have great durability, would not wear fuzzy and would stand all the tests of the laundry . . . it is no overstatement to say that an expert can hardly distinguish between 'Himalaya' and silks that cost $1.00 to $1.50 a yard. [6]

Magazine editors discussed fabrics with the same language they used to describe dress styles. As one fashion editor described, "The samples of the new fabrics illustrated on this page were selected as those which will be the smartest and most fashionable for spring" and put significant resources into printing color plates of new designs.[7] They knew that consumers chose carefully. Lilla Bell Viles-Wyman cared about her fabrics and included swatches of her choices in her journals.

Fashion influenced colors as well as design: Viles-Wyman wrote that "the present rage is for Black & White" and soon thereafter bought material that was black with a white stripe. Texture was also important—as a tactile object, fabric has to appeal to the touch. A magazine spread on the latest fabrics for 1910 described how "the materials showing a ribbed effect are specially in vogue, as well as those in basket weaves."[8] Jean Gulrich remembered her mother touching the fabrics in the store, claiming "she only wanted the softest ones."[9]

While home sewing remained a given in most women's lives, textile producers and retailers used pricing, variety, style, color, and quality to sell their goods. While businesses competed for customers among themselves, they did not have to justify why women should buy fabric in the first place. Adult women were assumed to have a basic knowledge of different materials, weaves, and textures, and retailers did not presume to teach consumers the basics. These dimensions of the fabric trade would change, however, as sales dropped after the First World War.

SEWING MACHINES

If the fabric trade with its mind-boggling variety played an important role, sewing machines made up another significant sector of the home dressmaking industry. First introduced for home use in the 1850s, hand-cranked and then foot-powered sewing machines gained rapid acceptance in American homes. Marguerite Connolly argues that the sewing machine was vital to middle-class life in the late nineteenth century, saving women hours of work.[10] Manufacturers marketed their machines as a way to sooth family tensions, reduce women's drudgery, and save money and time. The machines were touted as a fitting piece of furniture for a middle-class home (some models folded into attractive wood cabinets) and appealing to feminine taste. Trade cards showed flowery pictures, placid homes, and happy seamstresses.[11] Retailers used middle-class values to sell their goods, arguing that machines were a route to domestic harmony, since mothers would spend the time and money saved on their family and home.

Once they had convinced Americans that a sewing machine would contribute to the family economy and quality of life, producers and retailers competed with each other for consumer dollars. Price was, as always, an important selling point. While a sewing machine was a significant expenditure, many households saw it as a worthwhile investment that would help the woman of the house save money in the long run.[12] Unlike textiles, however, machine manufacturers often had to convince the man of the household to make the

investment. After the dissolution in 1877 of what was essentially a cartel created by patent protection laws, machine prices slowly fell. In 1856, a Singer cost
about $125 when the average annual income was $500. By 1902, consumers
could purchase a *Minnesota* brand machine for $23.20 from the Sears, Roe-
buck & Co.[13]

Machines were accessible to working-class families from fairly early on. According to an 1875 study of about 400 white, working class families in Massachusetts, 34 percent owned sewing machines.[14] Singer sold machines on an installment plan, suggesting that families could make the payments easily as
women earned and saved money using the new purchase. Women who did not
have their own machines often had access to those owned by relatives and
friends. In some ways, sewing machines were especially desirable for working-
class women. After all, they provided a way to make a living in an accepted
feminine line of work. An undated pamphlet claims that "[a] respectable
woman, black or white, without a cent to pay, can get a machine from any lead-
ing company that will enable her to support herself and dependent children or
friends."[15] As condescending as this might be, it nonetheless underscored the
reality of the types of work available to women at the time.

Singer Sewing Machine Company, the world's first multinational corpora-
tion and the giant of the industry, also acknowledged that working-class women
were major customers and encouraged training on sewing machines as a means
to get a job. The instruction booklets that accompanied Singer machines emphasized the role of sewing machines in the lives of working-class women. One
argued, "[A] girl who has been properly trained in the use of a Singer Machine
is not only able to save herself and family much money and time, but is equipped
to quickly earn her own living, should she require to do so, in one of the great
sewing industries."[16]

Sewing machines crossed ethnic and racial lines as well, often representing
American culture. Jane Simonsen describes how a particular Native American
couple in Nebraska owned a sewing machine along with their stove and rocking
chair in their frame house. The couple, who were Omaha but had converted to
Christianity, had received funds from the Women's National Indian Association, an organization of white women focused on assimilating Native women
through "model homes" and Anglo-style domesticity. For these white reformers, sewing machines were part of a lifestyle that represented "civilization" and
domestic industry.[17] Likewise, in her study of women in the Southwest, historian Sarah Deutsch writes that sewing machines were among the "female cen-
tered items" acquired by Hispanic families in the early twentieth century. [18]
Whether or not the machines represented "civilization" to the women who actually used them, or were merely a convenience, we do not know.

TISSUE PAPER PATTERNS

Along with textiles and sewing machines, a third pillar of the home dressmaking industry was the paper pattern. Tissue paper patterns had first been commercially developed by Ebenezer Butterick, a tailor, in the 1860s. A decade later, his company produced almost six million patterns annually.[19] By the 1880s, several firms competed for consumers. Some of the biggest names were Butterick, Demorest, and McCall. During the early twentieth century, several other firms and publishers tried their hand at pattern design and marketing, including the Woman's Home Companion, Sears, Roebuck, Vogue, and Pictorial Review.

When they could assume a regular customer base, pattern companies promoted their products on the basis of style. Advertisements emphasized the variety and attractiveness of their designs, and magazines that sold patterns took pains to show off their distinctive fashions. The *Woman's Home Companion* depicted one pattern as "the most stylish design of the season," and the *Delineator* described a model as a "stylish waist, uniquely designed."[20] The flexibility and variety inherent in patterns was also a major selling point. Turn-of-the-century Butterick patterns often came with a subtitle explaining the variations one could employ, such as the ""Ladies' Surplice Blouse-Waist (to be made with a high or v-neck, full-length or elbow sleeves and with or without the peplum and revers.)[21] Lengthy descriptions of the patterns discussed the appropriate uses of the garment and suggested a variety of fabrics, colors, and trims.

While style was important, price and convenience mattered as well. In the early twentieth century, Sears, Roebuck offered very inexpensive patterns for 5 cents, claiming that they were offering them "without any idea of profit." This was clever marketing, as the minimum order was 50 cents and they expected a woman to choose a pattern along with her dress goods.[22] Anecdotal evidence suggests that a wide variety of customers bought sewing patterns, either for individual use or to bring to a dressmaker.

The mainstream pattern companies did not address the race of their customers, although the women portrayed in illustrations and, later, photographs were invariably white. Publications intended for an African American readership, however, also discussed patterns and styles. The Colored American Magazine offered fashion advice and sketches "designed exclusively" by a Mme. Rumford of New York City who gave detailed advice to "the Ladies of Fashion" as to the cut of the new shirtwaists and the latest fabrics and trim.[23] Her sketches evoke the style used by the Delineator—showing multiple views of a shirtwaist and variations on skirts—but it is not clear whether her designs were available as commercial patterns or whether they were intended to serve as guides to skilled home dressmakers who could cut their own from an illustration.

When home sewing was the norm, the magazines and catalogues selling the patterns assumed a high degree of skill by the reader. At the turn of the century, many patterns were a dizzying maze of dashes and dots as the outlines of different pattern pieces were drawn over each other.[24] Once the seamstress had divined the pattern pieces she wanted, traced them onto paper, and cut the paper shapes, she would follow instructions for the most efficient way to lay those paper pieces on her fabric to cut. Patterns became easier to use over time. By the 1890s, many patterns included a seam allowance so the user did not have to calculate it herself, and by the early twentieth century, some patterns were more recognizable as blueprints for garments, but these changes were not used as a major selling point. Whether or not their patterns were simple to use, the pattern companies did not emphasize ease of use as part of their marketing strategies in the late nineteenth and early twentieth centuries. While the different companies had to persuade customers to buy their particular brand, they did not have to convince women to buy patterns in general.

MAGAZINES AND BOOKS

Women's magazines, whether multi-purpose or specifically focused on sewing, promoted sewing through regular articles, advice, and products.[25] Magazines aimed at women had been available for much of the nineteenth century but were usually aimed at an elite audience who could afford high subscription rates. By the 1890s, however, the magazine industry relied on advertising revenues and could therefore afford to charge fairly reasonable subscription and single-copy rates, making mass market magazines available to the middle class.[26] Together with low prices, an expanded postage system, higher literacy rates, and urbanization, the 1890s began a growth period for women's as well as general-interest magazines.

Women's magazines were especially good sellers, with higher circulation rates than the general-interest publications. In February 1904, the *Ladies' Home Journal* was the first U.S. magazine to have more than a million subscribers. Of the ten magazines with the highest circulation in 1916, six were aimed at women and focused on or included material on sewing: *McCall's, Pictorial Review, Woman's Home Companion, Delineator, Ladies' Home Journal,* and *Woman's World.*[27] Because of their high circulation rates, these magazines attracted advertisers like ants to a picnic. Companies knew that not only did many women

turn to magazines for advice, they also often made household spending decisions. A 1917 analysis of advertisers in Butterick magazines showed that a range
of products, from furniture to toiletries to food, were advertised; 12 percent of
the ads were for clothing and 2.9 percent were for piece goods.[28]

The popular women's magazines at the turn of the century were arrayed
along a spectrum of interests but all included some discussion of sewing. Some,
such as the *Delineator, Pictorial Review,* and *McCall's* were published by pattern producers, whereas others such as the *Woman's Home Companion* and the
Ladies Home Journal ran regular columns on dressmaking advice. Most columns assumed a rather high level of expertise, but some targeted less experienced sewers by emphasizing the ease of making particular garments. These
columns provided guidance for making new styles, often using the patterns supplied by the particular magazine, and promoted themes such as thrift and individuality as an incentive to sew.

This sewing advice ranged from information on the latest styles to instructions for making over old dresses. For years, the core of the *Delineator* was a
feature on the latest fashions, most of which, at least through the First World
War, were elaborate, tight-fitting confections with all kinds of ruffles, braid,
fringe, and contrasting underlayers. The magazine gave little attention to the
difficulties of sewing and rarely acknowledged that its designs might challenge
the average home dressmaker. Other magazines were more forgiving. Diana
Sturgis, the long-time editor of the "What to Wear and How to Make It" column in the *Ladies' Home Companion,* offered advice and responded to readers
who expressed difficulties with their sewing projects. One tip implied that readers had trouble cutting cloth correctly:

> It is very important to cut linings and dress-goods on the same thread of the goods. If
> one is cut straight way and the other ever so little on the bias, they do not receive the
> strain alike, and soon become awry.[29]

Other suggestions often concerned what sort of materials to choose, what
colors were most useful, and how to get the best fit.

Columnists consistently wrote features aimed at saving money. A *Delineator*
column called "Dressing on Dimes" aimed at thrifty use of fabric, and "What
to Wear and How to Make It" regularly gave advice on making over old dresses
to be more fashionable. Sturgis announced at one point:

> Let it be taken for granted at the outset that those who are reading these cogitations
> are on the lookout for some suggestions that can be inexpensively carried out. Ex-
> pense, to be sure, is a relative term. . . . Still, we will keep within the bounds of
> moderate expenditure as more likely to suit the majority at all times . . . .[30]

Sturgis regularly answered letters that asked how to use fabric from an older garment to make something new, or what sort of dress was most useful if the reader could only afford one new outfit. Judging from the anxiety evident in the letters, much of her audience was most likely lower-middle-class or even working-class women: they would be the most eager for advice on how to fit in to a middle-class aesthetic. There was a clear understanding that readers looked to the magazine's sewing advice to help them get the most from their limited resources.

While they took customer support into consideration, and individual editors may have been sensitive to the pressures of clothing costs, the primary goal of magazines was to present themselves as avatars of fashion. Publishers that printed how-to books had a slightly different set of needs and strategies. There was significant overlap, however, as some texts and how-to guides were published by familiar names like Butterick and McCall. Textbooks intended for use in school sewing and home economics classes were consistent through the 1910s, offering basic outlines of necessary skills and their use in the household. The methodical structure of these books is reflected in one published in 1913: "After the various stitches and seams have been learned, the pupil's knowledge is applied to the making of small articles and miniature garments. These small garments are an excellent preparation for the making of the full-size clothing in the upper grades."[31] A survey of a number of sewing texts shows a standard progression from basic skills to assembling garments, with limited discussion of why the reader might choose to sew in the first place.

Publishers saw a market for instructional books aimed at adults as well. Books such as Butterick's *The Dressmaker* gave illustrated instructions for making garments and showed how to adapt paper patterns for different figure types. The step-by-step instructions included in these manuals supplemented the patterns sold by the same companies. Another book offered very detailed instructions on different kinds of seams, linings, sleeves, etc, while assuming the reader was working with a commercial pattern. Lesson 304, "Routine of Making a Skirt," explained that "practically all skirts are made according to a well formulated, closely followed routine. The following guide will prove of value, as each step has been carefully explained in detail in the lessons given for reference."[32] The skirt lesson contained thirty separate steps, starting with "obtain the necessary skirt measurements" and finishing with put on hangers," with each step referring to various lessons covered elsewhere in the guide.[33] The very existence of these guides acknowledges that women did not always understand every step the pattern asked them to follow.

While these guides offered detailed instructions, they rarely discussed why women should sew to begin with. The preface to *American Dressmaking Step by Step* explains that "the woman who knows practically nothing about sewing or dressmaking must be taught from the beginning," yet does not question whether nor explain why the reader should make the effort.[34] Publishers recognized a market for sewing advice manuals but took home sewing for granted.

FACING THE CHANGES IN HOME SEWING

The people and companies that presumed that women would always sew at home were in for a shock. Economic and social factors such as industrial production practices, demographic shifts, contraception, and women's increasing presence in the workforce had a significant impact on those sectors of the economy that relied on traditional behavior. Following World War I, trends which had begun before the war accelerated. More women were working outside the home, and ready-made clothing was both cheaper and better fitting than prior to the war. Home sewing went into a marked decline, but many women continued to sew out of necessity or pleasure. To reach those women and to convince old customers to return to the fold, sewing-oriented businesses were forced to rethink their assumptions and strategies.

A survey of department stores by the Bureau of Business Research at Harvard showed that until 1920, sales of fabric kept pace with sales of ready-made clothing. However, as of 1920, the balance tipped and people bought less fabric and more clothing.[35] Another survey, done in-house for Singer Sewing Machine and using figures from the federal government, noted that between 1924 and 1927 alone, retail sales of cotton fabric dropped 27 percent.[36] At the same time, annual sales of factory-made dresses rocketed from under 500 million dollar's worth in 1914 to over a billion dollar's worth five years later.[37]

Why such a drastic change? One reason was a matter of design. Women's clothing had changed dramatically by the 1920s, and the simpler and less fitted designs—such as the straight lines of "flapper" dresses—made it easier to buy stylishly fitting dresses off the rack.[38] These straight lines combined with shorter hemlines meant that less fabric went into each dress, and fewer details and a looser fit required less work to make, resulting in lower costs to the manufacturers and cheaper retail prices.

The causes were demographic as well. By the 1920s, more women than ever, especially from the middle class, were working outside the home. In 1870, women made up 14 percent of the paid workforce, a figure that grew to 20 percent by 1910 and 22 percent by 1930.[39] Higher education became more of a possibility among the middle class and female graduates found work in pink-collar jobs, giving them more disposable income to spend on ready-made clothing, dress codes to meet, and less time to spend sewing. In addition, a lower birth-rate meant less sewing for children by even full-time homemakers.[40]

This decrease in sewing was part of a larger socioeconomic trend in which households produced less and purchased more. All sorts of goods and services, from bread to entertainment, had become commercialized and clothing was just one element of this pattern. As people bought more items instead of making them at home, fewer women wanted or needed to sew—especially those in the middle class who could afford to buy off-the-rack clothing and preferred to spend money instead of time.[41]

This is not merely a story of declension, however. Not all women changed their habits. Many continued to sew at home, especially those who lived in rural areas where they were less likely to work for wages; had limited access to factory-made clothing; and often maintained more traditional family roles. In fact, one study found that many rural women sewed *more* in the 1920s than they had earlier.[42] After all, the new designs that were cheap to manufacture were also easier to make at home! It was still more expensive to buy clothing than to make it, so poorer women, young women, and girls, all of whom had less disposable income, were more likely to sew as well. Others sewed for non-economic goals such as charity. Many women preferred to sew because they did not like the new styles, found store-bought clothing to be poorly made, or enjoyed sewing as a creative outlet. Still, home dressmaking declined overall in the 1920s and it was in the interest of sewing-goods manufacturers to encourage home sewing. The question was how to promote a traditional activity in a society that was rapidly inventing new roles and behaviors for women.

NEW BUSINESS STRATEGIES

Changing consumer habits threatened industries that were invested in traditional behaviors.[43] Now that home sewing could no longer be assumed to be the norm, businesses had to adjust their marketing and sales practices. In an effort to regain customers and rescue their falling profits, some of these industries promoted a return to long-established gender roles, asserting that sewing was central to being a good mother and wife. Other approaches were based on adapting services and products. Firms assumed that women needed more training or wanted patterns that were easier to follow. Other tactics involved changing the image of home dressmaking and presenting sewing as easy, fun, and modern. Advertisements implied factory-made clothing was shoddy, expensive, and unimaginative. Some businesses sought to regain the affections of lost customers, while others focused on new recruits. In many ways, the industry chose to encourage women to sew by emphasizing supposedly natural feminine traits such as love of fashion, maternalism, and household thrift.

However, these companies were ultimately more interested in selling goods than in reforming society. After all, the people who made marketing decisions were also living in a context of social change. As a result, sewing-related businesses were flexible in their choice of tactics and arguments. They assiduously promoted traditionalism when it was convenient, but they also managed to use the very nature of the changes around them as selling points. They sought to accommodate customers by offering better prices, products and services, and by encouraging home sewing as modern—a means to earn extra money and express creativity. To a certain extent, retailers and advertisers acknowledged the changing lives of their customers and sought to accommodate new ideas about women's work and place in the home. The people calculating how to appeal to a shrinking pool of customers evidently wanted to appeal to women's sense of identity but did not want to alienate their customer base by seeming out of touch with social change.

These ideas were not new: firms had promoted all of these aspects of sewing in the past. The difference was that when sewing was no longer an automatic assumption, sewing-related businesses had to push harder, in any way they could, to convince women to sew. One of the ways the sewing-related businesses sought to regain customers was by blatantly associating home sewing with motherhood. Singer, for example, was eager to convince women that, even if they purchased clothing for themselves, at the very least, they ought to sew for their children. Singer machines were touted as ideal for a busy yet loving mother. One advertisement cried:

> "Mother - Let *me* sew!" Even a child is tempted by the ease of sewing with a modern Singer Electric . . . Mothers are finding this Singer Electric the quick and easy, inexpensive way to have more clothes for the children. . . . [44]

Singer published a series of how-to books written by Mary Brooks Picken, a sewing expert who had her own dressmaking school and taught "Economics of Fashion" at Columbia University. In *How To Make Children's Clothes the Modern Singer Way*, Picken described children's clothing as easy to make, appealing to natural maternal instincts and important to child development. Her introduction proclaims, "The mother who knows the treasured virtue of good taste will consider it as important to cultivate good taste in clothes in her children as good manners and correct speech."[45] The book would serve two purposes: it would teach women to sew and it would help them raise their children according to middle-class standards.

Children's clothing was portrayed as considerably easier to sew than a dress for an adult woman. A 1923 article in the magazine *Inspiration* exuberantly declared:

> Spring sewing is bound to have a fascinating aspect when looked at from the romper point of view, for when a romper suit for a wee lad or lassie who is the pride of the household is the point in question, sewing most certainly cannot assume a foreboding nature.[46]

The author conceded that it was easy enough to buy such things, but that when shopping "for the dearest little one in perhaps the whole wide world," mothers would naturally want to buy the best outfits which were inevitably too expensive. The solution? Make your own, preferably using patterns by McCall, *Woman's Home Companion*, or *Pictorial Review*.

Inspiration was, not coincidentally, put out by the Woman's Institute of Domestic Arts and Sciences, which had an obvious interest in encouraging the joys of homemaking. To persuade women to subscribe to correspondence classes in sewing and cooking, the organization put out the message that those skills helped women provide a nurturing environment for their families. A do-it-yourself guidebook published by the Woman's Institute entitled *Home Sewing Helps* argued that "plenty of well-made articles for home, self and family, which bespeak womanly pride and forethought, are assets in every home. . . ."[47]

Part of being a "good" housewife was clothing one's husband. While men's clothing had been the first to be absorbed by the ready-to-wear industry in the nineteenth century, some women had continued to make men's shirts. Some businesses sought to expand this niche market with kits that had the pieces already cut out and the hardest part, the neck and collar, pre-assembled. An advertisement for the kits claimed, "Women, who have learned how simple it is to make men's shirts with ready-made neck bands and how much better and more economical such shirts are, are very glad that they can perform such a service for the men of the family."[48] This sort of kit was appealing because it was a compromise—women could get the credit for making their husband's shirts while not having to do all of the work.

What if the potential customer did not feel a need to sew in order to prove her maternal or spousal skills? Another common strategy used to interest consumers was to emphasize that sewing could be easy, if one had the right supplies and equipment. In this light, women and girls were giving up too soon if they bought their clothing. Technology helped sewing machine manufacturers, largely because they could now make small motors to drive the machines. Singer emphasized the hours saved by users of these new electric machines: 20 minutes spent sewing a yard of straight seam by hand became a miraculous

20 seconds on a Singer Electric.[49] They had used the same argument of saving time to entice their earlier customers, who went from sewing all seams by hand to using hand-crank or treadle machines. Now, modern science was to be harnessed by the housewife once again. The argument was that with such savings of time, sewing was no longer work at all, eliminating one more excuse for not sewing for your family.

The new patterns were also easier to follow than their antecedents. Butterick's "Deltor" instruction sheet, first patented in the U.S. in 1919, led to the company's reputation for simplicity. Soon, Butterick pattern envelopes read: "The Deltor, enclosed with this pattern, shows you with pictures how to lay it out, put it together and finish it, so that it retains all the style and beauty of the original model." [50] A number of women interviewed for this project recalled Butterick's clear instructions; Edith Kurtz remembered that her mother found Butterick patterns "easy to follow."[51]

Paper patterns became even easier to decipher in just a few years. In 1921, Butterick rival McCall patented a way to print near-photographic quality images and instructions on the pattern pieces themselves. Also printed on the patterns were "Four Reasons why every woman should use the new McCall Pattern". Reason number one,"the instructions are clearly printed on every piece of the pattern. No more puzzling perforations", referred to competitors' products which had perforated numbers on each piece. The McCall pattern pieces are in fact clearer to read and handle. Whether the changes would live up to their promise to eliminate "that home-made look" is harder to discern.[52]

Publishers were also eager to promote the joy of sewing, and magazines ran regular features on quick and easy projects. The straight and loose styles of the 1920s, which helped make ready-to-wear clothing successful, were also easier to sew and magazines encouraged women to try out the new silhouettes with articles like "Straight Cuts to Style—Without any dangerous curves to plague the home dressmaker."[53] This emphasis on the ease with which women could sew, complemented by the magazine's advice, may have encouraged some readers: one reader thanked the *Woman's Home Companion* for its "pretty and practical" patterns.[54] Another letter writer remarked, "The dressmaking hints . . . are very interesting and helpful to inexperienced sewers like myself."[55] The campaign to render sewing less intimidating achieved considerable success.

This emphasis on ease could be misleading, however, and did not always acknowledge or address the difficulties faced by poorer or more isolated women. For example, many rural areas were not yet linked to municipal power grids. Others may not have had the cash to electrify their homes or replace a perfectly satisfactory treadle machine with a new electric model. The new patterns were of no use to women who could not afford them in the first place; sharecropper's wives in Texas could rarely afford to buy new patterns, and instead shared them amongst themselves.[56] While the new styles were easier to make when one had plenty of yard goods, it could be especially tricky to convert an older dress into a modern style. The buzz about the "new, improved" face of sewing products demonstrates the urban middle-class slant of the majority of these businesses.

Another strategy intended to convince women to return to their sewing machines was to focus on the individuality of homemade clothing and to emphasize women's "natural" desire to be attractive. The December 1923 issue of *Inspiration* included an article entitled "Husbands, Unlike Trains, Don't Always Stay Caught." A Dr. Frank Crane reminded women that their appearance was important in keeping their marriages healthy. He noted, "My point is that the woman who is careless about her appearance when she and her husband are alone is adding to her chances for unhappiness." While the commentary did not mention sewing per se, much of *Inspiration* was oriented toward sewing skills.[57] The same organization published a series of advertisements containing supposedly true stories of women who had changed their lives by sewing. In one such ad, a woman wrote:

> As I look back now, I can see that I was so busy with the baby and the housework that I wasn't giving as much attention to my clothes and myself as I did when I was single. And I don't care what the poets say—no man is going to love a woman with the same old fervor of the sweetheart days unless she keeps herself attractive.[58]

She found the means to make herself desirable again—and therefore save her marriage—by learning to sew her own clothing.

Other companies claimed that store-bought dresses were numbingly boring. Singer declared that home sewing would rescue women from the "endless duplication" of factory-made dresses, arguing:

> All women want to be "well dressed"—which means the attire most becoming to their personality. To accomplish this is real Art, for it implies a knowledge of draping the figure, of harmony in color and the colors best harmonizing with personality. This knowledge is the stock in trade of the highly paid dress designers, but it is innate to most girls.
>
> If properly taught in the use and productive value of a Singer machine and its appliances, the young woman can not only be well dressed but have the pride of individual dress-creation suited to her personality, and this at minimum cost, without tiresome shopping for suitable 'ready-to-wear' garments. . . . [59]

Butterick made similar claims; anyone could buy something, but a more discerning woman would prefer a home-made dress. Butterick, Singer, and other firms were eager to encourage the notion that home dressmaking was a way to acquire individuality and style 8211; and thereby feminine attractiveness.

While magazines ran articles on how sewing at home was an easy way to have original clothes, advertisements belied their true identity as profit-driven vehicles. As one scholar writes, "The magazines' twin missions as profit-making firms and advisors to women could sometimes operate at cross-purposes."[60] This was evident when articles on sewing were published adjacent to advertisements for ready-made clothing. Take, for example, an article promoting a pattern for a slip-on dress, described as "one of those comforting adaptable patterns that turns out a pretty frock," printed directly next to an advertisement for a mail-order catalog featuring blouses and dresses.[61] The advertisement and article are the same dimensions and feature similarly styled and sized images. A reader who sewed regularly and liked the pattern design might not have been distracted by the advertisement, but it is easy to imagine someone weighing the time and energy needed to make a unique dress versus the expediency but expense of buying one.

Most likely, expense was a significant factor for our hypothetical reader. While firms and trade organizations insisted that women were naturally maternal or drawn to fashion, they could not ignore an even more basic reason why women had sewn for decades: to save money. In order to cajole women into sewing, businesses had to appeal to this basic rationale. Even as it expanded its reach, ready-to-wear clothing was still more expensive than items sewn at home; women could make equivalent or even better-quality dresses for up to two-thirds off the price of a store-bought dress.[62] If women did not earn wages, sewing remained a way that they could make a significant contribution to the family economy.

Businesses were well aware of the economic reasons for sewing and promoted the savings affected by using their products. In this case, they were perhaps more sensitive to questions of socioeconomic class than usual. Magazines ran regular columns on how to keep expenses down through sewing and sold patterns for inexpensive designs. The *Woman's Home Companion* claimed that its "Economy Dress" included

> all the essentials of smartness—printed crepe silk, a circular skirt generously wide, long flowing sleeves. And if you make the dress yourself the cost is less than $11. To be exact, the findings total $10.95. Or, if you have an old chiffon waist or tunic, scratch seven-eighths yard of chiffon from your shopping list and your purchases will come to only $9.32.[63]

The writer included a detailed list of necessary supplies and their cost, and then added, "Of course it couldn't be done if it wasn't for the fact that this dress has a circular skirt that doesn't waste the goods."[64] Such a blunt discussion of thrift may seem counter to the interests of the magazine, which, after all, sought to sell advertising space, but the editors were also keenly aware of the needs of their readers and evidently believed that a frank discussion of economical sewing would serve them well.

This set of circumstances gave a new twist to marketing strategies. Much advertising was directed at middle-class consumers, who were the ones with money to spend, but it was working-class women who were the most likely to make a significant portion of their clothing. A study in 1919 by the Bureau of Municipal Research of Philadelphia found that families with an income of less than $2,000 a year tended to wear more home-made than store-bought clothing.[65] In 1927, another survey claimed that 90 percent of respondents sewed because of "economy." Most of these women were in families in which the annual income was between $2,000 and $3,000. In 1927, the average yearly salary for all industries, including farm labor, was $1,380.[66] Therefore, women in families earning *over* the national average still found it helpful to sew in order to conserve resources, making it even more likely that women in families with smaller incomes felt considerable pressure to sew. Home dressmaking industries needed to do more to address the interests of women who were concerned about their home finances, whether they were working class or middle class.

Sewing machine companies had been attuned to the cost and class dimensions of their product from the beginning and they continued to promote the long-term benefits of investing in a machine when sales began to dip. Singer's instructional booklets often spoke of the lower cost of home sewn items. One booklet asked consumers to

> think of the saving effected—with only the cost of materials involved, the average home made dress costs only about one-third the price of a similar dress ready made. And the materials purchased are usually of far better quality, which means they give better service.[67]

But many women did not have to be reminded that a machine, if affordable, could save hours of work and a considerable amount of money. A sewing machine was a great help to poor women who had no choice but to make all of their family's clothing as well as work in the fields or for wages. Inez Adams Walker, an African American woman who sewed for her children during the 1920s, told an interviewer, "I had four girls. And before I was able to get my machine, I made them dresses on my hands. Get a needle and thread and made them on my hands."[68] Since Walker had little choice but to sew to clothe her girls, it was simply a question of how long it would take. At a time when the vast majority of black women in that area worked in the fields chopping cotton, a sewing machine could make a huge difference in their quality of life. Machine producers and retailers would have been remiss had they not been keenly aware of the class and racial dimensions of selling their product.[69]

While sewing as a cost-saver was essential to working-class women, it was an issue for middle-class women as well who were often responsible for household spending but depended on their husbands to make the bulk of the family income. By emphasizing the thrifty nature of sewing at home, magazines and producers could appeal to the fact that home sewing gave women a degre of control over family finances.[70] A Singer manual bluntly described this scenario, claiming that "a large part of the family income is usually spent by the woman and her knowledge of how to plan and make proper clothing for the family has a great influence on the purchasing power of the income."[71] The industry was careful not to provoke too much thought about household power dynamics, however, preferring to argue that the resulting thrift would help women fulfill their domestic roles.

Another population that had limited funds to spend on clothing was girls and teenagers. Magazines and producers used cost-conscious marketing to attract young consumers, who, even if they came from a middle-class family, would have had little money to spend. The Girl Scout magazine *American Girl* encouraged girls to try easy projects such as making slips and nightgowns. One installment of the regular feature, "Let's Talk About Clothes," focused on undergarments and reads, "As a matter of fact, if you don't mind work (and by that I mean sewing), you can save a little money on your underwear by making it yourself."[72]

Home economics books and magazines aimed at teenaged girls often included advice on budgeting. *American Girl* described a "typical" girls' clothing budget as

> drawn up in collaboration with the Altman School and College Bureau which is constantly working on these problems and really knows what girls need, like and buy. It indicates a general minimum. Some girls will want more. It would probably be possible to get along with less. And it can be varied to suit the individual, locality or special circumstances.[73]

These advertisements and articles embraced thrift, presenting cost-consciousness as a virtue to be admired and desired by teenaged girls. *American Girl* regularly included articles about girls who wanted a new dress for a party and who cleverly made their own instead of pestering parents who might be unwilling or unable to buy one.[74] One author claimed she could think of nothing

> more satisfying than to be the clever girl who can make it herself—a new party dress, for instance, when a party comes up unexpectedly that you just have to have a new

dress for, or lots of simple summer dresses that you can make for very little and that do cost a lot when you have to buy them.[75]

Sewing was promoted to cash-poor teenagers as a means to obtain a degree of financial independence and style. For this particular group, their age largely defined their access to clothing. Companies like Singer that were interested in promoting sewing or groups like the Girl Scouts that wanted to appeal to girls identified thrift as a virtue.

A number of firms poured resources into sewing education while claiming to improve women's quality of life. Singer supplied schools with sewing machines for decades and the instructional booklets that accompanied each machine include photographs of girls and young women sitting in Singer-filled classrooms in schools and colleges around the country. One booklet, published in 1923, insisted that "no matter what station in life a woman may occupy, she should at least understand the elementary principals of sewing, but to those who have the ambition to cultivate skill in machine sewing there is a world of happiness at hand."[76] It did not hurt that women who learned to sew on a Singer were more likely to buy one, too.

Pattern companies also put significant resources into sewing education, betting that if girls were taught to sew they would continue to do so as adults. The *New York Times* supported this tactic, stating in one article that there were more than 16 million schoolgirls in the country who were all potential customers.[77] Butterick and McCall supplied public schools with textbooks that claimed sewing—including, of course, learning to use patterns 8211; was crucial to girls' future home life. Butterick created a "School Department" and participated in curriculum conferences.[78] An in-house document claimed that Butterick "is active in school work and has what is considered one of the best prepared books on the teaching of sewing that is being requisitioned for use in schools everywhere."[79]

The same companies encouraged girls to sew by introducing an element of competition. Butterick organized a series of contests for girls, with the finalists' designs judged by "experts" in New York and awarded prizes.[80] Florence Epstein recalled winning a prize in a Butterick contest in the early 1920s. At 89 years old, she still remembered winning a "pretty purse" when she was twelve. Clearly, these companies made an impact, impressing their brand names on the minds of future customers.

In addition to pursuing these and other strategies independently, sewing businesses joined forces to promote common interests. To a certain degree, they were already working together. Magazines and how-to books hawked machines and patterns, fabric shops ran sewing classes on Singer machines, and pattern companies had long described the latest fabrics to use with their designs. Still, as the pool of women who sewed at home shrank, businesses made concerted efforts to cross-pollinate.

One obvious way for firms to take advantage of the audiences at each other's disposal was to increase advertising. Until sewing began to decline in popularity, the big pattern companies had offered their goods solely through their *own* magazines and through designated vendors around the country. As of the 1920s, however, there is evidence that they bit the bullet and began advertising in magazines that they did not control. For example, Pictorial Review, Butterick, and McCall started advertising in Crowell-Collier magazines, publishers of *Woman's Home Companion*, as well as *The American Magazine, Colliers,* and others.[81]

Other sewing-related companies, such as Corticelli Silks and the Spool Cotton Company, increased their advertising expenditures around the same time. The Woman's Institute was among the seventy-five top sources of advertising revenue for Crowell-Collier in 1922.[82] Of course, without evidence of other factors influencing decision making, it is impossible to fully understand a rise in advertising budgets. Still, it is likely that dramatic jumps in advertising spending, such as the 700 percent increase in expenditures between 1913 and 1922 by the Armory Brown Company, a Boston-based textile firm, is an indication that textile producers felt it necessary to reach customers by new means.[83]

While advertising in each other's publications was one way for companies to try to work together to increase interest in sewing, another more overt form of cooperation was to form a trade association to determine problems and coordinate strategies. Butterick helped form the National Costume Art Association in the late 1920s, which then became part of the National Retail Dry Goods Association based in New York. One strategy promoted by this umbrella organization was to focus on customer service. Butterick argued that customers were not to blame, and, in fact, were eager to sew. Instead, it was the producers and retailers who had failed customers by not providing sufficient support. An internal document in the Butterick archives argued that the heart of the problem was that stores were not accommodating customers. Stores were urged to hire a "consulting costume artist" who could help customers with their sewing projects. The author claimed that while women and girls were eager to sew, they

> need a little guidance whether it be in selecting becoming styles and fabrics, cutting out their first few dresses, in fitting or adjusting the nearly completed dress, or in some sewing operation; and it has been proven that they are willing to pay for such help because with it they can now have dresses which are as attractive and becoming as any.[84]

The *New York Times* praised these collaborative efforts, noting in 1926 that home sewing "has been an industry lacking in coordinated effort to maintain and stimulate it by those who manufacture the products it absorbs.[85] The article noted that the National Costume Art Association, which at press time included twenty companies, was reaching out to women's clubs, the Y.W.C.A., and charities. Plans were in the works for further school outreach and national dressmaking contests. These efforts were intended to rekindle and support what producers claimed were innate desires in women. According to the Butterick documents, "Most women and girls are deeply interested in individuality, good taste and beauty;" retailers just had to work together to harness those naturally female inclinations.[86]

Throughout this revamping of marketing strategies, sewing businesses, and interested media found themselves in an incongruous position. They were largely urban entities promoting an activity that was becoming a predominantly working class and rural art. A *New York Times* article in 1923 praised a network of Home Dressmaker's clubs in Wisconsin, remarking on how "farm women" saved thousands of dollars by making their own clothing.[87] A few years later, the *Times* praised the "one section of the feminine population that is holding out against utter uniformity," citing a home economist from Indiana who claimed that

> farm girls dress better, with more distinction than the city girls, and that they do it on less money. It can hardly be said that they are less subject to the insidious influence of film flappers, for they get into town often enough. They must be more individualistic, more dependent on their own resources, and inclined to develop along lines of their own choosing.

The article then asked whether these talents extended to other dimensions of women's lives: "Does their superiority, one wonders, extend to other things? Do they also cook better, keep house better, manage husbands and children better?"[88] The article does not appear to ask these questions in an ironic tone. We have an example, then, of a New York City institution comparing its own readers to rural women and finding the out-of-towners more feminine, creative, and resourceful.

For businesses, however, this admiration of rural women's resourcefulness was more practical than ideological. After all, home dressmaker's clubs bought a sizable amount of fabric, patterns, and machines. While they found themselves encouraging urban women to behave like their rural counterparts, sewing businesses were providing ideas and access to urban styles to women who lived far from the centers of fashion. Catalogues and magazines sold ready-to-wear garments but also provided inexpensive and up-to-date patterns and fabrics to women who had little access to shops and fashionable dressmakers. One scholar argues that rural women (as well as urban working-class women) used sewing as a way to conform to urban middle-class standards of dress and appearance. [89] The businesses and media that encouraged urban women to behave like rural women also provided the means for rural women to look like women in New York, including the possibility for them to dress like "film flappers." It was sales, not the resourcefulness or femininity of rural women, that attracted businesses' attention.

CONCLUSION

Sewing-related businesses sought to harness cultural values to ensure continued demand for their goods. One "product" they promoted was the transmission of gender roles to girls and women. As they simplified sewing products, promoted education, and publicized the cost benefits of home dressmaking, businesses urged women to rediscover the "domestic virtues" associated with sewing. They romanticized motherhood and homemaking and promoted the domestic work of rural women as desirable to the general population. By doing so, businesses helped to transform domesticity into a product that they could sell to women and their families.

Such a message might reassure the many women who needed no convincing to buy sewing goods and sway those who would otherwise buy ready-made clothing. At the same time, the people making marketing decisions, designing patterns, and writing articles 8211; many of them women with home economics degrees—were not operating in isolation. They recognized the powerful changes influencing women's decisions and saw in them ways to garner customers. If they believed that their customerhad changed from a rural homemaker to a woman who worked in an office she was offered patterns and fabric for appropriate office wear and a speedy electric sewing machine. After all, this customer made her own money—there was no more need to appeal to a husband to pay for that Singer.

These businesses faced an uphill battle. As workforce participation, access to birth control, increasing urbanization, and commercial culture changed the way women behaved, home dressmaking was most popular in rural areas and among women who needed to save money. As a result, many businessmen and journalists found themselves trying to convince middle-class urban and suburban women that they should behave like a rural, lower-income group.[90] It is not surprising that producers of fabric and related products would move to encourage sewing, but when this promotion dovetailed with notions of femininity and motherhood, the businesses were selling more than sewing machines or patterns. To speak of sewing as a "domestic virtue" while planning to harness such activity to bolster sales is to see sewing as both a private, inherently feminine domain and as a commodity.

NOTES

1. "Would Teach Girls To Make Dresses: Dry Goods Buyers Lay Loss in Cloth Sales to 'Neglect of Domestic Virtues'," *New York Times*, 19 January 1926, 2.

2. "To Help Increase Sewing in Homes, Plans Have Been Laid for a Cooperative Campaign Having This End in View," *New York Times*, 7 March 1926, 19.

3. United States Thirteenth Census, Manufacturing, 1910, reel 2 of 2, 25, and United States Fourteenth Census, Manufacturing, 1920, reel 2 of 2, 169.

4. Sears, Roebuck & Co. *Catalog No. 111*, 831 & 845.

5. Sears, Roebuck & Co. *Catalog No. 111*, 831, 845, 848 & 869.

6. Advertisement for Fred Butterfield & Co., *Woman's Home Companion* (March 1910): 69.

7. Grace Margaret Gould, "Street Fabrics for Spring," *Woman's Home Companion* (March 1910), 82.

8. Grace Margaret Gould, "Street Fabrics for Spring," *Woman's Home Companion* (March 1910): 82.

9. Jean Gulrich, telephone conversation with author, 7 April 2001. Mrs. Gulrich was born in the mid-1920s.

10. Connolly notes, however, that a machine could only do so much. She writes that "despite these high hopes, the sewing machine failed to fundamentally transform the task of home sewing. While it could produce a faster, more secure seam than those produced by hand, the machine could only perform certain sewing tasks. Moreover, the sewing machine could not help at all with the difficult tasks of cutting and fitting garments." "The Transformation of Home Sewing and the Sewing Machine in America, 1850–1929," 46–7.

11. See for example *Singer the Universal Sewing Machine*, advertising pamphlet/trade card, 1901, Joseph Downs Collection of Manuscripts and Printed Ephemera, Winterthur Museum, Garden and Library.

12. 348 Brandon, 121, and Derks, 68. A number of scholars have studied the history of the sewing machine industry and its effects on women's work and the economy at large. Some focus on the machine industry themselves: Ruth Brandon's *A Capitalist Romance: Singer and the Sewing Machine* (Philadelphia & New York: J. B. Lippincott Co., 1977) provides an overview of the Singer empire along with insight into the founder's salacious personal life Others such as Joan Severa locate sewing machines in the social history of fashion.

13. Figures from *Sixth Annual Report of the Bureau of Statistics of Labor* (Boston: Wright & Potter State Printers, 1875) 436, cited in Connolly, 69.

14. Statistics from the *Sixth Annual Report of the Bureau of Statistics of Labor* (Boston: Wright & Potter, State Printers, 1875) 436, cited in Connolly, "The Transformation of Home Sewing and the Sewing Machine in America," 69.

15. *The Sewing Machine Business As It Is To-Day*, undated pamphlet, New-York Historical Society, 1. Judging from the prices it quotes the pamphlet is probably from the late nineteenth century.

16. *A Manual of Family Sewing Machines*, (New York: Singer Sewing Machine Company, February 1914 & November 1914), 2.

17. Jane Simonsen, *Making Home Work*, 80.

18. Pauline Reynard, *A Century of Home Sewing*, 53, unpublished typescript, folder 6, box 1, Singer Sewing Machine Company records, and Sarah Deutsch, *No Separate Refuge: Culture, Class, and Gender on an Anglo-Hispanic Frontier in the American Southwest, 1880–1940* (New York: Oxford University Press, 1987), 38. Deutsch also notes that the machines were popular: by 1930 about 90 percent of Hispanic women in one county owned a sewing machine; 188.

19. Nancy Page Fernandez, "Innovations for Home Dressmaking and the Popularization of Stylish Dress," *Journal of American Culture* 17 (1994): 23–33, 27. For an overview of the development of the pattern industry, see Carole Anne Dickson, "Patterns for Garments: A History of the Paper Garment Pattern Industry in America to 1976," Ph.D. Dissertation, Ohio State University, 1979 and Joy Spanabel Emery, "Dreams on Paper" in Burman, 235–253. Scholars have taken different positions on the role of the pattern industry pattern industry. Claudia Kidwell, Margaret Walsh and Fernandez claim patterns "democratized" clothing, giving ordinary people access to fashionable clothing; see Kidwell, *Cutting a Fashionable Fit: Dressmakers' Drafting Systems in the United States* (Washington, DC: Smithsonian Institution Press, 1979) and Walsh, "The Democratization of Fashion: The Emergence of the Women's Dress Pattern Industry," *Journal of American History* 66 (1979): 299–313. However, in *The Female Economy: The Millinery and Dressmaking Trades, 1890–1930* (Urbana and Chicago: University of Illinois Press, 1997), Wendy Gamber sees the growth of easy-to-follow patterns as detrimental to independent dressmakers.

20. Marie Jonreau, "The New Spring Shirt-Waists," *The Woman's Home Companion* (April 1900): 36 and "Fashions of Today," *Delineator* (October 1898): 413.

21. "Fashions for February, 1898," *Delineator* (February, 1898): 159.

22. *Sears, Roebuck & Co. Catalogue No. III*, 858. This was a good price—four years earlier, a Butterick pattern for a similar item cost about 20 cents.

23. Mme Rumford, "The Prevailing Styles for Early Summer," *The Colored American Magazine* (June 1901):130.

24. See for example the fold-out pattern included in the October, 1903 Harper's Bazar.

25. Several scholars have addressed the role magazines played in women's lives and debate how magazines can be used as historical sources. For two such studies, see Jennifer Scanlon, *Inarticulate Longings: The Ladies' Home Journal, Gender, and the*

Promises of Consumer Culture (New York: Routledge Press, 1995) and Matthew Schneirov, *The Dream of a New Social Order: Popular Magazines in America, 1893–1914* (New York; Columbia University Press, 1994).

26. The new rates were about $1 a year or 5–10 cents per issue. In "Old Homes in a City of Perpetual Change, Women's Magazines, 1890–1916," *Business History Review* 63 (Winter 1989): 715–756, Mary Ellen Waller-Zuckerman argues that working-class women would not have been able to afford a new magazine but may have read issues that had been "passed along," 720–21.

27. Waller-Zuckerman, "Old Homes in a City of Perpetual Change," 751. The other magazines on the list were the *People's Home Journal,* the *Saturday Evening Post, Cosmopolitan* and *Collier's.*

28. Analysis in Mrs. John Doe, *A Book Wherein for the First Time an Attempt Is Made to Determine Woman's Share in the Purchasing Power of the Nation* (New York, 1918), chart reproduced in Waller-Zuckerman, "Old Homes in a City of Perpetual Change," 738.

29. Dinah Sturgis, "Hints to Home Dressmakers II" in "What To Wear and How to Make It," *Ladies' Home Companion* (June 1895), 10–12, 10. Cutting fabric "on the bias" means diagonal to the weave, which makes it hang in an attractive way but also requires more fabric.

30. Dinah Sturgis, "What To Wear and How To Make It," *Ladies' Home Companion* (May 1893): 8.

31. Anne L. Jessup, ed. *The Sewing Book, Containing Complete Instructions in Sewing and Simple Garment-Making for Children in the Primary and Grammar Grades* (New York: The Butterick Publishing Co., 1913), 3.

32. Lydia Trattles Coates, *American Dressmaking Step by Step, containing complete, concise, up-to-date, and comprehensible instruction in Sewing, Dressmaking and Tailoring* (New York: The Pictorial Review Company, 1917, second edition, 1920), 235.

33. Coates, *American Dressmaking Step by Step,* 235 & 237.

34. Coates, *American Dressmaking Step by Step,* preface.

35. "Sewing at Home Decreases as ''Ready-Mades' Gain Favor - but Survey by Bureau of Home Economics Discloses Rural Women Still Ply the Needle," *New York Times,* 18 December 1927, 6.

36. Reynard, *A Century of Home Sewing,* 63.

37. Reynard, *A Century of Home Sewing,* 63. Exact figures are $473,888,000 in 1914 and $1,200,543,000 in 1919.

38. There is debate as to exactly why the styles changed so much during this time. Most fashion historians would agree however that it was a combination of factors, including changing roles for women, including increased interest in sports and the concomitant fashions; the catalyst of the war, including rationed fabric and the demand for ease of movement for female ambulance drivers and nurses; and the influence of a few particularly influential designers such as Paul Poiret and Coco Chanel. James Laver's *Costume & Fashion, A Concise History* (London: Thames and Hudson, 1969, reprinted 1988) provides an overview of these changes.

39. Mary Beth Norton and Ruth M. Alexander, eds., *Major Problems in American Women's History* (Lexington, Massachusetts: D.C. Heath & Co., 1996), 284.

40. In *The Grounding of Modern Feminism* (New Haven: Yale University Press, 1987) Nancy Cott addresses how changing demographic, educational, cultural and work patterns affected gender relations. I have applied some of her data and theories to home sewing in particular.

41. See for example Mabel Hastie and Geraldine Gorton, "What Shall We Teach Regarding Clothing and Laundry Problems," *Journal of Home Economics* 18 (March 1926): 127–133.

42. Hastie and Gorton describe a study undertaken by the Education Section of the American Home Economics Association that found, in part, that 65 percent of rural respondents (compared to 17 percent of urban women) made more clothing in their homes in 1925 than they had three years earlier; see p. 131.

43. There is a diverse literature on the cultural ramifications of consumerism. Some scholars such as Kathy Peiss, Nan Enstad and James Livington tend to see consumption as a means of expressing identity and subjectivity, whereas others such as Sara Deutsch remain wary of the way consumer goods can be used to coerce and change cultures. Still other scholars such as Susan Porter Benson examine how gender and class hierarchies are reenacted in environments devoted to consumerism such as the department store. See Nan Enstad, *Ladies of Labor, Girls of Adventure: Working Women, Popular Culture, and Labor Politics at the Turn of the Twentieth Century* (New York: Columbia University Press, 1999), Kathy Peiss, *Cheap Amusements: Working Women in Turn-of-the-Century New York* by Kathy Peiss (Philadelphia: Temple University Press, 1986), James Livingston, "Modern Subjectivity and Consumer Culture," in Susan Strasser, Charles McGovern and Matthias Judt, eds., *Getting and Spending: European and American Consumer Societies in the Twentieth Century* (Cambridge: Cambridge University Press, 1998), 413–429, Sara Deutsch, *No Separate Refuge: Culture, Class, and Gender on an Anglo-Hispanic Frontier in the American Southwest, 1880–1940* (New York: Oxford University Press, 1987) and Susan Porter Benson, *Counter Cultures*.

44. Advertisement for Singer Sewing Machine Co., *Fashion Service* (Fall & Winter 1929), inside front cover.

45. Mary Brooks Picken, *How To Make Children's Clothes the Modern Singer Way* (New York: Singer Sewing Machine Co., 1927), 1. Picken ran the Woman's Institute before moving to New York.

46. Awilda Fellows, "Rompers in Fascinating Variety," *Inspiration* (March 1923): 5.

47. *Home Sewing Helps: Ideas and Instructions That Make Possible the Development of Many Lovely Garments and Articles of Use in the Home* (Scranton, PA: Woman's Institute of Domestic Arts & Sciences, Inc., through the International Educational Publishing Company, 1925), 2.

48. Advertisement for Merchandise Service, *Inspiration* (March 1926): 14.

49. *A Manual of Family Sewing Machines* (New York: Singer Sewing Machine Co., 1923), inside front cover.

50. Pattern #1449, "Frock for Women and Young Girls" (New York: Butterick Pattern Company, circa 1925).

51. Kurtz, interview.

52. McCall Pattern Company, Printed Pattern #5044, for a Ladies' and Misses' Negligee, ca 1925.

53. "Straight Cuts to Style - Without any dangerous curves to plague the home dressmaker," *Women's Home Companion* (February 1922): 32.

54. Mrs. L.G., Connecticut, "Dear Editor," *Woman's Home Companion* (December 1924): 134.

55. Mrs. A.D.B., Nebraska, "Dear Editor," *Woman's Home Companion* (May 1920): 160.

56. Sharpless, *Fertile Ground*, 97.

57. Frank Crane, "How I Like a Woman to Look," reprinted from the *American Magazine* by special permission, *Inspiration* (December 1923): 10–11.

58. Advertisement for the Woman's Institute of Domestic Arts and Sciences, *Woman's Home Companion* (January 1922): 61.

59. *A Manual of Family Sewing Machines* (New York: Singer Sewing Machine Company, 1923), 14. Singer Company records.

60. Waller-Zuckerman, "Old Homes in a City of Perpetual Change," 755.

61. "Button On or Tie About" and advertisement for Bella Hess & Co., *Woman's Home Companion* (February 1922), 84. As the first promotes a *Woman's Home Companion* pattern, perhaps they are essentially both advertisements, only for different uses of time and money.

62. Katherine Cranor, "Homemade Versus Ready-Made Clothing," *Journal of Home Economics* 12 (May 1920): 230–233, 230.

63. "Clothes You Can Afford," *Woman's Home Companion* 50 (January 1922) 63.

64. "Clothes You Can Afford," 63.

65. Bureau of Municipal Research of Philadelphia, *Workingman's Standard of Living*, 3–11, cited in Connolly, "The Transformation of Home Sewing and the Sewing Machine in America, 1850–1929," 213.

66. Scott Derks, ed., *The Value of a Dollar: Prices & Incomes in the United States 1860–1999* (Lakeville, Connecticut: Grey House Publishing, 1999), 163.

67. *A Manual of Family Sewing Machines* (New York: Singer Sewing Machine Company, 1923), 14, Singer Sewing Machine Company records.

68. Sharpless, *Fertile Ground, Narrow Choices*, 97.

69. Sharpless cites a survey that claimed that 95 percent of black women picked cotton and 81 percent chopped and hoed the plants, compared to 89 percent and 69 percent respectively for the same jobs for white women, 166.

70. In *When Ladies Go A-Thieving: Middle-Class Shoplifters in the Victorian Department Store* (New York: Oxford University Press, 1989), Elaine Abelson describes how middle class women "had virtually no control over money. A woman's allowance or pocket money was generally a gift bestowed, not something to which she was entitled", 166. While Abelson describes an earlier era, many of the same dynamics were at work in the 1920s.

71. A *Manual of Family Sewing Machines* (New York: Singer Sewing Machine Company, 1929), 2, Singer Sewing Machine Company records.Singer Company Records.

72. Hazel Rawson Cades, "Let's Talk About Clothes," *American Girl* (July 1926), 27.

73. Hazel Rawson Cades, "A Clothes Budget," *American Girl* (September 1929), 25.

74. See for example Camille David, "A Party Dress for a Princess," *American Girl* (November 1924), 20–21, 46.

75. Helen Perry Curtis, "Anyone Can Make It," *American Girl* (July 1928), 17–18.

76. A *Manual of Family Sewing Machines* (New York: Singer Sewing Machine Company, 1923). 14, Singer Sewing Machine Company records.

77. "To Help Increase Sewing in Homes, Plans Have Been Laid for a Cooperative Campaign Having This End In View," *The New York Times*, 7 March 1926, sec. 2, 5.

78. Anne L. Jessup, ed. *The Sewing Book, Containing Complete Instructions in Sewing and Simple Garment-Making for Children in the Primary and Grammar Grades* (New York: The Butterick Publishing Co., 1913)

79. Ruppell, *The Story of Butterick*, section 3, 20.

80. "Prizes are Awarded to Girl Dressmakers," *New York Times*, 29 December, 1928, section 9, 2, and Ruppell, *The Story of Butterick*, section 3, 20.

81. Crowell-Collier Co., *National Markets and National Advertising* (New York: The Crowell Publishing Co., 1922), 142.

82. Crowell-Collier Co., *National Markets and National Advertising*, 52.

83. Crowell-Collier Co., *National Markets and National Advertising*, 63. Armory Brown spent $7,300 on advertising in Crowell-Collier publications in 1913 and $51,250 in 1922.

84. Ruppell, *The Story of Butterick*, section 7, 14.

85. "To Help Increase Sewing in Homes . . ."

86. Ruppell, *The Story of Butterick*, section 7, 14.

87. "Wisconsin Home Dressmaking," *The New York Times*, 29 July 1923, sec. 7, 4.

88. "Farm Girls and Pretty Clothes," *The New York Times*, 15 December 1926, 6.

89. Joan M. Jenson and Sue Davidson, eds. *A Needle, A Bobbin, A Strike: Women Needleworkers in America* (Philadelphia: Temple University Press, 1984). Jenson, in her introduction, argues that sewing was in fact a means of social conformity and that "patterns helped women conform to national dress norms", 13.

90. Industries experienced a range of effects from changing consumer habits. While the textile industry, for example, could redirect its products to the ready-to-wear market, domestic sewing machine manufacturers were less flexible. A number of firms went out of business before the turn of the century in part because of the structure of the overall industry, but a second wave of buyouts, consolidations and closures took place in the 1920s. For details, see Grace Rogers Cooper, *The Sewing Machine; Its Invention and Development* (Washington, DC: Smithsonian Institution Press, 1976), 160–162.

5. CLOTHING FOR SPORT

Home Sewing as a Laboratory for New Standards

At 53, Frances Willard, leader of the Women's Christian Temperance Union, learned to ride a bicycle. When she rode her two-wheeler 8211; which she named Gladys—she wore a tweed suit, the skirt hem three inches from the ground, and walking-shoes. In her 1895 book, *How I Learned to Ride the Bicycle,* Willard questioned women who claimed their conventional dress was comfortable and wrote that "reason will gain upon precedent, and ere long the comfortable, sensible, and artistic wardrobe of the rider will make the conventional style of woman's dress absurd to the eye and unendurable to the understanding."[1]

Women who crafted sleeveless dresses and shorter skirts often tested the boundaries of accepted taste. There were, however, circumstances which warranted unusual clothing and which therefore accustomed people to new designs. The clothing made and worn for sports such as cycling, swimming, and gymnasium exercise shows how home sewing interacted with new behaviors, changes in sewing-related businesses, and transforming cultural patterns. These garments offered women the chance to determine the parameters of acceptable appearance and dress. The physicality of newly popular sports demanded a genre of costume that challenged prevailing ideas of decorum and women's fragility. Through the process of inventing and adapting clothing to suit new activities, both women and the fashion industry helped to produce a new conception of what it meant to be feminine.

This chapter explores the role of invention and negotiation in the development of a new category of clothing. It argues that the novelty and marginality of clothing for sport provided a space in which women contested notions of modesty and appropriate bodies, behavior, and appearance. An interactive relationship between producers and consumers emerged in which the choices women made helped reinvent twentieth century femininity. Moreover, while affluent and middle-class women had the most time for sports, this athleticism was accessible to working-class women as well. As these new activities redefined notions of propriety, some of the distinctions between white, middle-class women and the working women against whom they had defined their respectability were challenged as well.

While sports outfits became available ready-made, many women sewed their own. Schools and other institutions that supported women's sports often expected participants to make their own gym suits, and women who wanted to make bicycling or bathing ensembles had the approval and support of pattern producers and magazine editors. With fewer rules to follow, home dressmakers could take risks with the designs for clothing for bicycling or swimming that they might not have taken with their other garments. By sewing their own outfits, women had the most control over design, how they could move while playing their sport, and how they would be perceived.

CHANGING VIEWS OF WOMEN AND SPORT

Among the changes in gendered behaviors of the late nineteenth and early twentieth centuries was a growing acceptance of women's participation in athletics and physical culture and a gradual re-thinking of the meanings attached to the female body. A new understanding of health and leisure, tempered with caution, informed ideas of proper female behavior. It was increasingly common to see women at beaches, in single-sex gymnasiums, on the recently invented bicycle, playing tennis and golf, fencing, and walking in the woods. Once discouraged, girls now were encouraged to be "athletic" and seized opportunities to play and exercise at schools, playgrounds, and settlement houses. This new physical culture infused and informed the emerging concept of the "New Woman."[2]

Even as sport and "physical culture" became increasingly accepted, they remained problematic. [3] Although some experts encouraged women to exercise, others warned of its dangers. Well into the twentieth century, magazine articles which praised healthy "modern girls" would in the same breath ask,

"Are athletics a menace to motherhood?" Too much exercise, especially unsupervised, could threaten a girl's future health and fertility; the "free out-of-door life, so priceless when properly conducted, may prove to be the path to pain and weakness, if not to permanent invalidism."[4]

At the very least, writers argued, too much sport could leave women with masculinized bodies. Contemporary fiction and magazine articles expressed a fear that sport would toughen women, either in specific physical ways or by behavioral changes. In Edith Wharton's *The Age of Innocence,* set in the 1870s, a society matron complains that a younger woman's hand was too large due to "these modern sports that spread the joints."[5] Either because they were invested in the same values or in self-defense, exercise proponents eagerly assured readers that athletic women would not develop hard muscles or other "masculine" traits. An 1890 article promoting fencing warned against the dangers of too much tennis, claiming that among aficionados "big, knotty biceps are found to have become all too prominent in a white, rounded arm, and gloves for the left hand refuse to fit over the broadened palm."[6] Another article glowingly praised a new women's health club but assured readers that the club's gymnastics instructor was not at all the typical athlete, with specimen biceps and iron integuments, according to the popular notion, but a thoroughly womanly and refined personality," thereby implying that she would not threaten the femininity of her pupils.[7]

Still, the concern for health could also serve as an argument for greater acceptance of women's participation in sports. In 1850, the *Massachusetts Teacher* warned that girls would not be "fit" mothers if they did not exercise.[8] Proponents of calisthenics such as Catharine Beecher claimed that gentle stretches and push-ups against a table would render women healthier for childbirth and housework. Etiquette books proposed that mild exercise was good for women's health. One manual from the 1860s claimed that "calisthenics, and the Indian sceptre, as taught on the improved scale by our present professors, are also highly beneficial as exercises," and that "ladies of every age" who participated "gained increased strength and stature, improved in the state of their health, and added grace, ease, and firmness to their motions."[9] Exercise was therefore acceptable as long as it promoted health and preserved feminine qualities such as grace and posture. It might even encourage a "rosy glow" which would make young women more attractive to appropriate men.

During the 1870s and 1880s, schools and colleges began to teach physical education, and seaside and mountain vacations became more affordable. By the 1890s, innovations such as the bicycle became wildly popular. A day trip to the beach was accessible to people of all income levels. Contemporary articles about Coney Island described how both rich and poor enjoyed the beaches although they did note a "descending scale of fashion" among the beach resorts.

Meanwhile, private gyms and colleges were oriented more toward the middle and upper classes.[10] Organizations such as settlement houses created to address the needs of working people offered sports activities as well. The ideas of femininity and respectability central to white, middle-class ideology therefore affected any woman who joined in the discussion over clothing for sport.

Sports became increasingly associated with ideas of modernity. Athletics offered new sources of personal gratification and social interaction, based more on consumption and entertainment than production and traditional class and family ties. Charles Dana Gibson created the famous "Gibson Girl" images that epitomized for many Americans the "New Woman." He often critiqued Victorian control of women in his illustrations and portrayed women involved in sport. It was just one example of how the New Woman" was becoming heavily intertwined with the new physical culture.

WHAT TO WEAR?

As sports and leisure became increasingly common, women began to ask what could be worn which would preserve modesty and femininity yet allow for ease of movement and comfort. While mainstream clothing changed relatively slowly, clothing for sport, in its specificity and novelty, was open for debate. Moreover, given its marginality, it was considerably less threatening. Starting around the 1870s and accelerating through the turn of the century, cultural vehicles such as magazines and etiquette books recognized that sports required a re-thinking of clothing design. Articles in mainstream publications asked what women should wear for specific activities and fashion magazines offered suggestions and images. Meanwhile, schools and clubs proposed their own uniforms, and etiquette writers, dress reformers, fiction writers, and sports enthusiasts joined the discussion.

Many women found that their clothing did not accommodate new physical activities, and so embraced a series of innovations that defined a new form of clothing that was appropriate yet practical.[11] Unlike the dress reform movement, marginalized since its beginnings in the 1840s and '50s, clothing for sport engaged a wide variety of women in a discussion about their relationships with their garments. At a time when mainstream women rarely challenged fashion's dictates, the novelty of sport offered an opportunity to rethink women's clothing. Meanwhile, the idea that some clothes were worn only for play made them less of a threat to anyone who perceived them as challenging traditional women's styles. Embodied in the new activities and the clothing worn for them was a changing and problematic concept of femininity, one that allowed women's bodies new freedoms while not offending prevailing ideas of modesty. As women considered what they thought was appropriate, useful, and comfortable; as they read magazines describing sports clothing; as they chose patterns and sewed garments; and as they wore the garments to participate in leisure activities, they both questioned and embraced inherited ideas of appropriate dress and behavior.

Clothing for calisthenics embodied this process of innovation. Early calisthenics manuals show women in ordinary clothing, but later, a specific "gymnasium costume" emerged. Female students wore the earliest gym suits at colleges and schools that issued instructions to incoming students (and their mothers) for making a suit. The designs for such suits were hardly uniform; some specified a dress with separate bloomers, some attached bloomers to a blouse with a separate skirt, and some required no skirt at all. In 1883, the gymnastics instructor at Mount Holyoke College issued written directions for a suitable "Gymnastic Dress" (a dress worn over bloomers) complete with a specified length of seven inches above the floor. Many years later, in 1908, Mount Holyoke was still offering detailed instructions. By then, they were for a suit with a divided skirt, including the exact dimensions of the split and the crotch. The seamstress was to first make the more familiar skirt and then turn it into two gusseted legs.[12]

A variety of businesses entered this debate. Magazine articles asked what made a good sports outfit, offered a variety of options, and acknowledged the potentially conflicting issues of comfort, aesthetics, and modesty. Pattern companies sold designs intended to be interpreted in different ways, allowing readers to create their own definitions of what was appropriate and feminine. In addition to everyday styles such as skirts, blouses, coats, and undergarments, the *Delineator* marketed patterns for gymnasium suits, walking and biking skirts, and knickers to wear under skirts for "all outdoor sports."[13] An entire spread on "New Styles for Bicycling," introduced one outfit as "a new three-piece cycling skirt . . . combined with a perfectly adjusted jacket in a most pleasing and up-to-date cycling costume that is equally appropriate for golfing and general outing wear."[14] The magazine and the pattern company behind it sought to convince women that such clothes and activities were socially acceptable. It was, after all, in the interest of business for these companies to promote sports and sports clothing as desirable.

The patterns described in the *Delineator* allowed for a great deal of personal interpretation, each offering numerous options for the final garment. A "Misses and Girls' Bathing Costume," made using pattern #6894, could have long or short sleeves, a high or scoop neckline, an optional Bertha, and loose or gathered leg openings, with "the pattern providing for each of the styles."[15] A similar suit came with eleven separate pieces of printed tissue paper so that an individual could make the top and attached bloomers with her choice of long or short sleeves, high or scoop or v-neck, Bertha, skirt, and peplum.[16] Pattern #1727, for a "Ladies' Gymnastic Costume," could be made "high-necked with a standing collar or open-necked with a sailor collar and with elbow or full-length sleeves." A "practical and becoming gymnastic costume," it was shown in "navy-blue serge and trimmed with black braid" but could be made in numerous other combinations of color, trim, and fabric. No matter what fabric and style the reader chose, Butterick promised it would be "exceedingly comfortable for wear while engaged in gymnastic exercises."[17]

The pattern industry recognized that women would have a variety of requirements for their sport clothing and produced designs with a great deal of room for personal interpretation.[18] But what choices did women make as they sewed these garments? One example is an actual suit in the collection of the Costume Institute at the Metropolitan Museum of Art. Home-made of navy blue wool, the one-piece gymnastics costume bears a striking resemblance to the Butterick pattern #1727 described above. The person who made it chose a sailor collar and long sleeves.[19] The Costume Institute recognized the similarity to the Butterick pattern and referred to the magazine in the collections record. It is very possible that the costume was sewn according to the *Delineator* pattern or one like it. The person who made this suit may have preferred long sleeves to short, and the low neck to a high one, or those design elements may have been required by her school or club. She used the corresponding tissue pieces to cut her fabric and sewed her suit accordingly.

The blue suit is woolen, but women chose from a range of fabrics, adding another dimension to their ability to shape their own garments. A costume at the Hermitage Museum in Ho-Ho-Kus, New Jersey is made of black silk with elbow-length sleeves and long bloomers.[20] It has a separate skirt that hooked on to the waist. While silk is lighter in weight than wool, as well as cooler and nonitching, the skirt nonetheless added more layers of cloth around the legs. This design demonstrates a different interpretation of what was appropriate for gymnasium use.

EMANCIPATION AND TREPIDATION

Gymnastic costumes provide valuable insight into the process of invention, negotiation, and interpretation of sports clothing at the turn of the century, but gym suits were almost always worn in private, single-sex settings. In comparison, bicycling clothing, even more than bathing costumes, was intended to be worn in public and therefore triggered especially intense discussion. The invention of the "safety bicycle" with brakes and soft rubber wheels in the mid-1890s meant that bicycling, previously a rather macho sport, was now marketed to and acceptable for women. Moreover, unlike colleges or private clubs, the bicycle was accessible to working-class women as well, who could rent a bicycle in a park for the afternoon.

Many, including Frances Willard, saw bicycles as offering new mobility and freedom to women. Willard called her bicycle an implement of power" and wrote that through bicycling, she "found a whole philosophy of life."[21] In addition to being worn in public, the designs for bicycling clothing were also rather daring. While bathing and gym costumes included bloomers, they were often hidden under a skirt. Now, some women wore bloomers or knickers, without the skirt on top, in plain view. The new clothing, like the activity itself, was associated with modernity and independence.

Advertisers took advantage of these associations and used rhetoric of liberation to sell their merchandise. Magazines teemed with advertisements for bicycles, bicycle cloth, cycling corsets, skirts, and knickerbocker suits. Knickers or knickerbockers were pants that extended below the knee, were worn with stockings, and were narrower than bloomers. Magazines like the *Delineator* offered numerous skirt designs as well as knickerbocker suits, and women were left to make their own decision as to which style to choose.

Manufacturers and merchandisers explicitly connected bicycling to modernity and freedom. An advertisement for Victor bicycles in the May 1895 *Ladies' Home Journal* compared images of a woman sitting at a spinning wheel to a happy cyclist and offered the following verse: "The Spinning Wheels of days gone by / Give way to Spinning Wheels that fly / And damsels fair to lightly tread / The graceful Victor now, instead."[22] Another ad claimed "Physicians recommend bicycling. Dame Fashion says it is 'good form.'" This overruled two common objections to women's athleticism: perceived threats to feminine health and appearance. Furthermore, the ad promoted daring costume styles when it offered a women's bike with a high bar that was "especially designed for the many ladies who prefer to wear knicker-bockers rather than cumbersome skirts."[23] A third advertiser associated its products with the dress reform movement. A Sterling Cycle Works ad read, "For Bloomers: Ladies who cycle in bloomers will find The Sterling the ideal Bicycle. Very light; very strong; very easy running."[24] One can interpret these advertisements as co-opting and cheapening the language of independence, but nevertheless, they promoted athleticism as a modern activity.

This association of sports clothing with freedom was not just a retail strategy. Dress reformers were vocal about the opportunities offered by sport or "outdoor" costume. What they had failed to popularize with arguments of health and gender politics now gained adherents through sports. Willard was certain that the costume worn for bicycling would serve as the test case for dress reform ideas and finally "convince the world that has brushed aside the theories, no matter how well constructed, and the arguments, no matter how logical, of dress-reformers."[25] Another woman wrote excitedly that liberating dress was preferable to economic or political independence and influence:

> Talk about the emancipated woman! The right to earn her own living on terms of equality with man, to vie with him in work, sport or politics, to vote, to hold office, to be president as well as queen and empress, would never bring the blessed sense of freedom that an outdoor costume, sans trailing skirts and entangling folds and plus a short skirt and bloomers, gives to the average woman . . . [26]

While many would have objected to her hyperbolic suggestion that freedom in dress was preferable to economic or legal independence, her words make evident how thrilling it must have felt to wear such clothing. Sports gave women the opportunity to experience and discuss the meaning, design, and feel of their clothing in a way previously left to women seen as oddballs or radicals.

"ANY DESIRED LENGTH"

Still, women felt some trepidation when it came to actually wearing pants for bicycling, so the pattern companies, eager to sell the new styles, came up with discreet alternatives. With articles such as "New Styles for Bicycling," the *Delineator* offered the consumer numerous designs—skirts that had extra pleats so they acted and looked divided; divided skirts that were full enough to look undivided; and even divided skirts, such as pattern #2044, which had an extra flap of fabric to cover the split in front. Style #2044 was billed as a "Ladies' Divided Cycling Skirt, having deep side-plaits at the back and the division in front concealed by lapped gores (to be worn on diamond or drop-frame wheels and to be in any desired length)." It was described as "a decidedly stylish divided cycling skirt planned on simple, graceful lines . . ."[27] The design description noted that the "division" of the skirt is hidden, while the illustration showed it in two lengths. Evidently, the pattern designers sought to reach readers who were shy about wearing a divided skirt but who were less reluctant to be seen in shorter hems.

A suit that follows this basic design demonstrates how from the back, the skirt functioned like pants, allowing for easier pedaling, yet from the front, it looked like a skirt.[28] Other women wore knickers with a skirt over them. At least one manufacturer offered ready-made suits with a matching removable skirt for "stylish women everywhere." The bicycle costume cost $7.50, the skirt, $2.50 extra.[29] An article in *Outing* magazine suggested that women might consider bringing a matching skirt with them on cycling trips "for use when approaching the unappreciative and hypercritical civilized communities where its use is no great hardship and going without transgresses custom."[30] Two identical examples of such a costume are in the Costume Collection at the Metropolitan Museum of Art; custom made for two sisters, the skirts are wool while the knickerbockers are linen (perhaps they wore the warmer skirts in cooler weather).[31] Judging from the good condition of the skirts, it is possible that the knickerbockers were worn regularly, the skirts put aside.

However, either because of budgets or personal taste, not everybody wore the latest look in bicycle clothing when they rode. Two cyanotypes from the turn of the century show a woman, dressed in a skirt and shirtwaist, climbing onto a bike with a diamond frame (or "man's style") as a friend steadies the bike. The second photo shows her riding confidently down the field, her skirt bunched up around the crossbar, exposing her stockings and high boots.[32] The magazines do not show this slice of reality; the elegant women in advertisements wear knickerbockers on a high-frame bike and skirts on a drop-frame or "ladies'" model. Contemporary etiquette writers would have fainted dead away to see her expose her stockings. Nonetheless, she had evidently decided it was acceptable to wear what she did.

Delineator patterns for bicycling skirts explicitly stated that the consumer could make the skirts "in any desired length."[33] This element of choice is very much in keeping with the idea that the unfamiliar realm of sport and sport clothing allowed, even required, a significant degree of improvisation. Even basic designs were contested and discussed. As styles were conceived and chosen as appropriate and respectable by the media and by retailers, women could make their own suits or purchase different versions.

All of these activities involved a re-thinking and an invention of basic styles of clothing and their relationship to the female body. They also involved a re-consideration of *whose* body could even be "respectable." Because they had more time for leisure and the resources to spend on special outfits, white middle-class women were responsible for much of the re-definition of femininity due to sports and sport clothing, but working-class women, white and African American, were active participants. Just as their appearance and behavior had long served as a foil for the definition of middle-class respectability, the fact that they now participated in some of the same leisure activities, and dressed in some of the same styles to do so, demanded a re-thinking of that respectability.

While etiquette manuals and magazine writers assumed a middle-class reader, working women were eager participants in this growing sports culture during the late nineteenth century. In a study of the history of women in sports, Susan Cahn writes that "young black and white women of small or average means for the first time found significant opportunities to engage in athletic activities, from basketball and baseball to tennis and track and field."[34] Working-class women enjoyed recreational opportunities after the turn of the century in the form of community leagues, settlement houses, schools, and Y.W.C.A gymnasiums, pools and summer camps.

The national Y.W.C.A. offered summer camps for working or "industrial girls" well into the teens. Photographs from the camps show happy-looking girls in swimsuits, bloomers, and middy blouses. One camp held a "Health Pageant" whose "purpose was to set forth in a symbolical [sic] way, right ideals about living, eating and clothing." The pageant included women representing allegorical goddesses called "Zeal, Knowledge, Good Taste, etc." The Y.W.C.A. newsletter wrote that of those who acted and watched

> most of these girls are Industrial girls . . . they took keen interest in the sports, which were portrayed and in the kind of clothing which Good Taste approved for sport wear. They were enthusiastic over the sport shoes and the clothes which lent themselves to the best advantages that could be had from outdoor sport.[35]

Because of their financial situation, working women were more likely to make their own clothing for sports. In the Y.W.C.A. photos, the young women's blouses are not uniform, which suggests that they were told what type to buy or make but were not given exact details. The blouses all follow a general style but vary as to sleeve length and decoration, two things that often varied according to sewing patterns. The same degree of variation is apparent in a different photograph, taken in 1915, of a basketball team at the National Training School for Women and Girls, which was a school for African Americans in Washington, DC.[36] Neither image guarantees that the young women pictured sewed their own outfits, but the variety in their dress suggests that at least some of the garments were made at home.

Many of the young women in those pictures probably *wanted* to buy their sports clothing. Like clothing not meant for sport, homemade sports clothing had its pitfalls and could be a sign of poverty. In fact, because it was intended to be what twenty-first century marketing would call a "performance garment," homemade sports clothing could prove especially problematic. When Mary Ellen Coleman Knapp attended high school in St. Louis in the early 1920s, she wanted to take swimming lessons because she considered swimming to be "modern." Her mother, who could not afford the $1 regulation suit (Knapp's father was a streetcar conductor), made one of grey poplin with bloomers. The very first time Knapp got in the pool, the water was unable to drain from the densely woven fabric and she sank to the bottom. The (female) swim instructor had to rescue her and run her finger under the bloomer elastic to let the water out. Knapp was mortified, and repeated her request for a store-bought suit. Instead, her mother made buttonholes around the bottom of the bloomers to provide drainage.[37] It is unlikely that Knapp appreciated her mother's ingenious solution to the problem. Vividly told to her daughter-in-law years later, Knapp's story illustrates the creative and frugal dimensions of home sewing as well as the drawbacks. For some women, sewing sports clothing was an exciting way to enjoy a degree of agency in the design of their clothing, but for others, it was a painful reminder of class status.

CHANGING DEFINITIONS OF MODESTY

While women were gradually willing to try new garments, they had hardly abandoned older ideas about propriety and modesty. Most were still wearing corsets (sometimes even to swim) and opaque tights. A constant theme in advertisements and articles is the importance of protecting feminine modesty and attractiveness. This concern often manifested itself in terms of esthetics or decoration but also extended to the actual construction of a garment. Since many of the designs for sports involved divided skirts or bloomers, which were the most shocking, manufacturers stressed their "grace" and convenience.

This anxiety over bloomers is evident in an 1889 article describing a women's athletic club. The female author, who was clearly enthusiastic about women's participation in sports, nevertheless demonstrated some ambivalence about the design of the club uniforms. The costume consisted of a dark blue blouse and divided skirt or bloomers, the "severance" of which, she noted carefully, was "scarcely perceptible." After a long and detailed description of the construction of the bloomers, she decided that "the effect obtained is extremely good, granting all the necessary freedom to the legs and presenting, at the same time, a graceful and modest garment."[38] It was thus important, even in a publication devoted to sport and in an article praising women's participation in athletics, to convince readers that both the activity and the clothing worn for it did not threaten ideas of feminine bodies or "graceful and modest" clothing.

In addition to articles, patterns, and advertisements, fiction provided another arena for discussing the relationship of athleticism to femininity. Ellen Gruber Garvey discusses the role of fiction in teaching women "correct" bicycling etiquette. Most of the magazine stories she describes involve a young woman returning to the home after a brief rebellion. Such stories, she contends, "contained" the threat posed by the mobility and perceived sexual nature of the bicycle. In one such story, the girl dresses as a boy to go biking, is discovered by a suitable boyfriend and switches to female clothing. Another describes a young woman who rebels against a strict father; she tells her father that "girls ride them things . . . in trousers and breeches like men." The father claims such attire is not "commonly decent," but she rides off anyway.[39] (According to Garvey, her rebellious behavior was acceptable to readers because of the parochial attitude of the father.) In both stories, there is a degree of uncertainty about what behavior and dress is acceptable.

In addition to their concerns about the radical nature of pants, or where to wear such clothing, most women did not want to reveal the contours of their bodies. This was especially true when it came to bathing costumes. Both etiquette books and retail catalogs emphasized the modest nature of the fabric out of which bathing suits were made, and some emphasized modesty over comfort or mobility. One etiquette book instructed readers that "bathing calls for a costume of some material that will not cling to the form when wet. Flannel is appropriate, and a heavy quantity of mohair also makes a successful dress, as it resists water and has no clinging qualities."[40]

The 1908 Sears, Roebuck & Co. catalog addressed the same concern, offering three models of women's bathing suits, all with skirts, attached bloomers, and short puffy sleeves, to be worn with dark stockings, described as "very pretty" and not "clinging to the figure."[41] Despite such hopeful promises, a photograph of bathers in the Maine surf shows that suits similar to those in the Sears catalog did in fact cling.[42] It is impossible to know whether the suits in the photograph were made at home or purchased, but homemade suits of similar design would have the same problems. It may be that this soggy reality was a secondary concern, and that both retailers and consumers presumed that it was nonetheless necessary to use yards of wool fabric to at least claim the right balance of modesty and practicality.

Articles advocating women's involvement in sports reminded readers that the new activities and clothing need not compromise their delicacy. One *Delineator* article claimed that while sports "give the body perfect freedom of action and engender a courageous spirit, they detract nothing from that womanliness which is always woman's greatest charm."[43] The same piece described outfits for different sports as "trim," "graceful and comfortable," "jaunty," and "attractive." The writer was determined to reduce the perceived threat to femininity posed by athleticism while encouraging readers to buy Butterick patterns for the new designs.

Pattern designers were well aware of the anxiety surrounding sports clothing. Some addressed these concerns with decoration and cuts that followed trends from mainstream fashion. Gym suits were trimmed with silk bows, bathing costumes with nautical insignia. Some gymnasium suits had extra fullness in the bust in the blousy "pouter pigeon" style of the early 1900s.[44] At other times, cycling, golf, and tennis styles were more "mannish" with their straight ties and boater hats. Another, more disconcerting trend was to design garments to resemble children's clothing. The sailor collar, a design associated with children's play suits, is found repeatedly in both bathing and gymnasium costumes. Perhaps encouraging grown women to dress like little boys and girls was a way to reduce the threat of their changing behavior. Unlike the functional elements of the clothing, these stylistic choices did not engender much discussion or debate. Perhaps the feminizing details, winks at cross-dressing, and childish styles reassured both wearer and spectator that the wearer was harmless enough.

Questions of modesty continued to be part of the discussion about sports clothing, but the boundaries of modesty shifted dramatically after the First World War.[45] By 1916, a male author writing for *Outing* was ready to dismiss the idea of modesty altogether. He compared the relative merits of skirts, bloomers, riding breeches, and knickerbockers for walking and hiking. There was no longer any need to blush over the description of bloomers. In fact, he dismissed all options except for knickerbockers, writing, "They have all the virtues and none of the vices [of other styles]. On the woman of average build they look neat and trim, mask rather than exaggerate or display the figure . . . They are the thing to use for every reason."[46] Bifurcated garments for sport were no longer a threat but a given. At least some of that change had come about because women had sewn and worn designs that challenged previously held ideas of modest dress. They had helped develop a standard language of what sports clothing should be and had helped to influence popular conceptions about what women should wear.

CONCLUSION

The novelty of women's sports opened up a space in the discussion of women's clothing, and in that space, women and the fashion industry negotiated different representations of femininity. Advertisers, retailers, magazine writers, and pattern makers played a significant role in this ongoing discussion by offering opinions, playing to women's desires and insecurities, and providing multiple options. Women, however, were the ones who actually wore the styles—and made many of them—so their views were central to the process.

Because many of the contested sports outfits were sewn at home, sports clothing offered another outlet for women to use sewing skills in a creative way. Because the sports clothes were for a specific purpose—and for most people, not a terribly serious one—they allowed home dressmakers to take risks they might not have taken with their "real" clothing. Pattern designs and sewing advice gave women quite a lot of choices, an experience that consumers then sought out for other garments. Sport clothing gave home dressmakers agency in the process of negotiating ideas about women's behavior and bodies. However, as sport clothing became mainstream, it was increasingly available for purchase. Those close-fitting knit bathing suits, for example, were often made in industrial settings. As their clothing for sports became more accepted, women lost some control over how they would look at the beach or in the gym.

At a time when sport posed a challenge to notions of womanhood, clothing for sport both smoothed and exacerbated the paradox of "sporting women." Throughout this period, the clothing worn for sport displayed what can be seen as a social ambivalence over changing gender ideals. The tension between traditional female roles and bodies and modern ideas of womanhood manifested itself verbally in the rhetoric used by advertisements, articles, and patterns, and visually in the form of images and actual clothing. This is not to suggest that the new clothes themselves caused changes in femininity, although it is arguable that the clothes helped women experience their bodies in new ways. However, the process through which the clothes were invented and popularized helped women, along with a diverse fashion industry, re-think what it was to be feminine. At a time of significant gender flux, the tension between traditional female roles and bodies and modern ideas of womanhood was created, negotiated, and at least partially resolved through the discussion and appearance of clothing.

NOTES

1. Frances E. Willard, *A Wheel Within A Wheel: How I Learned to Ride the Bicycle, With Some Reflections By The Way* (1895; Bedford, M.A., 1997), 38.

2. In *American Beauty* (New York, 1983), 135, Lois Banner claims that women who had access to college education, professions, or who "claimed the prerogatives of husbands and fathers" were first viewed with suspicion and labeled "advanced" during the 1880s. By the 1880s, as their numbers grew, they were seen as less of a threat and were labeled "new." Banner, 146.

3. A number of authors have written about the perceived health risks of sport, especially to reproduction. For example, Caroll Smith-Rosenberg and Charles Rosenberg write of the preoccupation with women's reproductive health and the idea that the body was a "closed system" with a finite amount of energy in their article "The Female

Animal: Medical and Biological Views of Women and Their Role in Nineteenth-century America," in *From 'Fair Sex' to Feminism: Sport and the Socialization of Women in the Industrial and Post-Industrial Eras,* ed. J.A. Mangan and Roberta Park (London, 1987), 13–37. It is now known that female athletes who reduce their body fat ration to extremely low proportions stop menstruating, but it is highly unlikely that Victorian-era women were exercising to that extreme. It is much more probable that poor women would have had insufficient nutrition or body weight to become pregnant or maintain a healthy pregnancy, yet these doctors and writers were predominantly concerned with middle-class women's reproductive capacity.

4. Annette Parry, M.D., "The Athletic Girl and Motherhood," *Harper's Bazaar* (August 1912), 380.

5. Edith Wharton, *The Age of Innocence* (New York: Appelton & Company, 1920), 27.

6. Margaret Bisland, "Fencing for Women," *Outing* (February 1890), 342.

7. Eleanor Waddle, "The Berkeley Ladies' Athletic Club," *Outing* (October 1889), 58–9.

8. "Some Defects in Education," *Massachusetts Teacher* 3 (1850): 67& 68, cited in Roberta Park, "Health, Moral and Strong: Educational Views of Exercise and Athletics in Nineteenth-Century America," in *Fitness in American Culture: Images of Health, Sport, and the Body, 1830–1940,* ed. Kathryn Grover (Amherst, M.A. and Rochester, N.Y., 1989), 123–168, 139. Park also notes that Darwin's theories influenced the move to support exercise for women.

9. Anonymous, *Etiquette for Ladies and Gentlemen; or, The Principles of True Politeness, To which is added The Ball-Room Manual* (London: n.p., n.d. [1860]), 82–3.

10. "To Coney Island," *Scribner's Monthly* (July 1880): 357.

11. Women had been working in long skirts for centuries, but as middle class women became interested in sports, they led the search for a new style of clothing. However, working-class women were very much a part of this innovation.

12. Warner, "Clothing the American Woman for Sport and Physical Education, 1860 to 1940: Public and Private," 69 and 73–4.

13. The *Delineator* is especially interesting in that it appears to have had a diverse readership, and promotional materials for the *Delineator* claim that it reached women from a range of economic classes. It was relatively inexpensive, ran ads for sibling magazines in Spanish, German, and French, and included numerous ads for "respectable" ways for "ladies" to earn money. Souvenir of the Butterick Exhibit at the Pan-American Exposition (New York, 1901), 2, in the collection of the Hagley Museum and Library, and "Remarks on Current Fashions," *The Delineator* (May 1890): 361.

14. "New Styles for Bicycling," *Delineator* (October 1898): 484.

15. "Fashions for May," *Delineator* (May 1894), 500.

16. "Fashions for May," 483 & 485. Physical pattern studied at the Butterick Archives, New York.

17. "Up-To-Date Bicycle and Gymnastics Fashions," *Delineator* (August 1898): 165–167.

18. This design was in fact intended for use as a bathing costume, but strongly resembles the gymnastics costumes. Lady's Bathing Costume, Butterick Pattern Company Pattern #6838, May 1894, Butterick Company Archives, New York.

19. Gymnastic costume, American, 1890s, 1981.149.10, gift of the Jacqueline Loewe Fowler Costume Collection, Metropolitan Museum of Art.

20. Gymnastic costume, American, ca 1904, 84.16.9ab, Hermitage Museum.

21. Willard, *A Wheel Within A Wheel*, 73 and 25.

22. Advertisement for Overman Wheel Co., *Ladies' Home Journal* (May 1895): 30.

23. Advertisement for Columbia Bicycles, *Ladies' Home Journal* (May 1895): 30.

24. Advertisement for Sterling Cycle Works, *Ladies' Home Journal* (May 1895): 30.

25. Willard, *A Wheel Within A Wheel*, 39.

26. Mary Sargent Hopkins, "Out of Doors," *The Ladies' World* (February 1896): 10, cited in Warner, 159. Some women did in fact wear gymnasium suits for purposes other than sport, notably for travel, see for example Lillian Schlissel, *Women's Diaries of the Westward Journey* (New York: Schocken Books, 1992), 141.

27. "New Styles for Bicycling," 484.

28. Bicycle costume, American, ca. 1908, 72.20.1ab, gift of Mr. John Noble, Museum of the City of New York.

29. Advertisement for Edward B. Grossman & Co., *Ladies' Home Journal* (April 1896): 29.

30. William J. Whiting, "Skirts or What? Should the Woman in the Woods Wear Skirt, Bloomers, Riding Breeches, or Knickerbockers?" *Outing* (October 1916): 33.

31. Bicycle costumes, American, ca 1900, CI.55.41.5ab, gift of Miss Mathilde E. Webber, Metropolitan Museum of Art.

32. Photographs of Mary Elizabeth Rosencrantz, also known as "Aunt Bess," ca 1895–1900, 2002.001.0083 and 2002.001.0084, Hermitage Museum.

33. "Ladies' Bathing Dresses," 43, and "New Styles for Bicycling," 484.

34. Susan Cahn, *Coming On Strong: Gender and Sexuality in Twentieth-Century Women's Sport* (New York, 1994), 36.

35. "The Health Pageant," *War Work Bulletin* (25 July 1919): 2.

36. Photographs of camp attendees in "Laboratories of Work, Worship and Play—Summer conferences," *Blue Triangle News* (July 1920):2–3, photograph of basketball team in Cahn, *Coming On Strong*, 86b-c.

37. Knapp, interview. Mary Ellen Coleman Knapp was Mary Knapp's mother-in-law. As an adult, the elder Knapp made clothing for her family and recognized that while it wasn't very stylish it was of better quality than she could purchase ready-made.

38. Waddle, "The Berkeley Ladies' Athletic Club," 61.

39. Garvey, "Reframing the Bicycle: Advertising-Supported Magazines and Scorching Women," 87.

40. Cooke, *Social Etiquette or Manners and Customs of Polite Society*, 425.

41. Sears, Roebuck & Co., *Catalog* (Chicago, 1908), 1112.

42. Bathers at Ocean Park, Maine, August 1906, photograph in private collection.

43. "Dress for Summer Sports," *Delineator* (June 1894): 670.

44. Gymnasium costume, ca 1904, 84.16.9ab, Hermitage Museum, and Gymnasium Costume, American, ca 1905, 63.186.5ab, gift of Miss Margaret D. Leverich, Museum of the City of New York.

45. I agree with McGovern (see note #63) that this was neither an immediate change nor caused entirely by the war. Nevertheless, many fashion historians do cite the war as at least having some effect on changing clothing styles.

46. Whiting, "Skirts or What?," 33.

EPILOGUE

"Pincushions have come out of hiding. Sewing is in fashion once more."[1]

By the 1920s, many women who ten years earlier would have hesitated before purchasing clothing for themselves and their children were doing so regularly. The combination of simple fashions and cheaper production methods (including, of course, low wages paid to sewing operatives) and social changes such as smaller families and more work for women outside the home meant that the ready-to-wear industry was on a roll. Many women continued to sew throughout the 1920s because of economy and personal tastes, but ready-to-wear had become a permanent fixture. Inexpensive and attractive garments were accessible to increasing numbers of women who now had more options as to how they would clothe themselves and their families.

This gradual but significant trend was shaken, however, in 1929. Hit by the Depression, many families had to reconsider their financial options. The economic horizon had changed dramatically and so did household budgets. Alice Kessler-Harris argues:

> For many women, reduced incomes meant less money for recreation and more necessary activity in the home. Women increased their services to household members, making up for lost income by substituting their own labor for the goods and services

they had previously purchased. Activities like sewing at home, preserving fruits, and canning vegetables increased.[2]

The Depression highlighted the importance of women's domestic labor to a household economy. Under these circumstances, sewing was once again valuable as a set of skills that may not have generated income but were central to preserving it. Anecdotal evidence reflects this shift. Roberta Thourot's husband was employed as a teacher, but he made under $1,000 a year, so she needed to sew to save money.[3] Likewise, Marian Goodman had to sew during the Depression because she couldn't afford "new things."[4] Sewing was also a way for women to earn money, especially if their husbands were unemployed. When Virginia Yans' immigrant parents were living in the Bronx during the Depression, her mother worked as an assistant dress designer to support the family when her husband, a baker, could not find work.[5] As the *Woman's Home Companion* spun it, sewing was "back in fashion."

Just as it was a survival strategy for individuals and families, sewing was also part of the macroeconomic plan to improve the national economy. The Federal government, which had assiduously promoted sewing through extension programs before the Depression, included sewing in the New Deal. Relief efforts and the Works Progress Administration included work that paid women for their sewing skills or offered sewing instruction to poor families. Peggy Terry remembered learning to sew in a camp for migrant laborers in Texas, telling an interviewer, "See, we didn't have anything. And they showed us how to sew and make dresses."[6] Eliza Champ McCabe, an African American teacher who was shut out of white schools because of segregation, got work sewing for the WPA in Washington State. McCabe helped the white woman who sat next to her because "she didn't know how to do a thing, but she had to be on WPA, just as I did."[7]

Sewing-related businesses saw a complex silver lining in the new economic reality. After a decade of devising strategies to combat the pull of ready-to-wear, sewing industries were faced with consumers who had an incentive to sew but little disposable income and spare time. The *Woman's Home Companion*, which by then had an arrangement with Butterick, reminded readers that sewing was a way out of their difficulties despite the demands on their time:

> Poof to the idea that you, an efficient business woman, haven't time to make any of your own clothes. It is only a matter of planning and that's your forte.
>
> If you are looking for the will to show you the way, consider what a good Triad pattern can do for you. It can give you three different outfits along the simple lines you crave. It can set you up with exactly the right colors. It can stretch your clothes budget to include a new accessory or two—these widestrapped black calf shoes per-

haps or the neat bow-trimmed kid pumps. And it can accomplish all this with a minimum of effort, since cutting these designs from one pattern is so easy.[8]

The Depression made a frank discussion of cost-saving measures part of the standard patter of the magazines. The domestic adaptations forced by the Depression were familiar to women who had sewn regularly before the crash. Anyone who had sewn to save money, recut hand-me-downs, dress for a job, or stretch a household budget would recognize the new emphasis on thrift brought on by necessity.

However, women also perceived sewing as a creative skill, not just one that helped them get by. Yans notes that while her mother did not want her and her sister to sew professionally, she nonetheless "used [sewing] as a skill that could allow her daughters to have a positive sense of themselves and their appearance."[9] While its economic role now grew in importance, sewing continued to provide women with an expressive outlet, a means to exert control over how they were perceived. Florence Epstein, whose father had hemmed her skirts while she stood on a table, enjoyed making stylish clothing throughout the Depression. In 1935, she was recently married and working for her husband's dry cleaning business in Rochester, New York. She was secure financially, but sewing was a way to have very stylish things while enjoying the process of making them. At a time when many people felt they had lost control, help with details such as how they could dress themselves and their families was a great help.

The crisis of the 1930s renewed interest in sewing, but these changes were not permanent. Despite the Depression, war shortages, and the emphasis on domesticity in the 1950s, the emphasis on sewing never returned to the levels it had enjoyed before the 1920s. Women continued to work outside the home and to spend less time on domestic labor. While many women continued to sew, ready-made clothing became the norm.

As sewing became less crucial to a domestic economy, it continued to resonate with cultural understandings of feminine labor. The decline in home sewing generated anxiety because it was a reflection of larger changes—many of which were threatening to those invested in traditional gender and family roles. In 1920, one advocate of home economics education asked:

To what extent does the housewife contribute to the income by her work in the home? If the housewife does her own sewing, cooking, washing, or other housework, her labor is a means of increasing the income . . . . A trained woman who has a business or profession may desire to continue her work outside the home and have her housework done. By doing so the actual income may be increased, but what will be the effect on the life in the home? It must be remembered that homemaking is a profession and should be recognized as such.[10]

Any sign that the home was declining in social importance troubled those who viewed homemaking as a profession or simply the most desirable focus of feminine labor. These institutions and individuals would continue to struggle to assert the value of women's domestic work. The more successful would be the ones who had an adaptable definition of what that work should be.

Institutions invested in home sewing would have to adapt to the changing definitions of women's work. In 1935, Ivol Spafford, supervisor of home economics education for the state of Alabama, published a textbook acknowledging that changing social trends demanded a new look at domestic education. Spafford began by asking, "Why should home economics be taught in the public schools? Is it because girls should know how to cook and sew, manage a home, and rear children, or is it because home economics has a contribution to make in the education of young people, whatever they may do?"[11] Spafford argued that a woman's decision to "have her housework done" might not be so disastrous after all. In a section called "The Challenge Ahead," he argued that given the changing role of women, there was a need to reevaluate the goals of home economics education:

> A knowledge of family life and home conditions is essential as a foundation for planning the home economics program, and there is no one answer because there is no one type of home . . . . The clothing needed today may be purchased ready-to-wear, but many women still do a great deal of family sewing. With increased leisure even more may do these things. Many girls should be taught to cook and sew, but they should be taught other things as well.[12]

Spafford's adaptive view of the future of home economics education—and therefore of women's domestic roles—illustrates the changing understandings of home dressmaking in American households during the late nineteenth and early twentieth centuries. Over this period, assumptions about home sewing shifted along with understandings of women's roles in and outside the home. For the women who could afford to buy at least some clothing, sewing became more of a hobby and less of a survival tool.

Experts like Spafford had to adapt their expectations regarding women's domestic work to changing times, but as he notes above, this is not entirely a story of declension. Even as some groups sewed less frequently, younger generations learned dressmaking skills. Women like Winifred Byrd learned to sew "out of necessity," and for many, sewing remained a central part of their domestic labor. Many women continued to sew throughout the 1930s, through the war years, and into the 1950s. During the 1960s and 1970s, sewing enjoyed a renaissance as an expressive craft (and one that was counter to the prevailing market economy).

Today, fabric stores display enticing pattern catalogs by Simplicity, McCall Vogue, and other companies. Sales in 2005 of electronic Singer sewing machines costing less than $200 were more than ten times what they were in 2004.[13] Like the women who came before them, people sew today for a wide variety of reasons. Some of those reasons are economic: a social services program in New Haven, Connecticut called Growing Through Sewing teaches sewing as a marketable skill to women recovering from substance abuse.[14] One graduate of the program sewed a last-minute prom dress for a neighbor who paid $50. Others are drawn to the creative dimension of sewing. A recent article in the *Wall Street Journal* quoted one young woman who sews because "everyone's starting to look like clones of each other," the same argument put forth by sewing proponents in the 1920s.[15] A diverse population has a wide variety of clothing needs and fabric stores in New York City sell material for saris, Muslim dress, and other culturally specific clothing. With inexpensive clothing so accessible and modern expectations of women's work as they are, it is unlikely that American home sewers will ever produce the volume of clothing that they did in the past—and why should they? But sewing maintains an appeal that is unlikely to disappear any time soon.

The reasons why women sewed in the late nineteenth and early twentieth centuries were colored by understandings of their roles in their family and larger community. Home sewing represented both traditional values and economic and cultural changes. Sewing was associated with thrift, discipline, ethnic and racial identity, domestic production, even sexual morality. As these values shifted over time, and as mass-produced clothing became more popular, the cultural meanings of sewing became more important. Sewing continued to represent traditional ideas about women and the home, but it also offered a tool for critiquing those older patterns. Sewing at home was still a way to save money, but that money afforded an increasing independence for women. A young woman's demure wedding dress doubled as an experiment in personal taste, and a homemade child's dress was a symbol of maternal love as well as a way to signal that a working mother had time for her family.

Sewing offers a lens through which we can gain a greater understanding of changing gender roles, class and race identities, educational priorities, business strategies, and domestic labor. Full of meanings about femininity, class, and work, home sewing is a fascinating way to interpret daily choices and larger social change.

NOTES

1. Ethel Holland Little, "You and Your Paper Pattern," *Woman's Home Companion* (January 1937): 47.

2. Alice Kessler-Harris, *Women Have Always Worked: A Historical Overview* (New York: The Feminist Press, 1981, 127.

3. Roberta Thourot, conversation with author, Oberlin, Ohio, 26 May 2001.

4. Goodman, interview.

5. Virginia Yans, email correspondence with author, 3 April 2001.

6. Studs Terkel, *Hard Times: An Oral History of the Great Depression* (New York: The New Press, 1970, new edition, 1986), 50.

7. Ruth Edmonds Hill, ed., *The Black Women Oral History Project* 8 (Westport, CT: Meckler, 1991) 361.

8. "Nine to Five and Five to Nine, A *Companion*-Butterick Triad for the business girl," *Woman's Home Companion* (January 1937): 43.

9. Yans, email correspondence.

10. Edythe P. Hershey, "Putting the Home on a Business Basis," *University of Texas Bulletin* (January 10, 1920, revised 1921), 13.

11. Ivol Spafford, *Fundamentals in Teaching Home Economics* (New York: John Wiley & Sons, 1935), 1.

12. Spafford, 5.

13. Anne-Marie Chaker, "It's Hip to Hem: Sewing Makes a Comeback as 'Project Runway,' Retro Fad Inspire a New Generation," *Wall Street Journal*, 1 November 2006, D1.

14. Joseph Berger, "These Stitches, In Time, May Save Some Lives," *New York Times* 1 October 2006,

15. Anne-Marie Chaker, "It's Hip to Hem."

INTERVIEWS

WINIFRED BYRD

Winifred Byrd was born in 1925 in Colorado Springs, Colorado where she lived until she married. Her mother, who had been trained as a teacher but could not find a school that would hire an African American woman, supported the family as a custodian after her husband was incapacitated by a brain tumor. Mrs. Byrd received a scholarship to Colorado College and worked as a medical technician for thirty years. We met at her daughter's home in New Jersey on May 24, 2001. In this excerpt Mrs. Byrd shares memories of how her family dressed well on a limited budget.

INTERVIEW WITH WINIFRED BYRD

Sarah Gordon: Anyway, so you were saying that your mom sewed because she had to.

Winifred Byrd: Yeah. And my fourth grade teacher she, she liked my mother evidently, because she would give her yard goods.

Sarah Gordon: Oh, OK.

Winifred Byrd: And my mother would make my sister and I dresses alike. We were, although we were two years difference, twenty three months difference in age, we were about the same size. And she was only a grade ahead of me, because her birthday came in January. So she was behind, well, yeah, she didn't go to first grade until she was seven . . . . And so this teacher, she, my mother would make these little dresses just alike, for us. And she did that, I can remember, she did that until I was like in maybe fifth or sixth grade, so . . . And then I started sewing. She showed me how. But the type of machine we had was that old pedal type. I remember running the needle through my finger once. You don't forget that. And then, I didn't, yeah, when I got ready, I made skirts and stuff for my sister and I when we were in high school. And then, and in college too.

Sarah Gordon: So your mom taught you when you were maybe . . .

Winifred Byrd: Eight or nine, that I can remember, yeah. And then when I got ready to graduate from ninth grade, well, she couldn't afford to get me a dress, but she had some, some material. And so I made a two piece dress out of that, to graduate in. And it looked nice. It looked as nice as anybody else.

Sarah Gordon: Was that part of a, did you have to make it for school?

Winifred Byrd: No, no, no. I made it so I'd look dressed up for graduation. Yeah. And then, when I got in high school, I took up pre-college, you know, so I didn't have time to take any of those classes, sewing or nothing. I didn't take them in high school.

Sarah Gordon: Interesting. So you had a more academic, college track

Winifred Byrd: More academic. And that's probably one reason I got that scholarship.

JANE DUNN

Jane Dunn was born in Orange, New Jersey in 1913 and grew up in New Brunswick and Highland Park, New Jersey. Her mother was a homemaker and her father, once a vaudeville star, directed physical education at the Y.M.C.A. She worked as a legal secretary for most of the 1930s before she married and raised two sons. We spoke on the telephone on May 2, 2001. Here Mrs. Dunn recalls the sewing talents of her mother and aunt.

INTERVIEW WITH JANE DUNN

Sarah Gordon: OK, did your, so, did your mom sew when you were little?

Jane Dunn: Oh yes.

Sarah Gordon: Do you remember? What did she make?

Jane Dunn: She must have made some things for herself. She was a very large lady and when my aunt came to visit, who was also a very large lady, the two of them used to sew together and help fit each other. And I got all the scraps to make doll cloths out of. And mother made me some very nice things that I recall.

Sarah Gordon: Really. Anything in particular that you remember, that you liked?

Jane Dunn: Well, she made me a lot of these little white dresses that had sort of a long torso and then an insertion where you could run a ribbon through to make a sash and below that a little skirt fluffed out. And it was, oh, some kind of a light cotton material.

Sarah Gordon: Sounds very sweet.

Jane Dunn: It was! I also remember one of those. I also remember that I had pink and blue sashes that ran, a satin ribbon about three inches wide, that ran through —

Sarah Gordon: Oh, that's wide.

Jane Dunn: - the eyelet type insertion and then tired in a bow in the back. I remember that, and I remember an outfit that my mother and my aunt together made. And it was a wool coat with some pleats on it and it had a gray fur collar, a caraco, I guess you'd call it, and a little muff to match. I remember that, early on.

Sarah Gordon: Right. That's nice. Did your mom, if she's making a coat, that's pretty sophisticated. That's, I think of coats as difficult.

Jane Dunn: Yes, well, they evidently were very proficient. That didn't phase them.

Sarah Gordon: Did they ever talk about how they learned? Or, you don't remember.

Jane Dunn: I don't have a clue.

Sarah Gordon: Did your mom, because she was so proficient, did she use patterns? Or did she make them? Do you remember if she -

Jane Dunn: Truthfully I don't recall, truthfully. As we discussed the other day, I guess patterns were very sketchy and a lot of people, you know, did their own, I think, just using basic measurements, things like that. I know many times my mother and my aunt and I would be shopping and we'd see something in the window, and my aunt would look at it and she would say, "Oh, I can do that!"

Sarah Gordon: Oh! Right! That's great, that's a real talent.

Jane Dunn: Yes.

MARGORIE DURAND

Margorie Durand was born in 1923 in Worden, Montana and was raised along with eight siblings on Montana farms with no indoor running water or electricity. Her family first owned a home but lost it after a devastating hailstorm and thereafter rented farms. After finishing Normal School Mrs. Durand taught math before learning to fly an airplane in hopes of joining the WACS during the Second World War. She later worked for the Navy in Seattle and for TWA. We spoke on the telephone on April 12, 2001. In this excerpt Mrs. Durand discusses how women would use patterns creatively and sew from high quality materials.

INTERVIEW WITH MARGORIE DURAND

Sarah Gordon: [Speaking of Durand's mother, Martha Eleanor Stromme Ewen] So do you remember, did she, she would make things for the whole family and everything, did she use —

Margorie Durand: All the baby clothes, all the little children's clothes. She could make the cutest dresses, she had the best ideas. I saw her make a dress for a neighbor, it was adorable. I see them in stores now I and I think "Mom wouldn't like that . . ."

Sarah Gordon: Not as good! Did she come up with all her own ideas, or did she use store patterns, or how did she do it?

Margorie Durand: Yes, she would use patterns. And what people do who sew a lot, is that they'll get parts of favorite patterns, and then they'll make up their own. Because that particular pattern fits someone well and then you use it, and you then can change either the top or the skirt or whatever you're going to do. So that's where they use their creativity.

Sarah Gordon: Where did she buy her things?

Margorie Durand: Sears, Roebuck catalog and Montgomery Ward catalog. Catalogs were well used.

Sarah Gordon: So it's all catalog, yeah. You can look at the catalogs now, the old ones, and look through them, from the 20s or the 10s or anything, in the library. So she, did she buy her fabric from the catalog too, or did she buy that in the town?

Margorie Durand: No, she bought it from the catalog.

Sarah Gordon: So everything.

Margorie Durand: I had silk blouses and wool crepe skirts to wear to high school.

Sarah Gordon: Wow!

Margorie Durand: See, when I look at the prices now and look at them I think gee, that was an everyday thing! Silk was very easy to do up, this is a . . . She always bought good quality stuff, because cheap stuff doesn't last.

Sarah Gordon: Right.

Margorie Durand: You're not going to waste your time sewing on cheap fabric. So you use good quality and it lasts, it comes out looking like new once it's washed and ironed.

FLORENCE EPSTEIN

Florence Epstein was born in Rochester, New York in 1912 to Jewish immigrants from near Bialystock, in an area that changed hands between Russia and Poland. Her father taught her to use a treadle sewing machine. After she married she helped run her husband's dry cleaning business. We spoke on the telephone on May 3, 2001. In the first excerpt Mrs. Epstein discusses how she began to be interested in sewing and used patterns. In the second she recalls how she received help from a neighbor with professional sewing skills.

FIRST INTERVIEW WITH FLORENCE EPSTEIN

Florence Epstein: I remember we . . . I mean, this was a class project. We made these middy blouses that we wore for graduating from grade school.

Sarah Gordon: Right.

Florence Epstein: And from then on, I started . . . You could pick up a piece of material for almost nothing . . . very little money, and I, that meant that I could make myself a dress any time I wanted a new dress.

Sarah Gordon: Right, right.

Florence Epstein: I didn't have to worry having money to go out and buy one.

Sarah Gordon: Right.

Florence Epstein: I could make one.

Sarah Gordon: Did you, were there certain, did you use pattern and things? Or did you just . . .

Florence Epstein: I always used a pattern.

Sarah Gordon: Yeah.

Florence Epstein: I, and the patterns always had detailed information on how to proceed.

Sarah Gordon: Right.

Florence Epstein: Specific instructions.

Sarah Gordon: Right. So you would just follow that.

Florence Epstein: And I remember, I used to especially favor Vogue—no, it was not Vogue. At that time it was Butterick.

Sarah Gordon: Uh-huh?

Florence Epstein: Butterick patterns.

SECOND INTERVIEW WITH FLORENCE EPSTEIN

Florence Epstein: I remember one thing. There was a woman, an Italian family living next door to us. And they had a lot of kids, they had . . . I don't know, boys and girls, and one of the girls was my age, and I used to pal with her. She was my friend. And her mother used to make buttonholes.

Sarah Gordon: Oh.

Florence Epstein: For the tailor.

Sarah Gordon: For money.

Florence Epstein: She was a professional buttonhole maker for the tailor. And she would do piecework. She would come home with a load of jackets or whatever it was that she would be working on. And whenever I needed a buttonhole, she would make it for me. It was a perfectly professional buttonhole.

Sarah Gordon: Wow. How much do you think . . .

Florence Epstein: I remember making a jacket that had a row of buttons down the front. And when she got through making those buttonholes the jacket looked completely professional.

Sarah Gordon: That sounds lovely.

PATRICIA GORDON

Patricia Gordon (no relation to the author) was born in 1919. When her father died when she was about twelve she, her mother, and her two sisters moved from Ohio to New Hampshire. She later studied at Smith College and received a Master's in Teaching from Harvard. While Mrs. Gordon claims she was never a natural at sewing, it was a "good thing" to have learned. We spoke at her home in Wallingford, Connecticut on May 7, 2001. Here Mrs. Gordon describes how her mother, a trained home economist, worked for a publicly supported program during the Depression.

INTERVIEW WITH PATRICIA GORDON

Patricia Gordon: And they had, in the high school home ec department, they had sewing classes for women. And women could, they could come in at any level, if, you know, they . . . and use the sewing machines and so forth. And my mother went, I don't remember how many nights a week she worked, but . . .

Sarah Gordon: So your mom taught there.

Patricia Gordon: She taught sewing there, in that instance, yeah. And it was a good thing for her too because she got to know quite a lot of . . . These women were, were not the same ones she played bridge with, you know. But they were, she enjoyed it.

Sarah Gordon: They were probably less well off.

Patricia Gordon: Yeah.

Sarah Gordon: They came to do this to learn the skills they needed.

Patricia Gordon: They needed to make some clothes, maybe. It's what she was doing at home.

MARIAN GOODMAN

Born in 1918, Marian Goodman grew up in Montana and South Dakota. As a young child she lived on an isolated forest station and later moved to town so she could attend school. She learned to sew very young. She recalled that during the Depression she couldn't afford new clothes, and during World War Two she couldn't find new clothes. After her husband retired she ran a small home business doing clothing alterations. She joined the conversation with Patricia Gordon. Here she recalls her distaste for her high school sewing classes.

INTERVIEW WITH MARIAN GOODMAN

Sarah Gordon: You said you did, you had had sewing classes in high school. Did you have to make anything—

Marian Goodman: Oh, yeah. Uninteresting things. You know, they make you baste everything first, and . . . Ah, I used to get so . . . 'cause I could make the garments they were trying to have us make twice as fast at home, but I had to go through all of this stuff in high school, yeah. Basting . . .

Patricia Gordon: They would stitch across pins if you put them in [unclear] . . .

Sarah Gordon: Right. But you don't have to.

Marian Goodman: I never liked sewing in school.

Sarah Gordon: You didn't like it. That makes sense, because you were ahead of the game.

Marian Goodman: It wasn't anything new to me, right. You had to take . . . You had to take half a year of sewing and half a year of cooking. The boys took manual training and something else I think.

Sarah Gordon: Woodshop or something. Electric—

Marian Goodman: I guess so.

Sarah Gordon: I've come across dresses that girls made in school. They had to make their graduation dresses. Did you have to do that?

Marian Goodman: No. We made aprons . . . I can't remember. Uninteresting things, I know that.

PATRICIA GORDON AND MARIAN GOODMAN

Later in the conversation Patricia Gordon offered an opinion as to why girls were taught to sew at a young age.

INTERVIEW WITH PATRICIA GORDON
AND MARIAN GOODMAN

Patricia Gordon: That's an interesting point and you were [addressed to Goodman], you were taught to sew at home and I'm sure that . . . I was taught in that school, I started school in Ohio, we, they started sewing in the fourth grade. They taught sewing from the fourth grade up, this goes back, you know, time back, I bet they don't any more, but I think they did this because, they didn't like to send anybody out who didn't know, you know. They felt that a girl really wasn't going to make it in that country if she couldn't sew.

Marian Goodman: If she couldn't. True.

Patricia Gordon: She couldn't keep house, she couldn't . . . And you couldn't tell when they opened those schools, how long a girl was going to stay in school. Sometimes a girl didn't even think about going to high school.

Marian Goodman: True.

Sarah Gordon: Right. So they started early.

Patricia Gordon: Yeah, yeah! Yeah, I think that must have been how it got started that way.

Marian Goodman: Probably.

EDITH KURTZ

Edith Kurtz was born in Illinois in 1904. She and two brothers grew up on farms in Illinois and Michigan; her father was what she called a "general farmer" and her mother ran the household. Mrs. Kurtz taught school, including high school math, before she married. During the Second World War she taught math to men who required more training before they became officers. We met in her room at Kendal at Oberlin, an assisted living facility, in Oberlin, Ohio on May 24, 2001. Here Mrs. Kurtz discusses how her mother skillfully re-modeled clothing.

INTERVIEW WITH EDITH KURTZ

Edith Kurtz: My mother made over everything I wore to go to college.

Sarah Gordon: Right.

Edith Kurtz: I had jumpers made up out of old dresses, and I had, well, I didn't wear skirts and blouses very much because I was not a figure to wear them. But, I never had anything brand new, and I didn't have very many of them.

Sarah Gordon: Did she make them over from . . .

Edith Kurtz: Made them over from things that I already had.

Sarah Gordon: So she renovated to look, to fix it . . . a lot cheaper . . .

Edith Kurtz: They were new to me. I remember one dress that I had that was really quite beautiful, that the sleeves had worn out. So she, she made dolman sleeves of a different color. It was, it was really beautiful. You had to buy some, some supplementary material to be sure, but the fabric was still good, so . . .

Sarah Gordon: Why not!

Edith Kurtz: Why not. And she was quite skillful at making, making things over to make me feel that they were something new and different.

Sarah Gordon: Right. That's a real skill.

Edith Kurtz: Yes.

Sarah Gordon: That's hard to do.

HELEN SCHWIMMER

Helen Schwimmer grew up in Toledo, Ohio where she was born in 1908. As a girl the family was hard hit by the Depression. She trained to be a nurse and medical missionary but became ill, and met her future husband while recuperating. Mrs. Schwimmer raised ten children in Michigan. We met at her home in Oberlin, Ohio on May 25, 2001. In this excerpt Mrs. Schwimmer recalls her frustration with her mother's exacting standards and reluctance to let her use the sewing machine.

INTERVIEW WITH HELEN SCHWIMMER

Helen Schwimmer: From when I was a little girl I used to sew all the time. When I was a little girl I used to be the child in the neighborhood who did the sewing. We used to have a little sewing club, even with the boys.

Sarah Gordon: Oh, really?

Helen Schwimmer: Even with the boys. And I can still remember buying . . . We used to be able to buy little small dolls, for twenty-five cents apiece, even with china heads on them, with eyes that moved. And we used to buy those dolls and I would make dresses for them. And I remember making that. But I never seemed to get much with my sewing because my mother would never let me sew on her sewing machine as I grew up.

Sarah Gordon: Why not?

Helen Schwimmer: Because she said I would break the sewing machine. This was coming on toward the, the, World War One, and the Depression, during the Depression. But I remember then, finally she let me sew on one. I was fourteen. I made my first dress.

Sarah Gordon: When you were fourteen. You made that on a sewing machine?

Helen Schwimmer: On the sewing machine.

Sarah Gordon: And you didn't break it?

Helen Schwimmer: No, I didn't break it! I have memories of ripping out all the time, though. Now I don't mind ripping out. I rip out mostly weaving and knitting, but I don't mind it. But at that time it used to kill me as a child. And my mother would never tell me, "just leave it go." It had to be done right.

Sarah Gordon: So she wanted, she liked . . . a stickler for details.

Helen Schwimmer: Yes. Yes. That's how I started in sewing. So that when I had five daughters I'd sew. I was well able to buy clothes until the second depression that came during World War Two, because that was a bad time for everybody, too.

Sarah Gordon: So you bought clothes before then?

Helen Schwimmer: I used to sew clothes and sew the same dress for three little girls, you know, at a time. They would be all dressed, dressed alike. I never sewed for myself. I used to buy my own clothes.

Sarah Gordon: Oh, that's interesting. Why, do you think?

Helen Schwimmer: I never was satisfied with them. Even now. Although I can make things over for myself.

SUSAN SEWS A SKIRT

I understand that many readers do not sew nor have they seen anyone else make a garment. While it is not necessary to be familiar with the specifics of sewing to appreciate my arguments, I decided to take advantage of the electronic publishing format and provide a photographic essay of the steps entailed in making a basic garment. My friend Susan Shaw, an artist and avid seamstress, agreed to make a skirt while I took photographs.

This exercise is not a historical reenactment. Susan made a contemporary garment with modern materials and tools. She used a sewing machine that dates from the 1960s, an efficient electric iron and modern components such as fusible interfacing. The point was not to re-create a sewing experience from another era but instead to show what the process of home sewing entails. Nevertheless many of the fundamental steps are the same as they would have been in the early twentieth century. Even the pattern that Susan used did not look dramatically different than the printed patterns sold by McCall's by the early 1920s. The most significant change has been in the styles of the garments, not the basic skills of sewing.

Watching Susan make the skirt underscored a number of ideas that I pursue in my book. For example, choosing to sew is a calculation of how we spend time, energy, and money. The skirt cost about $35 in materials and took about five hours to make, including shopping. Skirts are available for less than $35, so is it worth the time to sew? For Susan, it is in indeed worth the effort, at least some of the time. It is doubtful that an inexpensive ready-made skirt would be made of such a high quality material, and unlikely that such a skirt would fit her as well as the one she made. She was able to choose the colors and details that she wanted. Furthermore, while this particular design is conservative, Susan often sews to make things that are more unusual—see her cowgirl dress in the last frame of the essay for an example. Most important, this exercise reinforced that sewing is work and requires time, effort, money, and skill—but it can also be a pleasurable process with a gratifying result.

GLOSSARY

BASTING Basting stitches are large, loose stitches used to hold fabric in place while the seamstress sews the actual seams. They are a preliminary step in the process and should be removed when the garment is finished.

BATISTE Batiste is a soft, somewhat sheer fabric with a plain weave.

BERTHA A bertha was a ruffle sewn around the neckline and shoulders of a dress.

BIAS Cloth cut "on the bias" is cut at a 90-degree angle to the grain of the fabric. Designs that have the seamstress intentionally cut on the bias drape in a way that is attractive but difficult to sew. Fabric unintentionally cut in this way will not hang correctly.

BLOOMERS Bloomers were baggy shorts or pants. They were often knee-length but could be shorter, especially when worn with a bathing suit. The name comes from Amelia Bloomer, a nineteenth-century dress-reform advocate who suggested women wear loose, ankle-length pants under a knee-length skirt instead of long skirts.

DRAWERS   Drawers were women's bifurcated undergarments.

GINGHAM   Gingham is a yarn-dyed cotton fabric (as opposed to a printed fabric) with solid, checked, striped, or plaid designs, most commonly known in its checkered form. It is associated with rural America – such as Dorothy's dress in *The Wizard of Oz*.

GUSSET   A gusset is a triangular or diamond-shaped insert added to a garment, for example, in the crotch or underarms, which allows for more ease of movement.

MIDDY   Middy blouses were loose shirts modeled after sailor suits, with a square back collar and a front tie. The word comes from "midshipman." Middies were popular for both boys and girls but were also worn by adult women.

PEPLUM   A peplum is a short flounce added to the waist of a dress or jacket.

POPLIN   Poplin fabric is densely woven. Knapp's swimsuit did not drain water because of this tight weave.

RAW SEAMS   A "raw" seam would show where the fabric was cut and might unravel. A more polished way to finish a seam would be to make French seams, which entailed sewing up the same seam twice to enclose the raw edges inside. Most modern seams are "serged," which means that a special machine sews thread along the edge of the fabric to prevent unraveling.

SEAM ALLOWANCE   A seam allowance is the extra quarter- to half-inch of fabric needed on all sides of the cut fabric to allow sewing up the seams. Without such an allowance, the garment will be too small for the original measurements. Before the patterns included allowances, one had to remember to include them when cutting the fabric.

STROKED GATHERS   Stroked gathers are another name for "cartridge pleats," which are measured folds obtained by folding rows of stitches in parallel lines to make rounded pleats. Stroking between each pleat gave them a "cartridge belt" effect.

SURPLICE   In this context, a surplice-style garment has a neckline with a diagonal closing, similar to "wrap" styles of the late 20th and early 21st centuries. In another context a surplice is an ecclesiastical vestment.

TRIMMINGS   The world of fabric trimmings includes ribbon, braid, cording, tassels, buttons, etc. Many women would change the trim on a dress as part of a renovation. Contest judges were usually more interested in the garment's construction than added bells and whistles.

VOILE   Like batiste, voile is a fine sheer fabric usually used for making dresses and curtains. It can be made of a variety of materials, but eighth-grade girls used white cotton.

WAIST   The term "waist" meant what would today be called a blouse and was a general term for a woman's shirt. Shirtwaists, often white with decorative tucks or lace, were worn with skirts in the early twentieth century and became a popular alternative to a dress. They became one of the first mass-produced women's garments and were often produced in sweatshops like the Triangle Shirtwaist Factory.

Joan Severa, *Dressed for the Photographer: Ordinary Americans & Fashion, 1840–1900* (Kent, Ohio: Kent State University Press, 1995).

Webster's Ninth New Collegiate Dictionary (Springfield, Massachusetts: Merriam-Webster Inc., 1987).

BIBLIOGRAPHY

CONTENTS

- Primary Books, Articles and Toys
- Manuscript and Photograph Collections
- Museum Artifacts
- Business Records and Sewing Patterns
- Oral Histories and Personal Communications
- Government Documents
- Mass Market Periodicals
- Secondary Books and Articles
- Web Links

PRIMARY BOOKS, ARTICLES, AND TOYS

Anderson, Hattie E. "Making a Clothing Budget for Working Girls." *Journal of Home Economics* 20 (May 1928): 315–320.

Anonymous. *Etiquette for Ladies and Gentlemen; or, The Principles of True Politeness, To which is added The Ball-Room Manual.* London, n.p., n.d. [1860].

Bradley's Tru-Life Paper Dolls. Springfield, Massachusetts: Milton Bradley Company, 1914, 1916. Joseph Downs Manuscript Collection, Winterthur Museum, Garden and Library.

Brown, Clara. "Open Forum: Are We Justified in Teaching Clothing Construction?" *Journal of Home Economics* 15 (February 1923): 88–90.

Child, Lydia Marie. *The American Frugal Housewife (Dedicated to those who are not ashamed of economy).* 1833. Reprint, Bedford, Massachusetts: Applewood Books, [19–].

Clark, Sue Ainslie, and Edith Wyatt. *Making Both Ends Meet: The Income and Outlay of New York Working Girls.* New York: MacMillan Co., 1911.

Clark, Victor S. *History of Manufactures in the United States.* 3 vols. New York: McGraw-Hill Book Co., for Carnegie Institution of Washington, 1929.

Coates, Lydia Trattles. *American Dressmaking Step by Step, containing complete, concise, up-to-date, and comprehensible instruction in Sewing, Dressmaking and Tailoring.* 2nd ed. New York: The Pictorial Review Company, 1920.

A Conference on Manual Training. Boston: New England Conference Education Workers, 1891.

Cooke, Maude C. *Social Etiquette or Manners and Customs of Polite Society.* Boston, G. M. Smith & Co., 1896.

Cooley. Anna M. *Domestic Art in Woman's Education (for the use of those studying the method of teaching domestic art and its place in the school curriculum).* New York: Charles Scribners' Sons, 1911.

Cranor, Katherine. "Homemade Versus Ready-Made Clothing." *Journal of Home Economics* 12 (May 1920): 230–233.

Crowell-Collier Co. *National Markets and National Advertising.* New York: The Crowell Publishing Co., 1922.

The Dressmaker. New York: Butterick Publishing Co., 1911.

Fryer, Jane Eayre. *Easy Steps in Sewing, For Big and Little Girls, or Mary Frances Among the Thimble People.* Illustrated by Jane Allen Boyer. Philadelphia: Universal Book and Bible House, 1913.

Gladish, Nancy G. "Household Arts and the High School Girl." *Journal of Home Economics* 11 (November 1919): 488–497.

Glanton, Louise Phillips. "Does it Pay to Sew at Home?" *Journal of Home Economics* 15 (May 1923): 277–279.

Goodwin, Emma E. *Goodwin's Course in Sewing: Practical Instruction in Needlework for Use in Schools and at Home.* New York: Frank D. Beatty's and Company, 1912.

Gray, Greta. "Vocational Training for Girls." *The Journal of Home Economics* 11 (November 1919): 493–497, 495.

Hackley, E. Azalia. *The Colored Girl Beautiful.* Kansas City, MO. The Burnton Publishing Company, 1916.

Hall, Florence Howe. *The Correct Thing In Good Society.* Boston, 1902.

Hapgood, Olive C. *School Needlework: A Course of Study in Sewing Designed for Use in Schools*. Teacher's edition. Boston: Ginn & Company, 1893.

Hastie, Mabel and Geraldine Gorton. "What Shall We Teach Regarding Clothing and Laundry Problems?" *Journal of Home Economics* 18 (March 1926): 127–133.

Hershey, Edythe P. "Putting the Home on a Business Basis." *University of Texas Bulletin*. 10 January 1920, revised 1921.

Holt, Elizabeth G. "Negro Industrial Training in the Public Schools of Augusta, GA." *The Journal of Home Economics* 4 (October 1912): 315–323.

Home Sewing Helps: Ideas and Instructions That Make Possible the Development of Many Lovely Garments and Articles of Use in the Home. Scranton, PA: Woman's Institute of Domestic Arts & Sciences, Inc., in association with the International Educational Publishing Co., 1925.

Jessup, Anne L., ed. *The Sewing Book, Containing Complete Instructions in Sewing and Simple Garment-Making for Children in the Primary and Grammar Grades*. New York: The Butterick Publishing Co., 1913.

Johnson, Gertrude T. *Domestic Science, A Text in Cooking and Syllabus in Sewing, prepared for use in the Kansas City Elementary Schools, Yet eminently fitted for home work*. Kansas City, MO: The Burton Publishing Co., 1911.

Kellerman, Annette. *How to Swim*. New York: George H. Doran Co., 1918.

Kinne, Helen and Anna M. Cooley. *Clothing and Health: An Elementary Textbook of Home Making*. New York: The MacMillan Company, 1916.

Low, Juliette. *How Girls Can Help Their Country: Handbook for Girl Scouts*. 1913. Reprint, Washington, DC: Girl Scouts of the USA, 1972.

A Manual of Family Sewing Machines. New York: Singer Sewing Machine Company, February and November 1914.

A Manual of Family Sewing Machines. New York: Singer Sewing Machine Co., 1923.

Morgan, Mary H. *How To Dress A Doll*. Philadelphia: Henry Altemus Company, 1908.

Phelps, Elizabeth Stuart. *What to Wear?* (Boston: James R. Osgood and Co., 1873).

Picken, Mary Brooks. *How To Make Children's Clothes the Modern Singer Way*. New York: Singer Sewing Machine Co., 1927.

Scouting for Girls: Official Handbook of the Girl Scouts. New York: The Girl Scouts Inc., 1920.

Spafford, Ivol. *Fundamentals in Teaching Home Economics*. New York: John Wiley & Sons, 1935.

Thirteenth Annual Report of the Young Women's Christian Association of Brooklyn. New York: Young Women's Christian Association of Brooklyn, 1901.

Twenty-Five Years of Retailing, 1911–1936. New York: National Retail Dry Goods Association, 1936.

Watson, Edith B. "A Layette Project." *Journal of Home Economics* 20 (November 1928): 803–805.

Wharton, Edith. *The Age of Innocence*. New York: Appelton and Company, 1920), 27.

Webster, Jean. *When Patty Went to College*. New York: Grosset & Dunlap, 1903.

Willard, Frances E. *A Wheel Within A Wheel: How I Learned to Ride the Bicycle, With Some Reflections By The Way*. 1895. Bedford, Massachusetts, 1997.

Winchell, Cora M. *Home Economics for Public School Administrators*. New York: Teacher's College, Columbia University Bureau of Publications, 1931.

Yezierska, Anzia. *Bread Givers*. 3rd ed. New York: Persea Books, 2003.

MANUSCRIPT AND PHOTOGRAPH COLLECTIONS

Butterick Archives. Butterick Co., Inc. New York, New York.

Cambridge Sewing Club. Papers. Schlesinger Library, Radcliffe Institute for Advanced Study.

Crofton, Gabrielle Josephine. Diary. Hagley Museum and Library, Wilmington, Delaware.

du Pont, Francis Gurney. Papers. Hagley Museum and Library, Wilmington, Delaware.

Ellis, Blanche M. Diary. Downs Collection of Manuscripts and Printed Ephemera, Winterthur Museum, Garden and Library, Wilmington, Delaware.

Gamble, Elizabeth Chafee. Papers. Schlesinger Library, Radcliffe Institute for Advanced Study.

Jacob A. Riis Neighborhood Settlement Records. Manuscripts and Archives Division, New York Public Library.

Jenny Wren Club of Allston, M.A. Records. Schlesinger Library, Radcliffe Institute for Advanced Study.

Loop, Florence. Graded Sewing Exercises. Downs Collection of Manuscripts and Printed Ephemera, Winterthur Museum, Garden and Library, Wilmington, Delaware.

McBurney Family Photographs. Downs Collection of Manuscripts and Printed Ephemera, Winterthur Museum, Garden and Library, Wilmington, Delaware.

Miller, Margaret Motter. Papers. Downs Collection of Manuscripts and Printed Ephemera, Winterthur Museum, Garden and Library, Wilmington, Delaware.

1910 Sewing Circle. Minutes. Schlesinger Library, Radcliffe Institute for Advanced Study.

Photographs, ca 1895–1900. Hermitage Museum, Ho-Ho-Kus, New Jersey.

Vail, Georgiana. Diaries. Downs Collection of Manuscripts and Printed Ephemera, Winterthur Museum, Garden and Library, Wilmington, Delaware.

Viles-Wyman, Lilla Bell. Journal. Schlesinger Library, Radcliffe Institute of Advanced Study.

Wanamaker diary. Winterthur Museum, Gardens and Library.

MUSEUM ARTIFACTS

Bathing costume. Black and white wool. American, ca. 1870–73. 1979.346.18ab. Gift of the New-York Historical Society. Costume Institute, Metropolitan Museum of Art.

Bathing costume. Black cotton with white piping. American, ca. 1910. H75.415. Hermitage Museum, Ho-Ho-Kus, New Jersey.

Bathing costume. Black cotton with white piping. American, ca. 1910. 94.14.59. Hermitage Museum.

Bathing suit. Purple wool-silk blend. American, ca. 1915–1925. 1979.124.3. Gift of J. Robert Hoffman. Costume Institute, Metropolitan Museum of Art.

Bathing costume. Black silk. American, ca. 1900. 88.19.19. Hermitage Museum.

Bicycle costume. Cream linen. American, ca. 1908. 72.20.1ab. Gift of Mr. John Noble. Costume and Textiles Collection, Museum of the City of New York.

Bicycle costumes. Brown linen and wool. American, ca 1900. CI.55.41.5ab. Gift of Miss Mathilde E. Webber. Costume Institute, Metropolitan Museum of Art.

Girl's dress. White cotton batiste with lace, tucks and embroidery. American, 1914. 72.17.3. Gift of Mrs. Marie W. Fletcher. Costume and Textiles Collection, Museum of the City of New York.

Girl's dress. White cotton voile with net. American, 1918. 59.178.1. Gift of the Misses Anna S. and Helen Frankle. Costume and Textiles Collection, Museum of the City of New York.

Girl's dress. White cotton voile with lace and punched embroidery. American, 1920. 91.214.1. Gift of Harriet Lange Hayne. Costume and Textiles Collection, Museum of the City of New York.

Gymnastic costume. Navy blue wool. American, 1890s. 1981.149.10. Gift of the Jacqueline Loewe Fowler Costume Collection. Costume Institute, Metropolitan Museum of Art.

Gymnasium uniform. Cotton twill. American, 1929. 1980.193.1ab. Gift of Sadie E. Scudder. Costume Institute, Metropolitan Museum of Art.

Gymnasium costume. Black silk. American, ca 1904. 84.16.9ab. Hermitage Museum.

Gymnasium costume. Blue serge. American, ca 1905, 63.186.5ab. Gift of Miss Margaret D. Leverich. Costume and Textiles Collection, Museum of the City of New York.

Gymnastic costume. Black silk. American, ca 1904. 84.16.9ab. Hermitage Museum.

Gymnasium costume. American, 1890s. 44.66.1ab. Gift of Mrs. Henry James Spencer. Museum of the City of New York.

Sweater. Blue wool. American, ca 1895. 38.149.16. Gift of Mrs. John Hubbard. Costume and Textiles Collection, Museum of the City of New York.

Wedding dress. Cream silk, silk net and satin ribbon. American, 1916. Gift of Edna Maine Spooner. University of Rhode Island Historic Textile and Costume Collection.

BUSINESS RECORDS AND SEWING PATTERNS

Butterick Co. *Lady's Bathing Costume, Pattern #6838.* 1894.Butterick Archives, New York City.

Butterick Co. *Dress for Misses or Small Women, Pattern #8691.* Ca. 1916. Betty Williams Pattern Archive, University of Rhode Island Special Collections.

Butterick Co. *Frock for Women and Young Girls, Pattern #1449.* Ca. 1925. Author's personal collection.

Harper's Bazar. Fold-out pattern. October, 1903. Library of Congress.

A Manual of Family Sewing Machines. New York: Singer Sewing Machine Company Records, Hagley Museum and Library, Wilmington, Delaware.

McCall Pattern Company. *Ladies' and Misses' Negligee, Pattern #5044.* Ca. 1925. Author's personal collection.

Reynard, Pauline. *A Century of Home Sewing.* Unpublished typescript, 1951. Singer Sewing Machine Company Records.

Ruppell, G.A. *The Story of Butterick.* Unpublished typescript, 1929. Butterick Archives, New York City.

Sears, Roebuck & Co. *Catalog No. 111.* Chicago: Sears, Roebuck & Co. 1902.

——. *Catalog.* Chicago: Sears, Roebuck & Co., 1908.

——. *Catalog.* Chicago: Sears, Roebuck & Co., 1916.

——. *Catalog.* Chicago: Sears, Roebuck & Co., 1924.

The Sewing Machine Business As It Is To-Day. Pamphlet, n.d. New-York Historical Society.

ORAL HISTORIES AND PERSONAL COMMUNICATIONS

Byrd, Winifred. Interview by author. Tape recording. Plainfield, New Jersey, 24 May 2001.

Day, Jackie. E-mail correspondence with author. 31 October 2006.

Dunn, Jane. Interview by author. Telephone interview. 4 May 2001.

Durand, Marjorie. Interview by author. Tape recording. Telephone interview. 12 April 2001.

Epstein, Florence. Interview by author. Tape recording. Telephone interview. 2 May 2001.

Goodman, Marian. Interview by author. Tape recording. Wallingford, Connecticut, 9 May 2001.

Gordon, Patricia (Mrs. Herbert Pollock). Interview by author. Tape recording. Wallingford, Connecticut, 9 May 2001.

Gulrich, Jean. Interview by author. Telephone interview. 7 April 2001.

Knapp, Mary. Conversation with author. New York, New York, 27 March 2001.

Kurtz, Edith. Interview by author. Tape recording. Oberlin, Ohio, 25 May 2001.

McCoy, Kate. Conversation with author. New York, New York, 27 March 2001.

Nagle, Elizabeth. Interview by author. Telephone interview. 11 June 2001.

Orr, Dorothy. Interview by author. Tape recording. Ocean, New Jersey, 15 May 2001.

Schwimmer, Helen. Interview by author. Tape recording. Oberlin, Ohio, 25 May 2001.

Thourot, Roberta. Conversation with author. Oberlin, Ohio, 26 May 2001.

Yans, Virginia. Email correspondence with author. 3 April 2001.

GOVERNMENT DOCUMENTS

Alabama Polytechnic Institute, "Cooperative Extension Work in Agriculture and Home Economics, State of Alabama." Unpublished report. Auburn, Alabama: 1923. Alabama Cooperative Extension Service, Auburn University Archives.

Iowa State College of Agriculture and Mechanic Arts. *Education in Home Economics. Official Publication of Iowa State College of Agriculture and Mechanic Arts.* Ames, Iowa: 1917.

Nebraska State Department of Public Instruction. "Something About Sewing for Nebraska Girls." Series II, Bulletin No. 10. Lincoln, Nebraska: Department of Public Instruction, 1909.

New York City Department of Education. *Course of Study and Syllabuses in Sewing and Cooking for the Elementary Schools of The City of New York.* New York: New York City Department of Education, 1903, revised 1905 and 1911.

Office of Indian Affairs. *Outline Lessons in Housekeeping, including Cooking, Laundering, Dairying, and Nursing.* Washington, DC: Government Printing Office, 1911.

——. *Some Things that Girls Should Know How to Do, and Hence Should Learn How to Do When in School.* Washington, DC: Government Printing Office, 1911.

——. *Synopsis of Course in Sewing.* Washington, DC: Government Printing Office, 1911.

Rutgers University College of Agriculture Extension Service. *The Permanent Pattern. Extension Bulletin #58,* by Catherine Griebel. New Brunswick, NJ: 1926.

U. S. Department of Agriculture. *Present Trends in Home Sewing. Miscellaneous Publication No. 4,* by Ruth O'Brien and Maude Campbell. Washington, DC: 1927.

U. S. Department of Labor. Bureau of Labor Statistics. *Minimum Quantity Budget Necessary to Maintain a Worker's Family of Five at a Level of Health and Decency.* Washington DC: 1920.

U. S. Bureau of the Census. *United States Thirteenth Census, Manufacturing, 1910* and *United States Fourteenth Census, Manufacturing, 1920.* Bureau of the Census, Washington, DC, 1910 and 1920.

PERIODICALS AND NEWSPAPERS

American Girl
Blue Triangle News
The Colored American Magazine
Delineator
Fashion Service
Godey's Ladies' Book and Magazine
Harper's Bazaar
Inspiration
Ladies' Home Companion
Ladies' Home Journal
The Ladies' World
New York Daily Tribune
New York Evening Journal
New York Times
New York Tribune Illustrated Supplement
Outing
Scribner's Monthly
Wall Street Journal
War Work Bulletin
Woman's Home Companion
Yiddishes Tageblatt

SECONDARY BOOKS AND ARTICLES

Abelson, Elaine. *When Ladies Go A-Thieving: Middle-Class Shoplifters in the Victorian Department Store*. New York: Oxford University Press, 1989.

Banner, Louis. *American Beauty*. New York: Knopf, 1983.

Barnes, Ruth and Joanne B. Eicher. *Dress and Gender: Making and Meaning*. Oxford: Berg, 1992.

Bederman, Gail. *Manliness and Civilization: A Cultural History of Gender and Race in the United States, 1880–1917*. Chicago: University of Chicago Press, 1995.

Benson, Susan Porter. *Counter Cultures: Saleswomen, Managers, and Customers in American Department Stores, 1890–1940*. Urbana: University of Illinois Press, 1986.

Boris, Eileen. *Home To Work: Motherhood and the Politics of Industrial Homework in the United States*. Cambridge: Cambridge University Press, 1994.

Boydston, Jeanne. *Home & Work: Housework, Wages, and the Ideology of Labor in the Early Republic.* New York: Oxford University Press, 1990.

Bradfield, Nancy. *Costume in Detail, 1730–1930.* 1968. Reprint, New York: Costume and Fashion Press, 1997.

Brandon, Ruth. *A Capitalist Romance: Singer and the Sewing Machine.* Philadelphia and New York: J. B. Lippincott Co., 1977.

Brumberg, Joan Jacobs. *The Body Project: An Intimate History of American Girls.* New York: Random House, 1997.

Burman, Barbara, ed. *The Culture of Sewing: Gender, Consumption and Home Dressmaking.* Oxford: Berg, 1999.

Butler, Judith. *Bodies That Matter: On the Discursive Limits of Sex.* New York: Routledge, 1993.

Cahn, Susan. *Coming On Strong: Gender and Sexuality in Twentieth-Century Women's Sport.* New York: Free Press, 1994.

Cohen, Lizbeth A. "Embellishing a Life of Labor: An Interpretation of the Material Culture of American Working-Class Homes, 1885–1915." *Journal of American Culture* 3 (1980): 752–775.

Connolly, Marguerite. "The Transformation of Home Sewing and the Sewing Machine in America, 1850–1929." Ph.D. diss., University of Delaware, 1994.

Cooper, Grace Rogers. *The Sewing Machine; Its Invention and Development.* Washington, DC: Smithsonian Institution Press, 1976.

Cott, Nancy F. *The Grounding of Modern Feminism.* New Haven: Yale University Press, 1987.

Cowan, Ruth Schwartz. *More Work for Mother: The Ironies of Household Technology from the Open Hearth to the Microwave.* New York: Basic Books, 1983.

Davis, Fred. *Fashion, Culture and Identity.* Chicago: University of Chicago Press, 1992.

De Grazia, Victoria, ed. *The Sex of Things: Gender and Consumption in Historical Perspective.* Berkeley: University of California Press, 1996.

Degenhardt, Mary and Judith Kirsch. *Girl Scout Collector's Guide: 75 Years of Uniforms, Insignia, Publications & Keepsakes.* Leonard, IL: Wallace-Homestead Book Co., 1987.

Derks, Scott, ed. *The Value of a Dollar: Prices and Incomes in the United States, 1860–1989.* Lakeville, CT: Grey House Publishing, 1999.

Deutsch, Sarah. *No Separate Refuge: Culture, Class, and Gender on an Anglo-Hispanic Frontier in the American Southwest, 1880–1940.* New York: Oxford University Press, 1987.

Dickson, Carole Anne. "Patterns for Garments: A History of the Paper Garment Pattern Industry in America to 1976." Ph.D. diss., Ohio State University, 1979.

Elias, Norbert, and Eric Dunning. *Quest for Excitement: Sport and Leisure in the Civilizing Process.* New York: Oxford, 1986.

Enstad, Nan. *Ladies of Labor, Girls of Adventure: Working Women, Popular Culture, and Labor Politics at the Turn of the Twentieth Century.* New York: Columbia University Press, 1999.

Ewen, Elizabeth. *Immigrant Women in the Land of Dollars.* New York: Monthly Review Press, 1985.

Fernandez, Nancy Page. "Innovations for Home Dressmaking and the Popularization of Stylish Dress." *Journal of American Culture* 17 (1994): 23–33.

Formanek-Brunell, Miriam. *Made to Play House: Dolls and the Commercialization of American Girlhood, 1830–1930.* New Haven: Yale University Press, 1993.

Franklin, Penelope, ed. *Private Pages: Diaries of American Women 1830s-1970.* New York: Ballantine Books, 1986.

Friedman-Kasada, Kathie. *Memories of Migration: Gender, Ethnicity, and Work in the Lives of Jewish and Italian Women in New York, 1870–1924* Albany: State University of New York Press: 1996.

Garvey, Ellen Gruber. "Reframing the Bicycle: Advertising-Supported Magazines and Scorching Women." *American Quarterly* 47 (March 1995): 66–101.

Gamber, Wendy. *The Female Economy: The Millinery and Dressmaking Trades, 1860–1930.* Urbana and Chicago: University of Illinois Press, 1997.

Glenn, Susan A. *Daughters of the Shtetl: Life and Labor in the Immigrant Generation.* Ithaca: Cornell University Press, 1990.

Gordon, Sarah. "'Any Desired Length': Negotiating Gender Through Sport Clothing, 1870–1925." In *Beauty and Business: Commerce, Gender and Culture in Modern America,* edited by Philip Scranton. New York: Routledge, 2001.

Greene, Susan. "Service with Style: Indigo, Manganese Bronze, and Hoyle's Purple Dress Prints, 1800–1855." *Dress* 26 (1999): 17–30.

Grover, Kathryn, ed. *Fitness in American Culture: Images of Health, Sport, and the Body, 1830–1940,* Amherst: University of Massachusetts Press, 1989),

Guttman, Allen. *Women's Sports: A History.* New York: Columbia University Press, 1991.

Hewitt, Nancy A. *Southern Discomfort: Women's Activism in Tampa, Florida, 1880s-1920s.* Urbana: University of Illinois Press, 2001.

Higginbotham, Evelyn Brooks. *Righteous Discontent: The Women's Movement in the Black Baptist Church, 1990–1920.* Cambridge: Harvard University Press, 1993.

Hill, Ruth Edmonds, ed. *The Black Women Oral History Project.* 10 vols. Westport, CT: Meckler, 1991.

Hollander, Anne. *Sex and Suits: The Evolution of Modern Dress.* New York, Knopf, 1994.

Horowitz, Roger and Arwen Mohun, eds. *His and Hers: Gender, Consumption, and Technology.* Charlottesville: University Press of Virginia, 1998.

Horton, Laurel. *Mary Black's Family Quilts: Memory and Meaning in Everyday Life.* Columbia: University of South Carolina Press, 2005.

Hunter, Jane H. *How Young Ladies Became Girls: The Victorian Origins of American Girlhood.* New Haven: Yale University Press, 2002.

Hunter, Tera W. *To 'Joy My Freedom: Southern Black Women's Lives and Labors After the Civil War.* Cambridge: Harvard University Press, 1997.

Jenson, Joan M., and Sue Davidson, eds. *A Needle, A Bobbin, A Strike: Women Needleworkers in America.* Philadelphia: Temple University Press, 1984.

Jones, Lu Ann. *Mama Learned Us to Work: Farm Women in the New South.* Chapel Hill: University of North Carolina Press, 2002.

Joselit, Jenna Weissman. *A Perfect Fit: Clothes, Character, and the Promise of America.* New York: Henry Holt & Co., 2001.

Katz, Jane, ed. *Messengers of the Wind: Native American Women Tell Their Life Stories* New York: Ballantine Books, 1995.

Kessler-Harris, Alice. *In Pursuit of Equity: Women, Men, and the Quest for Economic Citizenship in 20th-Century America.* New York: Oxford University Press, 2001.

———. *Women Have Always Worked: A Historical Overview.* New York: The Feminist Press, 1981.

Kidwell, Claudia. *Cutting a Fashionable Fit: Dressmakers' Drafting Systems in the United States.* Washington, DC: Smithsonian Institution Press, 1979.

———. "Women's Bathing and Swimming Costume in the United States," *United States National Museum Bulletin* 250 (1968): 2–32 [repaginated as 169–200].

Kidwell, Claudia B. and Valerie Steele. *Men and Women: Dressing the Part.* Washington, DC: Smithsonian University Press, 1989.

Laver, James. *Costume & Fashion, A Concise History.* 1969. Reprint, London: Thames and Hudson, 1988.

Lazerson, Marvin. *Origins of the Urban School.* Cambridge, MA.: Harvard University Press, 1971.

Leavitt, Sarah A. *From Catherine Beecher to Martha Stewart: A Cultural History of Domestic Advice.* Chapel Hill: University of North Carolina Press, 2002.

Levine, Susan. "Workers' Wives, Gender, Class, and Consumerism in the 1920s U.S." *Gender and History* 3 (spring 1991): 45–64.

Livingston, James. *Pragmatism and the Political Economy of Cultural Revolution, 1850–1940.* Chapel Hill: University of North Carolina Press, 1994.

———. *Pragmatism, Feminism and Democracy: Rethinking the Politics of American History.* New York: Routledge, 2001.

Lomawaima, K. Tisianina. "Domesticity in the Federal Indian Schools: The Power of Authority over Mind and Body." *American Ethnologist* 20 (1993): 227–240.

Lynd, Helen Merrell and Robert S. Lynd. *Middletown: A Study in Contemporary American Culture.* New York: Harcourt, Brace and Co., 1929.

Mangan, J.A., and Roberta Park, eds. *From 'Fair Sex' to Feminism: Sport and the Socialization of Women in the Industrial and Post-Industrial Eras.* London: F. Cass, 1987.

Matthews, Glenna. *"Just a Housewife": The Rise and Fall of Domesticity in America.* New York: Oxford University Press, 1987.

McGovern, James B. "The American Woman's Pre-World War I Freedom in Manners and Morals." *Journal of American History* 55 (September 1968): 315–333.

Mihesuah, Devon A. *Cultivating the Rosebuds: The Education of Women at the Cherokee Female Seminary, 1851–1909.* Urbana: University of Illinois Press, 1993.

The Museum of Modern Art, New York. *The Hampton Album, 44 Photographs by Frances B. Johnston from an album of the Hampton Institute* (New York: Doubleday & Co., 1966).

National Association of State Universities and Land Grant Colleges. *The Land-Grant Tradition*. Washington, DC: National Association of State Universities and Land Grant Colleges, 1995.

Norton, Mary Beth, and Ruth M. Alexander, eds. *Major Problems in American Women's History*. Lexington, Massachusetts: D.C. Heath & Co., 1996.

Osaki, Amy Boyce. "A 'Truly Feminine Employment': Sewing and the Early Nineteenth-Century Woman." *Winterthur Portfolio* 23 (1988): 225–241.

Peiss, Kathy. *Cheap Amusements: Working Women and Leisure in Turn-of-the-Century New York*. Philadelphia: Temple University Press, 1986.

Pellegrin, Nicole. "Les Vertues de 'l'Ouvrage' - Recherches sur la Feminization des Travaux d'Aiguille (XVI-XVIII Siècles)" (The Virtues of Work: Research on the Feminization of Needlework (16th-18th Centuries). *Revue D'Histoire Moderne et Contemporaine* 46–4 (Octobre-Decembre 1999): 747–769.

Perrot, Philippe. *Fashioning the Bourgeoisie*. Translated by Richard Bienvenu, Princeton: Princeton University Press, 1994.

Rieff, Lynne Anderson. "'Rousing the People of the Land': Home Demonstration Work in the Deep South, 1914–1950." Ph.D. Dissertation, Auburn University, 1995.

Sagness, Arlene, ed. *Clothes Lines, Party Lines, and Hemlines*. Fargo: North Dakota Extension Homemakers Council, 1989.

Scanlon, Jennifer. *Inarticulate Longings: The Ladies' Home Journal, Gender, and the Promises of Consumer Culture*. New York: Routledge, 1995.

Schneirov, Matthew. *The Dream of a New Social Order: Popular Magazines in America, 1893–1914*. New York: Columbia University Press, 1994.

Schreier, Barbara. *Becoming American Women: Clothing and the Jewish Immigrant Experience, 1880–1920*. Chicago: Chicago Historical Society, 1994.

Schorman, Rob. "Ready or Not: Custom-Made Ideals and Ready-Made Clothes in Late 19th-Century America." *Journal of American Culture* 19 (1996): 111–120.

Severa, Joan L. *Dressed for the Photographer: Ordinary Americans and Fashion, 1840–1900*. Kent, Ohio: The Kent State University Press, 1995.

Sharpless, Rebecca. *Fertile Ground, Narrow Choices: Women on Texas Cotton Farms, 1900–1940*. Chapel Hill: University of North Carolina Press, 1999.

Simonsen, Jane. *Making Home Work: Domesticity and Native American Assimilation in the American West, 1860–1919*. Chapel Hill: University of North Carolina Press, 2006.

Shaw, Stephanie. *What a Woman Ought to Be and to Do: Black Professional Women Workers During the Jim Crow Era*. Chicago: University of Chicago Press, 1996.

Stansell, Christine. *City of Women: Sex and Class in New York 1789–1860*. New York: Knopf, 1982.

Strasser, Susan, Charles McGovern and Matthias Judt, eds. *Getting and Spending: European and American Consumer Societies in the Twentieth Century*. Cambridge: Cambridge University Press, 1998.

Strasser, Susan. *Never Done: A History of American Housework*. New York: Pantheon Books, 1982.

Sullivan, Joan L. "In Pursuit of Legitimacy: Home Economists and the Hoover Apron in World War I." *Dress* 26 (1999): 31–46.

Susman, Warren. *Culture as History: The Transformation of American Society in the Twentieth Century.* New York: Pantheon books, 1984.

Terkel, Studs. *Hard Times: An Oral History of the Great Depression.* New York: The New Press, 1970.

Turbin, Carole. *Working Women of Collar City: Gender, Class, and Community in Troy, New York, 1864–1886.* Urbana: University of Illinois Press, 1992.

Twenty-Five Years of Retailing, 1911–1936. New York: National Retail Dry Goods Association, 1936.

Ulrich, Laurel Thatcher. *A Midwife's Tale: The Life of Martha Ballard, Based on Her Diary, 1785–1812.* New York: Vintage Books, 1990.

Waalkes, Mary Amanda. "Working in the Shadow of Racism and Poverty: Alabama's Black Home Demonstration Agents, 1915–1939." Ph.D. diss., University of Colorado at Boulder,1998.

Waller-Zuckerman, Mary Ellen. "Old Homes in a City of Perpetual Change, Women's Magazines, 1890–1916." *Business History Review* 63 (Winter 1989): 715–756.

Walsh, Margaret. "The Democratization of Fashion: The Emergence of the Women's Dress Pattern Industry." *Journal of American History* 66 (1979): 299–313.

Warner, Patricia. "Clothing the American Woman for Sport and Physical Education, 1860 to 1940: Public and Private." Ph.D dissertation., University of Minnesota, 1986.

Welter, Barbara. "The Cult of True Womanhood, 1820–1860." *American Quarterly* 18 (1966): 151–174.

WEB LINKS

American Sewing Guild
Auburn University Digital Library
Butterick, McCalls, Vogue Patterns
The Hagley Museum and Library
The Hermitage
The Library of Congress
The Metropolitan Museum of Art
Mood Designer Fabrics
The Museum of the City of New York
The New-York Historical Society
The New York Public Library
The Palace of the Governors
The Schlesinger Library
The Tamiment Library & Robert F. Wagner Labor Archives

Spelman College
The University of Rhode Island Historic Textile and Costume Collection
Vanishing Georgia
The Commercial Pattern Archive at the University of Rhode Island
Winterthur Museum and Library
The Wisconsin Historical Society

ABOUT THE AUTHOR

Sarah Gordon received her B.A. from Oberlin College in 1993 and her Ph.D. in United States and Women's History from Rutgers University in 2004. She has published articles in *Beauty and Business: Commerce, Gender, and Culture in Modern America*, edited by Philip Scranton (New York: Routledge, 2001), the *Journal of Women's History*, and *Material History Review*. Gordon has taught at Rutgers and at SUNY Purchase College, teaching courses in U.S, public, and women's history, and has worked in a variety of public history contexts. She lives in New York City with her husband and daughter.

The author looks forward to discussing this book with readers. She can be reached at sarah@sarahgordon.net.

Printed in the United States
131384LV00001B/160-249/P

9 780231 142441